FEAR,
CONTROL,
and
LETTING GO

FEAR, CONTROL, and LETTING GO

How Psychological Principles and Spiritual
Faith Can Help Us Recover from Our Fears

RICHARD P. KRUMMEL, MDIV, PHD

WESTBOW
PRESS
A DIVISION OF THOMAS NELSON

WestBow Press books may be ordered through booksellers or by contacting:

WestBow Press
A Division of Thomas Nelson
1663 Liberty Drive
Bloomington, IN 47403
www.westbowpress.com
1-(866) 928-1240

The examples presented in this book are based on actual psychotherapy sessions. However, the details of the stories, including names, physical characteristics, and other identifying information, have been altered to protect the identities of the people involved.

ISBN: 978-1-4497-8244-3 (sc)
ISBN: 978-1-4497-8245-0 (hc)
ISBN: 978-1-4497-8243-6 (e)

Library of Congress Control Number: 2013900976

Printed in the United States of America

WestBow Press rev. date: 2/07/2013

5/06/13

Lois & Bob—
So very good to have shared
time with you in New York.
Peace be with you.

Richard

TO DEBBIE,
THE LOVE OF MY LIFE

CONTENTS

ACKNOWLEDGMENTS

The journey of writing and organizing this book has been a lengthy one that, at every twist and turn, was made easier by the consistent encouragement, acceptance, patience, and love of my wife, Debbie. The book also would not have its present form without the diligent, constructive feedback and editing of Woods Dixon during this past year. And, to all of my patients who have taught me so much over the years, I am grateful.

INTRODUCTION

I wrote this book as part of my lifelong work to establish a more intimate connection with the God who created me and who works daily in my life. I also wrote it to attempt to make sense of my environment and of the people who have been and are still in it. God does not move away from me, but I have often moved away from God or put something between us. As a psychologist, I have found that as we resolve our psychological issues we increase our potential to maximize the gifts of life and relationships that God has provided us. With these as our base, we grow as human beings and as spiritual beings.

When I look back on my life, I see two main themes. One is my search for the God of my being, and the other is the presence of fear in all its numerous variations and disguises. My fear has acted as a brake on my ability to connect with and to stay connected to God. My fear has taken the form of social inadequacy, anxiety about speaking in groups, worry about making mistakes, and numerous others. My fear of writing, printing, and making public the contents of this book have brought most of the fear themes in my life to the forefront—including the fear of being criticized. Fear has retarded my psychological growth for decades. It may not be obvious to others, but I know it, and so does God.

This book is complete because I decided—and God has continued to strengthen me in this decision—to live a life of faith rather than to exist in fear. This book is not perfect. Since its completion, I have thought of many changes I could make to improve it. Even as I wrote it, I knew it would not convey all of my best and most current thinking. I can criticize the book. Others can also criticize the book and me. But now, thanks be to God and to faith, I know I will be able to deal with criticism—not just survive it, but live on after it. I created my fear, and it wore me down like heavy chains thrown over my shoulders. God did not create the chains. I did. Because of God's help, they are no longer on my shoulders. I pray faith will keep them off.

While completing more than forty thousand hours of psychotherapy over thirty years with individuals, couples, and families, I realized that my fears and the themes in my life are not unique. I became aware that my path is a common one. It is a journey traveled by many. With God's support, I am able to help people grow, throw off their burdens of fear, and move forward. With my patients' help, I have also been able to learn and to progress. God gave me the people and the profession in which to develop. All I needed to do was to take advantage of the opportunities. I had to learn and practice ways to reduce my fear and increase my faith.

I grew up in a family of faith. Granted, there was a substantial amount of psychological dysfunction, but there was also much discussion and demonstration of the spiritual life. I am the third generation of ordained ministers in the family, all on my mother's side. My great-uncle Harold Lundgren was one of my grandmother's four brothers. Harold attended Colgate-Rochester Divinity School in Rochester, New York. He was ordained an American Baptist minister. Much of his ministry was with migrant workers in New Mexico, Arizona, and Colorado. When he visited the small town in northern Wisconsin where I grew up, the homecoming seemed similar to the return of the Prodigal Son in the Bible. Harold told wonderful stories and preached stirring sermons, all without notes of any type. He was a gray-haired hero to me—the man my grandmother and mother adored and whom I thought I was supposed to become.

My uncle Jim Palm was my mother's younger brother. Jim was athletic in a way I was not. He played football in high school, and I had problems dribbling a basketball. He was socially outgoing with many friends. I was shy and usually had one close friend at a time. He was also a man I wanted to copy, to be like, to have as a model. Jim also attended Colgate-Rochester Divinity School for one year, but when he found out that the books he was reading were written by theologians at Union Theological Seminary in New York City, he transferred there.

Jim was ordained a Presbyterian minister. Then he and his wife, Louise, left to become missionaries in the Philippines for eighteen years. When they returned every three to four years, even more fatted calves seemed to be killed for this returning Prodigal Son. I learned it was good to be a minister, to return home as a type of family hero.

As a child, I had long believed I would attend college and seminary as Harold and Jim had done. After college, I attended Crozer Theological Seminary near Philadelphia. After two years, Crozer merged with Colgate-Rochester, and I spent my last year at the same seminary my uncles had attended. During that time, I was a student minister. Even though I had completed all of the courses on pastoral counseling, I felt ill equipped to address the emotional issues of many individuals. Prayer was necessary to address their problems, but it was oftentimes not sufficient.

I wanted more skills, so I applied to several graduate schools to study counseling psychology. I chose the University of Nebraska because the program was accredited by the American Psychological Association. I planned to obtain a master's degree and then return to the ministry. I wanted to be part of a large church where I could work in family ministry doing counseling in a religious setting. While at Nebraska, the faculty invited me to stay to obtain a PhD. This was another example of God working in my life: preparing me for service, as well as reducing some of my fears.

After graduation I looked for jobs in Texas and accepted a position in Beaumont. God also led me to Beaumont so that I could meet Deborah, whom I married five years later. With Deborah, I was ready and not afraid. I knew deep inside that she was the one woman for me. Our lives and our psychological dynamics have been entwined ever since. Numerous times my fears have come to the forefront in our relationship, interfering with emotional intimacy and communication. On many occasions, Deborah has listened to me and loved me through my upsets, always accepting me, and always telling me what I needed to hear.

We all have some type of psychological baggage that interferes with our relationships with God, ourselves, and others. This baggage often takes the form of *core fears*—central themes in our lives that were learned early and have existed for a long time. The bad news is that they are old and habitual. The good news is that they are acquired and can be largely, but not completely, replaced by newer learning. The psychology of learning can illuminate this process as well as provide direction for change.

Society teaches us to believe that we can control outcomes—big consequences that are outside of ourselves. We are going to make things happen. Life slowly teaches us to recognize that we cannot control most of what happens outside of us. Spirituality teaches us to accept that so we can find peace within ourselves. We oftentimes separate one part of ourselves from the other parts and become disconnected and conflicted. We can learn to reconnect and find spiritual peace. Faith is necessary to find this peace.

In 1990, I was diagnosed with melanoma. It was my melanoma—my skin cancer—that got my attention and showed me that I was not in control of the outside world. I found out that I was not in control of the disease that had centered itself on a large mole in the middle of my back. Fortunately, the cancer was confined to just one area of skin that was excised. The experience resulted in a significant reorganization of my priorities. It led me to look at my needs as a human being and to examine the various control strategies I had developed over the years. These strategies kept me from feeling certain emotions, mainly fear, and provided me some sense—a false sense—of safety and predictability.

We all want some predictability and often learn to obtain it by using a variety of control tactics. Someone who grows up in a home where there are many secrets might continue to keep secrets in their marriage. Keeping secrets is what the person knows. It is familiar and safer than learning a new skill. Telling the truth, for example, will put the person on unfamiliar ground. Many of us are afraid of the unfamiliar and unknown. Doing something different will bring different consequences. Therefore, fear of unpredictable consequences causes us to avoid change even when the familiar is dysfunctional, inefficient, and ineffectual. Hopefully, the contents of this book will help some people to move into the unfamiliar.

PART 1

EARLY LEARNING

CHAPTER 1

HOW FEAR AFFECTS OUR LIVES

*I freed thousands of slaves. I could have freed thousands
more, if they had known they were slaves.*
—HARRIET TUBMAN

THE SONGWRITERS MAY BE CORRECT when they say "love makes
the world go round." However, it is just as true that fear will slow
it down. Love and fear seem to be in a delicate balance, with fear often
outweighing love. At times, it seems that fear is what drives people.
It may be fear that makes people's worlds go around and spin wildly.
If love is, in fact, the dominant force, then fear is running at a close
second. Fear will keep us from the relationships we want, achievements
we desire, and peace for which we yearn. It is the mismanagement of
our emotions, particularly of fear, that restricts growth and perpetuates
negative habits. What we are running from is running us, and what we
are usually running from is attached to fear. We run because we are
afraid of something, someone, or some event. We run because we fear

closeness. We run because we fear being *wrong*. We run because we fear failure. We run because we fear success. Possibly more than any other emotion, fear shapes the course of our lives. It can trap us in time, with unhealthy habits, removed from growth, faith, and intimate and conscious contact with God.

Growth is an inner journey, a journey that is walked only with God. Each journey is different. Our passage intersects with those of others and—if we are fortunate—some will parallel ours. On the journey, wherever we go, there we are. But many people do not look closely at who they are. They are afraid to do so. Like alcoholics who find other alcoholics at a party, people of fear find other people of fear. They stay with the familiar and change little. When we purge ourselves of unnecessary fears, we create space in our bodies, our minds, and our hearts so that love can flow in. Love does not cause wars. It does not cause low self-concept. And it does not cause resentments and desires for revenge. Love does not cause ulcers. Fear does. Love does not cause divorces. Fear does. Fear causes these and many other personal, familial, occupational, social, and international problems. Love is not impotent, but it is often overwhelmed by the presence of fear in all its numerous forms.

I know a man, a good man, who was sexually abused as a child by a priest. He did not tell his mother and father about the abuse because he worried they would not believe him. He thought the priest would harm him, and he was afraid of the pain his parents might feel. These fears inhabited the body of an eleven-year-old boy who was trying to make sense of the terrible incident. He kept his secret to himself and avoided his fears, but he still paid a severe price. During his adolescence, in an attempt to hide his feelings, he distracted himself by acting out sexually with girls. Perhaps he was also scared of being homosexual. The young man became promiscuous to "prove" to himself, and to others, that he was not gay. In college, his social activities distracted him from finishing his degree. For years he said he wanted to marry, but he never did. When an attractive woman walked by, he focused on her sexual parts and commented about them. He became emotionally stuck in fear as an adolescent boy.

Decades later, he was much the same: unmarried and watching women. Here was a man who was afraid to let go of something he had been practicing for forty years. If he continued to rehearse these behaviors, he would not learn anything new. With therapy and the love of his family, he confronted the bishop of the diocese where the abuse occurred. The process, the compassion of the bishop, and the removal of the offending priest from the priesthood helped this man a great deal—for a while. Then he returned to his fear and his habit of sexual immaturity. When asked if he planned to schedule with a therapist, he said he could not take the time because of work demands. When questioned if he intended to pursue a legal path with the diocese, he said he did not because he was afraid of what others might think of his intentions. He feared that people would think less of him if he was awarded money. This was an individual existing in fear rather than living truly and completely. The way he was managing his fear trapped him in his adolescence—thirty years in his past. This is a sad case, but it is repeated many times every day.

What Is Fear?

In our society there are many names and euphemisms for fear and for our responses to fear—words that do not sound so *bad*. These words include anxiety, concern, worry, trepidation, shyness, avoidance, and caution. These terms may sound better, but they still represent fear. To say we are "hesitating" is describing fear in a situation. Fear is related to terror, dread, desperateness, horror, fright, panic, and alarm. Shock and foreboding are also about fear, as are being scared or apprehensive. *Jumpy* and *tense* along with *edgy* and *uptight* are synonyms for fear. We use these other words and develop a variety of defenses in order to minimize fear.

No matter what name we use to describe fear, the same physiological reaction is involved. It is a physical arousal caused by the anticipation of something bad happening. Our heart rate increases, our breathing speeds up, and we may have sweaty palms. This is the classic *fight-or-flight response*, which is an adaptive response to fear that originated millions of years ago. The reaction allows us to focus our thoughts on the threatening object or person. The adrenaline surging through our bodies results in increased blood flow to the large muscles of our legs and arms and around our heart and lungs. If we have to fight, we are pumped and ready. If we decide to run, we also have the energy and blood flow for that. However, sometimes, instead of fighting or fleeing, we freeze. We become paralyzed or numb in the face of the fear object or situation.

Some level of fear is appropriate. It helps us to protect ourselves and to examine where and with whom we are safe. However, we do not need the intense fight or flight activation in most situations and for most relationships in today's world. Even so, it is part of our genetic structure and neurology, so it gets triggered. If we do not learn to manage fear well, we have responses that are inappropriate in certain circumstances.

Fear, Control, Ego, and Faith

Shakespeare may have been right when he wrote that "all the world's a stage, and all the men and women merely players." If that is true, the themes of the play could be fear, control, and ego. How we deal with, avoid, or change these themes determines the quality of our lives, our relationships, and our growth. In some social situations, we feel threatened when someone challenges our position on politics, theology, or how to set a table. Being threatened is related to fear—maybe an old fear of making a mistake. To deal with the anxiety we may attempt a control strategy such as belittling another person or her position. In doing so, we think that we are *right* and that she is *wrong*. We all know people who behave in this manner. We may not enjoy being around them because they do not compromise, do not hear us, and are difficult to connect with. Yet we oftentimes behave the same way. Behaving dogmatically and with self-centeredness will not lead to growth and fulfillment.

Control attempts are usually attached to self-centeredness and ego. They typically occur when a person is disconnected from their emotions and compassion for others. Manipulation to attain control in our lives can be obvious or subtle. A patient of mine was very upset with his prescription-abusing wife. His maneuvers did not work the way he intended. Coming home late to punish her did not work. Guilt and shame endeavors were unsuccessful. One day in my office he sat back in the sofa and said, "I've been doing this all backward. I've been praying for God's will in my life, but I've been praying for my will in her life." His efforts were keeping him from peace within himself, and they were not affecting his wife in any positive manner. "I don't have a problem on the job," he said to me, referring to his assertiveness and confidence in speaking up for himself. "I don't have a problem asking for what I want, meeting new people, or trying something different. But I haven't been able to do that with my family." It would have been reasonable to assume that if he exhibited these behaviors at work, he would be able to use them at home. In fact, he was capable. But he was also very afraid.

Growth in a career or in a familial situation requires a significant measure of faith. The more fear there is, the less faith there tends to be. If you are not particularly afraid of potential customers turning you down, you might require little faith to deal with fear. But if your fear is about your wife's continuing disappointment in you, you may need to pray for a lot more faith. Sometimes we trust too much in our own power and ability to control people and events. We work hard so that consequences happen more or less as we want them to happen. This belief in our power can increase our ego. If you think that you can make things happen, you do not need God. You do not need to call upon God for help, because you suppose that you can do it all. A parishioner I knew, who was very active in his church, said this: "My ministry puts me in a lot of places to do good or try to make things better. Then the Lord takes over."

Fear and Relationships

Life—when it is lived most fully—is about having meaningful relationships with God, ourselves, and others. The most fulfilling relationships involve being of service to others, giving rather than taking, and showing compassion. It is the mismanagement of fear in our lives that keeps us from living life completely. Many people are not living; they merely exist. Others feel lonely and hollow inside because their relationships are not satisfying. Some individuals are diminished spiritually because they behave with self-centeredness. It is with fear and control that we lose connection with (forget) who we are. It is with love and service that we learn (remember) who we are. Our problems do not begin with too much love. They begin and continue because of too much fear, too many attempts at controlling others, and too much ego invested in having things and people be the *right* way—our way.

Many, if not most, of the fears we have as adults are learned and carried over from our childhoods. For instance, a child's fear of rejection can manifest itself later in adulthood. In fact, a man I knew had a fear of rejection strong enough to prevent him from inviting a female friend on a date. He did not have the fears of an adult male. Rather, he held onto a forty-year-old's fears from his childhood when his parents were extremely critical of his academic efforts. This worry had become a theme in his life. If this man did not update his attitude and behavior, his childhood fears would continue to run his life. He has the opportunity to change his old habits and fears. If he does not, he will not individuate from his parents and the past. In essence, he will continue to live in his parents' house even though he physically moved out twenty years before.

A woman told me how frustrated and angry she was about her husband, who never threw anything away. He was afraid of not having something when he needed it. For example, he was fifty years old and still had the jeans he wore in college. He had not put them on in years because they were too small. Still, he couldn't manage to throw them away or even give them to Goodwill. This man seemed more attached to material "things" than to his wife. She was furious and said that she thought her husband was more concerned with his old and numerous golf shoes than with the state of their marriage.

Attempts at Control to Get Safety and Predictability

We possess a built-in need for safety in our lives. Safety for an infant is to be held by his parent. Safety for the pregnant mother is to visit her physician frequently. Safety for the child is to know her father will look under the bed and chase away the monsters. Safety for the father is to have a job and a home for his family.

Many of us do not experience much safety in adulthood because we did not have enough of it during our developmental years. If we have fears as children, we search for safety. We begin to copy or create control strategies such as manipulating, inducing guilt, whining, bullying, or avoiding conflict. We gravitate toward thoughts and activities that reduce our fear, at least temporarily. It is unlikely that we choose these strategies consciously. Instead, we start to use them if they work. We continue to practice using them, and then we become very good at it.

As we grow, we learn some very useful and adaptive behaviors. We also acquire some that are dysfunctional. But we are desperate when we cling onto them and do not realize that they have built-in limitations to change. We learn defenses and erect walls between ourselves and others—including God. Over time, we discover both healthy and unhealthy self-care strategies. However, after many years of use, unhealthy behaviors become worn and no longer provide the depth of safety that we want and need.

We realize that we can reduce our fear, for at least a little while, by engaging in behaviors that make future events more predictable. Infants learn that when they cry their mommies come to them to provide food, change a diaper, or sing a lullaby. Children learn to manipulate. They may whine over and over that they "need" a cookie. The parent may give in just to quiet the child. So the child discovers that whining results in cookies, and she continues to do it to get what she wants. Whining, manipulating, inducing guilt, and other similar strategies are often attempts at control. They are ways to increase the odds of getting what we crave and make future events more foreseeable. When the future is more predictable, we feel safer and have less fear. We learn to practice more and more control strategies, but there is one problem: we really cannot control people and events. If we could, each of us would be a god.

We can take good care or bad care of what occurs inside of us: our attitudes, emotions, and behaviors. Yet there are many variables operating outside of us, and these are very difficult to influence. Oftentimes, we cannot "fix" what is outside of us. We cannot "control" what is outside of us. Because externally oriented consequences are variable and frightening, it is important that we learn to positively manage what is within us. Control, true safety, peace, and well-being are inside of us, not outside of us.

Missed Opportunities

As we age and experience more of life, we may realize that something is missing—something that would provide the nurturance and care that deep inside we desire. Even so, we often prevent ourselves from changing. We do not always act upon the opportunities and invitations presented to us that offer more intimacy with others. We are afraid of the consequences of revealing our true selves. And these fears may have had such a long history that they become core fears that run our lives.

We can pray in great earnest and open our hearts to God. And then, at the first sign of internal or external conflict, we shut down and revert to our old patterns that are fueled by core fears. Our fear often overrides our faith. We are familiar with our fears; we have lived with them for years. We want to be close with God, but we may not practice faith building as much as fear building. It is a psychological principle that what we practice is what we make progress with. We might become very good at avoiding or disguising our fears because that is what we practice. Because we disguised our fears or were unaware of them, we remain stuck in our old patterns of handling fear. It is common sense that where there is no awareness, there is no change. We are given faith to deal with fear. We need faith because fear is so prevalent, occurs so often, and is created by us so often. Growth requires addressing our fears and having the spiritual faith to do so.

Some Fear Is Useful

Fear is an emotion that keeps us aware and allows us to take appropriate action. A mother will look often at her sleeping baby to make certain she is comfortable. Another mother may decide not to take her son to a birthday party when the hosting family is ill. Fear can help us take necessary care of ourselves and others.

Fear is a part of the human genetic code. It was programmed into us hundreds of thousands of years ago by our surviving ancestors. Those ancestors that had too little fear were eaten or killed before they could pass on their genes. There is much to fear today in the twenty-first century as well. Some examples are obvious, such as erratic drivers on the freeway. Some are subtler, or less immediate, such as the fear of a terrorist attack.

Thoughts are attached to all fears. Some thoughts are appropriate and some are foolish, contrived, and out of touch with reality. For example, an intelligent person may fear he is not smart. Consequently, he creates feelings of inadequacy and carries them around in a small, secret corner of his heart. Someone may be beautiful but believe that her nose is too large and fears being made fun of. Others are concerned their children will embarrass them or that their spouse will leave them. We believe the stories we create about ourselves, such as those involving our inadequacies and self-criticisms. We create many of our fears and continue to believe them, sometimes for a lifetime.

How did this process happen, and how did we get stuck in it? Just as importantly, how do we get out of it? Recovering from our past and updating to the present time period involves both psychology and spirituality. With psychology we can analyze our backgrounds and learn along with events, words, and actions that trigger a reaction in us. Psychological principles and techniques assist us with growth. Spirituality helps us to know we are not alone as we change. It teaches us that there is more to life than what is seen and touched. Spirituality is necessary for the full integration of all four parts of ourselves: the spiritual, intellectual, emotional, and behavioral. The next chapter and those that follow will trace the steps of our development and will describe the process of recovery, change, and growth.

CHAPTER 2

HOW WE LEARNED OUR
FEAR-BASED BEHAVIORS

In my family, we could normalize any abnormal event.
—FORMER PATIENT

THE FOUR PRINCIPLES

I N SOME OF OUR MOST important relationships, such as marriage and parenting, our goals are to show love and to be as vulnerable as small children. A child is not afraid to love or to approach others with delight. But what happens to that capacity to love, to be vulnerable, and to grow? Even as adolescents, we do not show love as we did when we were children. How do we change as we age?

During childhood many of us learn to be afraid of bullies, are embarrassed to speak in front of classmates, or fear the loss of a close friend. We have these fears and are sometimes taught by others how to deal with them. What we learn as children serves a purpose at that time, but may be inadequate later in life. If we hide from these fears and do not address them as we grow up, some of them may be present in adulthood. Consequently, we do not really *grow up*.

As children, we may misbehave in school and then fear that the teacher will call our parents. So when the phone rings it seems to be saying, "This is it. Here comes trouble. You're going to get it now." We have the fear within us. It is not in the phone. In actuality, the phone rings with the same tone and noise every time. We learned a fear response then and can learn a new response now. It is through this process that we come to fear the ringing. We manage it well now, or we mismanage it now.

When we are young, we grab onto something, someone, or some style that helps reduce our fears—at least temporarily. An image that comes to mind is this: being under water in a river with a tremendous fear of drowning. You reach up for the arms of people overhead, and in desperation, you clutch tightly. You are pulled from the water, but you grasp onto a huge snake that carries you up into a tree where it slowly strangles and eats you. Sometimes, the fear reactions we learn as children become very problematic—they can *strangle and eat* us. Just because you escape one fearful situation, it does not mean that you are safe and will remain safe. When we grab desperately we may be grabbing poorly.

We are not born with fearful, controlling thoughts and behaviors. When we are older we do not consciously decide to have strange worries and to spend much of our energy dealing with them. Moreover, we do not resolve to have thoughts and fears about inadequacy and negative self-talk. We do not decide who or what we will be afraid of or have anxiety about. We acquire these thoughts and behaviors as part of the natural learning process. This progression can be clarified by examining the *four principles of learning*.

PRINCIPLE 1: MOST HUMAN BEHAVIOR IS LEARNED

Most human behavior is not present at birth but is acquired later. A newborn may not be a blank sheet, a tabula rasa, as was once hypothesized. There are, in fact, parts of our neurology that are "hardwired," and this causes certain behaviors to unfold over time. One newborn differs from another in terms of activity level, size, speed of weight gain, and response to being held. Obviously, there is hardwiring that is present in an infant at birth. Otherwise, why would the infant suck to obtain nourishment? However, the infant is not born speaking English or being afraid of the bully down the street. These and most other behaviors—including our fears—are learned.

PRINCIPLE 2: WE LEARN BY INTERACTING WITH PEOPLE AND OBJECTS IN OUR ENVIRONMENT

A female patient of mine once told me the following: "It seemed I could never please my mother. Nothing was ever good enough. She told me my hair did not look good enough and my clothes did not fit right. If I cleaned my room, I heard about what I missed and not about what I did right. To her, I could not set the table right, or load dishes in the dishwasher right." This woman had learned about herself, her image, and her competency through interaction with her mother. She did not learn in a vacuum free of people. The daughter did not learn by sleeping but by actively engaging with others and objects.

If your two-year-old child moves around the kitchen when you cook, you will not want her to burn herself on the stovetop. You may tell her that it is very hot and that it will hurt if she touches it. Most children will look at you and nod their heads as if they understand. But some of them have not yet learned what *hot* means. So when you are not looking, the child might reach up and put her hand on the hot burner. Immediately she feels the pain and screams. When the child is calmer, you can tell her again that a burner is hot, that's why she got hurt, and she shouldn't ever touch it when it's hot. Yet again the child tilts her head as if she comprehends. Later on in the afternoon she wants to go outside and play. But you tell her that she cannot because it is too hot outside. For the next few days the child refuses to go outside at all. She is slowly learning what hot is, but she may still have it wrong. Children are not born knowing about temperatures just as they are not born knowing themselves. It is only through interaction with others and objects that we learn if we are adequate or inadequate, cute or funny-looking, and smart or are not quite as smart as the neighbor child.

Fears are learned in our social environment, and they are demonstrated with others in our social environment. The fears we have can keep us emotionally and behaviorally arrested during early stages of development. Our bodies may outgrow the clothes we wore ten or twenty years ago, but our fear reactions and habits may still be those we learned in the past, not changing much over time.

If we associate with spiritual people, we are likely to learn from them. We may copy what they do and become more spiritual. On the other hand, we may rebel and resist doing what they do, thereby weakening the spiritual connection within us. In either circumstance we learn by interacting with people. If we go to church when it is empty and quiet, we may learn to enjoy meditating or praying in silence. Alternatively, we may learn that we do not want to be alone in church because it is too quiet, or we are afraid to be close to God. Again, we acquired a path by interacting, this time with the church sanctuary.

Principle 3: The Behaviors We Learn Serve a Purpose

Behaviors are learned and maintained based on the consequences of the behavior. Consequences determine whether or not the behavior assists us in adapting more successfully. A behavior is learned when (1) a reward follows it, (2) when punishment is removed following it, or (3) when a punishment is given following it. After a child burns his hand on the stove, the heat becomes a punishment, and he stops touching the stove. He learns to avoid the appliance when it is hot.

If other kids call you clumsy when you play baseball, you may stop playing in order to escape the negative feedback. Escaping helps change your mood, and that could be the function of the behavior. Alternatively, you might tell the other children that they are also clumsy. They might agree, or at least stop being so hard on you, so that you learn to speak up for yourself. That behavior serves the purpose of improving your self-esteem. Therefore, the behavior results in a reward.

Over time, the experiences we have become the building blocks of stories that we create to describe ourselves. If our story is that we are good at playing sports, we play. If we are clumsy, we do not play. If we enjoy praying alone in church, we might make up a story explaining that it is easier to connect with God in church than somewhere else. Or we could create a story and an image of God embracing us; that might be very comforting. Individual experiences serve a purpose, and stories also have a purpose. Through this process, we assemble the basics of who we believe we are, how we view ourselves, how we believe others view us, and how competent we believe we are.

PRINCIPLE 4: BEHAVIORS BECOME HABITS

We do not need to think much, or be consciously aware of much, when we exercise a habit. We drive our car out of habit. We do not usually have to think about the amount of pedal pressure required to stop the car. We practice stopping thousands of times, and then we have car-driving habits. Since childhood, we may have told ourselves thousands of times that we are overweight, afraid of speaking in public, or not as smart as a sibling. We rehearse stories about ourselves over and over again.

Subsequently, they become habits of fear. Not only do habits steer your driving, but they also steer your life.

What we practice is usually what we become good at. We will not become perfect, but we will most likely become more accomplished. This is true if we are Olympic figure skaters competing for a gold medal. It is also true if we are working to lose weight or to become more peaceful and spiritual. If we want more spirituality, we must practice spirituality. If we desire more faith, we practice letting go of fear. If we would like to look in the mirror and see a person we love looking back at us, we need to practice saying loving comments to ourselves. It is not magic, and it is not difficult. But practice is needed. Specific practice strategies will be discussed in the sections on psychological and spiritual recovery.

Life will largely be run by our habits, so we must choose them carefully. It is difficult to be consciously aware all of the time. And it may not be useful or efficient in life to do so. Some habits, such as driving a car, can be useful. Unfortunately, many of our current habits are not learned in the current time period, but in our distant past. They are outdated, but because we continue to practice them, their strength is maintained. If you have a closet full of old jackets, boots, and sports equipment that you have not used in years, consider getting rid of them. These items take up space in your house—space that could be used for contemporary clothes and equipment. Similarly, our outdated habits take up space in our brains, in our behaviors, and in our lives. New and consciously chosen behaviors that make sense in your current life become stronger as you practice them. Novel behaviors can become strong enough to override old habits. Nevertheless, learned old habits, such as the fear of inadequacy, are programmed into our neurological makeup. They do not go away unless brain damage occurs.

What we learn as infants and children continues to operate within us in the background of our brains—just as computers have programs running unnoticed in the background while we work. We do not know about these old habits and stories until they begin to break down and cause problems. For example, a twenty-three-year-old man I know wanted to be an entrepreneur in the food business and eventually have his own restaurant. However, his mother said he ought to get a corporate job as his friend Johnny had done. "Johnny is making a really good salary," she said. She was salaried and understood salaried people, not entrepreneurs. The son reacted strongly, even overreacted, to what his mother said. As a result, he started skipping classes in college, did not study for tests, and was distracted. He was sabotaging himself and his dreams. Why? He was reacting as if he were eight years old and his mommy had said that he could not ride his bike by himself to the end of the street. She does not trust him, and she fears what might happen to him. She wants him safe at home. And now, at twenty-three, he is having the same reaction to his "mommy" that he had fifteen years ago. He learned this pattern by interacting with his mother, and they have practiced it numerous times over the years.

The Story of Erica

Erica had an eating disorder. She ate and then purged. Erica also ate food for comfort. When she had intense feelings and wanted relief she had dinner with her close friends, Mr. Ice Cream and Ms. Cookies. After years of this habit, she started attending a twelve-step program to change her behavior. She had successfully accomplished this when I met her. However, Erica's complaint at the time was that she was always angry at someone in her house. It appeared that she had substituted anger for eating and was using it as a comfort emotion.

The problem was that Erica's unresolved and underlying family-of-origin dynamics were fueling her symptoms of both eating and anger. One of the fundamental issues was about control. "In my childhood," she said, "I never got what I needed, not even affection, from my parents unless I begged for it and did not stop until they gave me what I needed. I was brought up to believe that I always had to look nice, that my appearance reflected back on the family." Erica's parents worked to control her behavior. They were afraid of what others might think or say about them if their daughter did not look or behave in a certain manner. Erica had learned her fear lessons well.

One morning when Erica came in to see me she had put her young daughter's hair in a ponytail and then taken her to school. She told her daughter in a demanding and intolerant voice that she had better not remove the ponytail. She was attempting to control her daughter out of fear just as her mother had done two decades before. My patient went on to say, "I've been living my life through my kids and husband. First I made food be my god, and then I made my husband be my god. Next I made my oldest be my god, and now I am all preoccupied with and focused on my daughter." Erica had made up a story about her life and roles in relation to the people around her. She was acting it out.

THE STORIES WE CREATE ARE OFTEN SCARY

None of us can read minds. I know I cannot. When someone talks to me I hear only what he or she says. Then I interpret based on my mood, experiences, beliefs, and emotions—including my fears. I do not infer based on what the individual *meant* to say. And what I hear may be different than what was intended. Oftentimes, we make up story lines or entire stories including plots and characters. These stories may be positive or negative, healthy or unhealthy, loving or fearful. In any event, we make them up from the recesses of our brains, and base them upon interpretations of our experiences. Many times the theme of the story is fear.

For example, another patient of mine, Dave, called his wife during the day while she was at work, but she did not answer the phone. Normally, when this occurred, Dave would become fearful and make up a story that she must be angry with him or that she was with other people who were more important to her than he was. He had inadequacies, a need for approval, and a fear of loss. Based on what he had learned in his psychotherapy sessions, Dave identified his needs and the fears attached to them. Rather than allowing his anxiety to grow and attempt control strategies—such as calling his wife's coworkers—Dave took a deep breath, said some affirmations, and practiced faith-talk. Within the half hour, his wife called him and explained that she was on a conference call and could not switch from it to answer his phone call. She said that she had telephoned as soon as the conference call finished and wanted to know if he would like to meet her for dinner at their favorite Italian restaurant. His initial fear was not founded on reality but on his learned responses and defenses to perceived neglect. The neglect had not even come from his wife but from his experiences before he met her. In therapy, Dave learned that he could not successfully run from what was within himself and that his fears were within him. In order to reduce our fears, we must explore ourselves, come to know ourselves, and be willing to change.

One day in therapy my patient, Mary, said, "I feel out of place with the people on a church committee. They know the who's-who and I don't. I know they want me on the committee, but what is it about me that they find likeable? I'm surprised that they do like me." She was not born thinking of herself with this doubt. It was learned, and now it is strong because she has been rehearsing it for many years. Mary recalled being shy—that is, fearful—as a child. Her recollection was that no one in her immediate family supported or encouraged her. Her mother was critical of her, and, similarly, Mary is critical of herself. If she is to change, she will need to learn to give herself the support that her mother did not provide her. But she is afraid to change or to believe in her own worth the way that the people on the committee do.

Examples of other fear-based patients include a white woman named Nancy who did volunteer work in a church. One of her responsibilities was to assist a black woman, Clara, with her errands because she was a widow and wheelchair-bound. Nancy's complaint was this: "Clara affectionately calls me her white daughter, and I really do enjoy helping her on Saturdays. But she makes too many plans for us after church on Sunday, and honestly I have other things I want to do. I have my own errands and need to get ready for work on Monday. But I don't want to turn her down. I don't want to disappoint her." I asked Nancy to consider the fact that sometimes it is necessary for people to be disappointed in us. It indicates that boundaries have been created. Disappointments and boundaries can then be discussed, and people can update their relationships. Moreover, none of us are perfect. We all make mistakes, and we can learn just as much from mistakes and disappointments as successes.

LIST YOUR FEARS

There are numerous types of fears: toward objects such as elevators, toward others because of abandonment or emotional harm, and toward God for our nonspiritual thoughts and actions. In the book of Genesis in the Bible, God gave Adam the authority to name "…all the livestock, the birds of the air and the beasts of the field" (2:20, New International Version, NIV). There is much symbolism in this act. It is not just God being benevolent and Adam showing creativity. In Old Testament days, when you named something, it meant that you had dominion over that thing or person. And with dominion came little or no fear. Similarly, if we name our fears and take time to write them down, we begin the process of reducing our fears by gaining intellectual and spiritual dominion over them. Frequently, I ask my patients to list their fears and to write them in sentences instead of single words. I have learned that most people compile lists of at least thirty—and sometimes as many as fifty—fears. Usually they are not aware of the majority of their fears. I asked a patient to do this. Part of her list included the following:

» I fear tomorrow.

» I fear I'll be wrong.

» I fear someone won't love me.

» I fear I'll be misunderstood.

» I fear I'll be left.

» I fear getting old and losing my looks.

» I fear being alone.

» I fear I'll be rejected.

» I fear people lying to me.

» I fear that I'll make bad choices.

» I fear I won't find another job making at least the amount I make now.

» I fear that I don't give enough to other people.

» I fear that I'm unlovable.

Fear is a natural human emotion. But an emotion, by definition, is not reasonable or logical—that is what thoughts are about. An emotion simply *is*. Fear is a survival emotion, necessary for us to protect ourselves. It helps keep us aware and on guard for danger. We do not want to have an absence of fear. That would be naive and foolish. On the other hand, we do not want to have too much fear.

My patient George did have a list of fears. He was afraid to say no to his wife because of a fear of disappointing her by his actions. So he deprived himself by giving her what she seemed to be asking for and ended up resenting her and himself. George was afraid of being alone, not being loveable, or not being loved for who he really was. After the divorce, he knew that he had been so desperate to have his wife love him unconditionally that he did not love himself unconditionally. George explained that when he was in college, if he botched an assignment and did not turn it in, he would freeze up and not complete any other assignments for days. He said that when he was a child, if he made one small mistake his father would harass him about it for weeks. The father never apologized, and George was always afraid. George's emotional paralysis was caused by fear.

He was anxious that he would not ever be able to catch up on his assignments. So he gave up.

A patient said, "My friend in golf plays one bad shot and that ruins that hole and the next several until he hits a good shot and that makes that, and the next two or three usually good." This golfer is carrying fear baggage from one hole to the next. Many people carry baggage from one day to the next, one week to the next, one person to the next, and one decade to the next. Fears are typically more numerous than we think and are very heavy baggage to support.

Chapter 3

The Illusion of Control

*People are only influenced in the direction in which they
want to go, and influence consists largely in making them
conscious of their wishes to proceed in that direction.*
—T. S. Eliot

I F CONTROL EXISTED, PEOPLE, PLACES, and things would be or would
do what we wanted them to—with little or no resistance. And they
would continue indefinitely until we sent them in a different direction.
Obviously, this is not true. We are taught that we can control and can
be controlled. The truth is much closer to this: we cannot control others,
and they cannot control us.

Control strategies take numerous forms. Any kind of abuse, whether
it is physical, sexual, verbal, or emotional, is an attempt at control. We
also endeavor to control others in the following ways: using guilt, yelling,
crying, whining, keeping secrets, threatening, demeaning, insulting,

nagging, lying, using passive-aggressiveness, procrastinating, victimizing, pretending to be ill, and playing roles such as victim and "poor me."

People make their own choices, even if they are made unconsciously. Sometimes their choices are in line with what we want done. However, this does not signify that we can control or change them. Additionally, people's choices are oftentimes not in accord with our own. We may be bothered by people's choices. And we may even have good intentions, such as getting someone sober, slimmer, or more educated. The fear of not having power, particularly over others, can lead to compulsions such as overeating, blaming, excuse making, drinking, shopping, exercising, volunteering, smoking, working, purging, bingeing, hoarding, and restricting food.

Sometimes we seem to have influence over others, and sometimes we even seem to *save* them from their own poor choices. But we are only able to accomplish this if they listen to us and then choose to follow our recommendations. So they run their lives. We do not. For example, I can control my car when I am driving. I cannot direct other drivers or what they may do to my car or to me. I can also control how motivated I am at work in my practice. However, I have no influence over the number of patients who get sick and may cancel an appointment, or the amount of appreciation I may receive at the end of a given day.

CONTROL AND NEEDS

We utilize control strategies because we are normal human beings struggling to have our basic needs met, one of which is safety. The opposite of safe is unsafe, and being unsafe is associated with the feeling of fear. In order to obtain more safety, we try to control people and things around us so that our interactions become more predictable. If future actions and consequences become predictable, the unfamiliar and unknown are minimized. Accordingly, more of our needs for safety are met.

Efforts to control have built-in rewards. With each perceived success at control, the reward impact becomes stronger. And if we practice anything long enough we become good at it. The only problem is this: most control is an illusion. People who practice control delude themselves. They are using up their valuable time, energy, and opportunities for growth.

If you have a normal need for connection with others—but fear being rejected—you may seek out someone to control by using guilt to get them to spend time with you. Or you may reject them first to avoid the fear. Some people use activities such as overeating or dieting to gain some sense of control, routine, or predictability. Others may use exercise, work, or shopping in their fear-based efforts to control something, be in charge, or have less fear. These human needs are normal. However, the way in which we meet these needs may be inhumane to others and to ourselves.

A divorced man I knew allowed his teenage daughter to repeatedly use his company-owned laptop because her Internet surfing had resulted in attacks by viruses that crashed her computer. He was afraid that if he did not allow her to use his laptop that she might spend less time with him. He believed that he could control certain outcomes (his daughter returning to his house) by continuing to give her Internet access. But by doing so, he perpetuated an illusion of control. He avoided his fear of confrontation and loneliness and put his own job in jeopardy.

A patient of mine and some of his friends used to play music together in a local bar just for fun. My patient said, "Bill is a nice guy until we get on the stage to play our music, and then he's a real pain. He wants to be top dog on stage." So Bill attempts to control the situation because he fears the band will not receive enough attention and do well unless he is pushy.

Another patient, Jacqueline, told me about her husband and his desire for respect from her. She explained how he tried to bully his way into receiving her respect instead of earning it. His bullying was a control strategy. The husband's parents had demanded his respect using control maneuvers, yelling, and threats. Ultimately, Jacqueline's husband tried to connect with her through these control strategies as well.

CONTROL STRATEGIES ARE LEARNED

Control strategies begin early in life—long before we know what they are or can even talk about them. But at that young age, we still have needs for attention and affection. We grasp at any approach that allows us to get our needs met without really knowing what we are doing. The intellect may not be operating, but emotions certainly are—especially fear. We may need connection with someone and then fear losing it because Mommy pays too much attention to our new baby sister. As a result, we might cry, refuse food, or hit the baby. We learn that those strategies get us the consideration that we need. The attention may be negative, but any attention is better than none. Consequently, we learn a rudimentary control strategy. Later on in life when we have the ability to ask for positive attention or to talk about our feelings, we instead may use a well-established control habit with energy and momentum behind it. So we do not change, but remain unaware.

Some fear is necessary, but too much fear will lead to desperate attempts to reduce it. Some fear, such as that of heights, is innate and present in infants. Control strategies are not innate. They are learned as we interact with people and things.

The problem with repeating a control strategy is that the more we practice, the better we become. This is all part of the *psychology of learning*. Too much practice of control tactics can lead to the development of compulsions—about others, ice cream eating, or shopping, for example. Before we even realize it, the habits and compulsions become part of our personalities. You may suppose "this is just me" and not believe that the personality characteristics that were learned can be changed. You may not know the origins of some of your fears. Therefore, the fear is not examined for what it is—instead, it is perpetuated. And then we continue the strategy while telling ourselves we cannot change. The manifestations of our unresolved childhood and adolescent fears are in our adulthoods.

I know a woman who had a friend, Jennifer, with a shopping

compulsion. Actually, it was more than just a shopping compulsion; it was also a buying compulsion. She shopped and bought numerous times each week. She frequented bargain stores that sold discontinued or damaged goods and would use any excuse to buy something. Jennifer would spend hours and hours in a store picking out things until her shopping cart was full, just to end up parking it near the checkout counter and buying a few items. Jennifer desperately needed a way to occupy herself so that she would not have to think and face her fears. The roots of her fear came from her childhood and anxiety about not ever fitting in. This woman is stuck in a compulsion process. She is developmentally arrested in her adolescence because she is still working so hard to fit in. She is not an adult at peace but an adolescent in conflict, and she is now in her fifties.

Most people try a control strategy at some point. Children use it with their magical thinking about the weather when they chant, "Rain, rain, go away; come again another day." Children will lie and say they are sick as a way to avoid completing chores, going to school, or doing some other activity. Adolescents try to control when they threaten not to remain friends with someone if that someone remains friends with someone else.

Like Napoleon, most of us will eventually meet our Waterloo—some event that reveals our powerlessness over people and situations. At that point, many of us learn that our old coping mechanisms, including the use of control, are not sufficient to keep us safe. Those who accept this fact are able to grow and move on. Those who do not accept it are trapped by old habits, control mechanisms, and fears. Then things become worse, not better.

The language in our society reflects and feeds our control orientation. For example, a husband once told me that he wanted to see a particular movie and said, "I'll see if I can talk my wife into going to the movie with me." At some unconscious level, he believed he had the power to control her thought patterns and her behaviors. He did not say, "I'll tell her why I want to go and ask her to go with me." That would have been a statement that recognized he does not control his wife. His attitude and behavior resulted in reduced communication and emotional intimacy with her.

Peace and Control

If we try to control someone else, we always feel fear at some level. We are afraid of losing that control and having the other person do what they want. This is a focus on trying to change the external—such as the other—and not a focus on changing the internal, which is us. We can have peace of mind only when we control ourselves, know ourselves, and relate to others with love and compassion.

Evelyn was a patient who was very concerned about what others thought. She had a significant fear of being left or rejected. She said that she used to be very shy and was always overly worried about what people believed about her. Evelyn avoided people, which led to negative self-talk, which in turn caused diminished self-esteem, which then lead to shyness and avoidance, which ultimately lead to negative comments by people who would then sometimes leave her. She was stuck in a circular trap. She felt like a dog chasing its tail. Eventually, Evelyn asked me if people could change their behaviors. I replied first with a question: "Can you learn to ride elevators even if you are afraid of them now? Of course you can." I further explained, "You can learn assertiveness even if you learned shyness first. It is the same as learning to drive a car even if you first learned to ride a bicycle."

Attempts at control strategies can produce serious consequences in intimate relationships. A husband and wife I once counseled had two dogs. One of the pets was a six-month-old puppy; he was a replacement for an older dog that had died the previous year. Both the husband and wife believed in appropriate training of the young dog, but the husband could be very demanding of the puppy. His actions bordered on abuse. The wife complained that sometimes her husband acted the same way with her. She explained that he seemed to equate obedience with love, whether it was with the dogs or with her. The husband had an agenda for the dogs and his wife. Unfortunately, the plan did not include patience or compassion. He was so entirely focused on the outcome that he became impatient. In his mind, if the dog and his wife loved him, they would do what he asked and do it swiftly. This is a type of control thinking.

In the couple's therapy sessions, it became clear that the husband's definition of love was very different from his wife's. When they argued about love there was no progress toward a resolution, because they were referring to two very different concepts. They came to the same impasse numerous times and walked away from each other, emotionally and physically. When each finally became willing to hear the other, they addressed the central problem. We wrote a definition of love to which they both agreed. It did not include obedience or domination. They began to make progress, to leave old behaviors behind, and to learn new healthy ones.

Control Strategies Are Self-Centered

What is the opposite of control? Acceptance is the opposite. Control involves a focus on the *self*, although it may look and sound like a focus on the *other*. The father who demands that his young son play Little League baseball—even though the son does not want to play and is not good at it—may want the boy to succeed and be social. At some level, even unconsciously, the father could aspire to have a son who he can be proud of. Perhaps the dad does not want to be embarrassed in front of other parents and wants to relive his success at sports.

Control involves disrespect and a violation of the boundary of others. We can utilize control when we over-identify with someone else. We have a self-centered idea of the way the child should be, the marriage should be, or the church volunteer system should be. We also believe that it should be our way, not someone else's. Control strategies usually involve an inflation of the ego.

A former patient of mine did not realize it at the time, but had been using self-focused control maneuvers for much of her life. When her life began to slowly unravel she said, "There can't be something wrong with me. I'm the one who always takes care of everyone. They're not supposed to take care of me." Playing the role also meant maintaining an illusion of control over others. She added, "I learned it from my dad. He worked to keep everyone calm in the family because he couldn't stand noise." As she became healthier and found balance in her relationships, she became less one-sided. She realized that people were treating her differently. One of her neighbors commented to her, "You must be feeling much less stressed, because you haven't been baking as much banana bread as you used to." My patient was shocked to learn her bread baking was a stress thermometer. She used to bake this bread as a diversion when she was anxious, sometimes as many as ten loaves a week!

BLAME IS A GAME

Sometimes control tactics take the form of blaming others. It is an immature defense characteristic of children, but is often employed by adults who are emotionally arrested. A patient once said, "I grew up in a house where somebody was always at fault. If the milk was spoiled, somebody was at fault and would be yelled at. So we learned to deflect, avoid, and even attack back. And I am that way with my children." This man did not learn to take responsibility in the household he grew up in. In therapy sessions with his wife, he often blamed her for the mistakes and emotions he had. But there is no change in blame. If we blame others for our problems, our feelings, or the way we were raised, we are not taking responsibility for ourselves. If we make excuses, we are doing the same. Our growth comes as a result of taking responsibility, and that frees us to change our present lives and our future lives. Blaming and excuse making keep us trapped in the past.

The quality of our lives and the level of peace that we experience are largely determined by the choices we make. If you want to go to college in New York, you have to go to New York. If you want to swim in the pool, you have to get wet. But you do not have to go to college in New York, and you do not have to swim. Those are the choices you make. There are no excuses and no blaming. You are responsible for the consequences of the decisions you make.

Trying to control other people is comparable to attempting to control the weather. Once in a while it may look like you can do it, but the reality is that you cannot. The focus can be on changing yourself—not the other. If you do not like the rain, you can say you are angry and shake your fist because you don't want it to rain. Nonetheless, you will not change the weather. However, talking about the weather and appropriately sharing your feelings can certainly change you for the better. Don't blame the rain.

Some fear is fine and not based on control. Some fear is necessary to keep us aware and alert in order to protect ourselves and our loved ones in a healthy manner. For instance, I had a patient, Thomas, whose boss told him that he would have to move to their central office in another state if he wanted to keep his job. This caused a lot of fear for Thomas. However, his fear was appropriate, and it did not result in any effort on his part to control anyone. For example, he did not blame his boss or try to sabotage work in the office. Thomas said, "I prayed about my problem, and I asked God to help me figure out what to do." He decided to tell his boss that he could not move and why. He chose to live in faith and identified five local job possibilities. Before therapy, Thomas would most likely have felt overcome with fear. Consequently, he might have tried to control his boss and become angry with himself. He probably would have eventually taken it out on his wife as well. Thomas had grown a great deal in one year.

Good Boundaries Are Not Control Attempts

Attempting to control others is not the same as having healthy boundaries. The first is manipulation, and the second is related to self-care. Like many parents, one couple I know has children who used drugs and alcohol irresponsibly enough that they had academic, professional, and legal problems. My patients said to me, "We now have a onetime get-out-of-jail-free policy. If they make that first mistake, we'll get them out. If they make any more they are responsible." This is not bad parenting, and it is not abandonment. Instead it is a healthy plan with good boundaries. This strategy also recognizes the reality of drug use and the recovery process. Moreover, from a psychological viewpoint, it acknowledges the cognitive differences among people. Your children may not learn the way you learn.

You may learn not to do something because someone has warned you about the negative consequences. Yet not all people have good visual imagery skills or auditory comprehension or a well-developed capacity to think in terms of sequences and consequences. Many individuals learn primarily through experience that must be repeated many times. Some young adults do not use drugs because they fear jail. On the other hand, some kids continue to use drugs because they behave as if jails do not exist. Many people who have attention deficit/hyperactivity disorder (ADHD), with or without the hyperactivity, or a related learning disability do not process information well enough to keep them from repeating the same mistakes.

A mother I knew spoke with her son as if she were talking to a clone of herself. She was reasonable, so she spoke reasonably to him—but reason, logic, and common sense were not his primary learning tools. He returned to live with his parents, at age twenty-one, after having left three colleges. This fact alone indicated there was a problem and that he was different from his parents: they had both attended one college all four years. When the son drove home in a beat-up old car with no driver's license or insurance, it also was a clue that he did not operate with reasonableness as his parents did. The mother learned that her son was on probation for a DUI, had not been paying his fine, and did not inform his probation officer that he was leaving the state. This alarming information should have provided a clue that simply talking with the boy about breaking some house rules—such as not stealing from Mom and

Dad—would not have an impression on him. The parents continued to talk reasonably, and the son continued to steal from them.

I work with many inattentive, impulsive, or hyperactive (ADHD) young adults who are missing something: vital chemicals in their brains that allow them to respect boundaries. Often these patients do well in the military. In the military they are told when to get up, how to dress, when to eat, and how to walk. All of these actions are performed under intense supervision and with accountability. However, when they return to civilian life they often deteriorate rapidly because civilian life is not structured enough to compensate for what is missing in their brains. You may not be able to change the neurological functioning of your adult child, especially if he or she does not want to take medications. Consequently, you may be left with changing yourself. Accept what you cannot change, and change what you can.

CHAPTER 4

THE FOUR PARTS OF PEOPLE

Work like you don't need money. Love like you've
never been hurt. Dance like no one is watching.
—RICHARD LEIGH AND SUSANNA CLARK

WE ARE COMPOSED OF FOUR parts: spiritual, intellectual, emotional, and behavioral. When the parts are aligned in one dimension—when they are all closely connected—our lives work well. We are in contact with God, with ourselves, and with others. It is then that we are at peace and have little fear. Any conflict between what is inside and outside of us is diminished or removed. One of the best ways to enjoy life is to have all four parts united. Watch children. They have fun because their four parts are not disconnected. When kids do an activity, they do only *that* activity. They do not think about the next activity or evaluate how they did on the previous one.

Unfortunately, many people have parts that are detached from one another. For example, a man knows that he will not die from apologizing to his spouse (the intellectual), but he is afraid to apologize (the emotional) and does not want to apologize because he has a habit of not apologizing (the behavioral). When we behave with high levels of fear, we do not live in faith (the spiritual). So the four parts are not in line. Like rooms in a house, people can subsist in four different rooms: disconnected from each other and not communicating. It is then likely that fear and old habits will continue, and a person will merely exist rather than live.

THE SPIRITUAL PART

The spiritual part of us is connected to the divine. We all have a divine spark within us. Some nurture that spark and it becomes fire. We are not the masters of the universe; we did not create it. It will exist when we are gone, as individuals and as a species. There is more to life than we can see. There is the *unknowable*. A part of me knows that. I call this God. I do not see God, but I have faith there is God. Many things have occurred in my life that were fortuitous, opportune, or simply well timed. Given the laws of probability, these events ought not to have happened to me at all. Instead, they came about at just the perfect moment—as I was asking for them—and often in exactly the form I needed. I do not call these *coincidences*; I call them *Godcidences*.

There is hunger for a connection with God within us. We cannot put it aside completely, and we cannot successfully run away from it. The hunger is within us, so it goes where we go. The spiritual dimension of our lives cannot be ignored without significant cost in terms of growth, peace, and caring. The spiritual part of us is the first to be neglected and weakened when there is a disconnection among the four dimensions. It is the first to be broken off—to be separated from the wholeness that makes us human. We do not see the spiritual; we experience it. We perceive it and are in contact with it when it is our focal point. We experience it when we have peace within ourselves even though there may be conflict around us. If we focus on money, we will not have the spiritual.

If we focus on resentment, we will not have the spiritual. If we focus on doing God's work, we open the door to the spiritual.

THE INTELLECTUAL PART

It is in the intellectual that we talk to ourselves and use our creativity and imagination to write beautiful music or to abuse ourselves with criticism and judgment. None of the parts can be ignored without substantial damage to the whole. The intellectual, like the spiritual, must be heard and be in balance with the other three parts. The intellectual is that part that makes sense of what we perceive and experience. It is also what some call "the perceiver" or "the observer" in all of us. It is wholly human. It is not where "I" exist; that is a function of all four parts. It is where we know what is knowable. It is also about our dreams for the future and about our memories from the past. These are the "what might be" and "what once was." These memories and dreams are more intense at times, such as when someone dies. It is then that we deeply experience what is happening, but also grieve, thinking about memories. And we realize that our dreams of future times may not occur.

THE EMOTIONAL PART

By definition, emotions do not inherently have intelligence or reflection. Emotions simply are. We do not think an emotion; we simply have an emotion. It does not have to make sense—it just is. However, by thinking, we can recreate an emotion that is attached to a memory—to an experience we once had. Even our emotions about events that have not yet transpired can trigger an emotion that we once had. When we look at our pregnant daughter, we may have the emotion of love for the future grandchild. Yet that is still the result of having loving memories of holding other babies. We may think about dating someone and worry that we will be rejected. That fear is related to other rejections or hurt experiences that we have had. The love memory will not cause us

39

problems, but the fear memory can lead to emotional immobilization, avoidance of new relationships, and perpetuation of old habits.

The emotional part of us does not exist in isolation either. Activation of the emotional has consequences for the body and for the other three parts. Love causes the body to relax, and the intellectual focuses on soothing and safe thoughts. The spiritual, because God is love, connects with the other parts. The opposite is true for the feeling of fear, which causes adrenaline to course through our bodies and increase our stress. The intellectual then focuses on these symptoms, the perceived source of fear, and the possible consequences related to fear. Hence the spiritual is diminished as fear increases. If a car is coming across the median of the highway and looks like it might hit your car, fear is a very good response to have. Fear can be adaptive and can help us live another day.

Having an emotion is similar to having a physical sensation in your body. A pain in your shoulder exists and means something. Emotions exist and mean something. So sit with it, and examine what it means. We are more likely to admit to a physical pain, such as a knee ache, than to an emotional one. If you limp and someone asks how you are, you certainly share what happened. We could do the same with our emotions because they are also another part of ourselves.

THE BEHAVIORAL PART

If you want to become good at golf, then practice golf. If you want to learn to speak Italian, take Italian lessons and rehearse speaking in Italian. If you are good at fear in all its forms, such as anxiety and worry, you have obviously completed many repetitions. And if you repeat an action or thought often enough it will become a habit. A reflex in our body, such as the knee-jerk reflex, does not require reasoning. Habits are a notch or two above reflexes because they also do not require thinking. Habits are rehearsed so often that—in the presence of some cues, such as certain people or situations—they simply happen. And, once established, they can exist for a lifetime. However, old and negative habits can be weakened by practicing new and positive habits. If you learn to ride a bicycle as a child and do not ride a bike again for thirty years, you retain the behavioral habits you had when you first rode. For example, you will still know how to balance and turn. If as a child you learn not to hug people but then practice hugging as an adult, there will still be neurological connections in your brain for "not hugging." Old habits are not unlearned, so they can at times reappear.

ESTABLISH THE CONNECTION

Getting and staying connected with ourselves involves an integration of the four parts. Part of our intellect's job is to determine what our needs and wants are and to be aware of the emotions we have at any given time. Our intellect can also help formulate a plan to assist us in achieving our goals. If we do not know where we are coming from, where we are now, and where we want to be, we will probably never get there. Our bodies carry out plans that are developed through the integration of our heads and our hearts. Since it is difficult to overcome fear, it is important to reach out to a power greater than ourselves for strength and support. Our faith, a spiritual value, completes the integration, or connection, of all four parts of ourselves. If we know what we want or need, and do our share of the work, God will complete the task. We become one inside of ourselves rather than having four parts struggling against each other. Where there is no struggle, there is peace.

I had a male patient who was a professional athlete. He did the golf circuit during the season. He had been very successful for several weeks one season, but then he hit a so-called cold spell. We discussed the possibility of fatigue. So I asked how long he had been on the road. He replied he had been traveling eight weeks. When I asked how long he thought he ought to be on the road at a time he said, "Normally it would be two or three weeks before I would need a break to regroup and to practice." He knew what he needed, but he was not giving it to himself. He said he thought he had to keep going. This patient practiced bad habits while being fatigued, and this gave him the cold spell. His career that summer was not a life-and-death situation in which he had to keep going or die. He pushed himself the way he would never have pushed a young son if he had been traveling with him. I told him that if he would not do this to a child, then what he was doing to himself was probably abusive.

Partway through the summer I met with my patient again. He was very tired, and he said he wanted to do a lot of sleeping. He added, "I'd like to go to some movies just to get away." Sleeping and eating are appropriate, but they are only part of the necessary formula. If you are hungry and in need of a good-sized meal, then eating one corner of a slice of bread will be moving in the right direction, but it will not be sufficient.

This young man was ignoring the basic principle of staying connected with all four parts of himself: to give yourself what you need so you will be in balance. We need to practice the appropriate behavior, use our intellect to see ourselves plan and practice that behavior, examine our emotions, particularly fear, and walk through the fear. And we need to have faith that God will take care of us. A golfer needs to practice a great deal (the behavioral part) so that he or she will develop muscle memory and swing easily. Practice provides confidence, which reduces anxiety (fear). Practice also allows us to visualize the right swing and to see the ball going where you want it to go. To do well all four parts of ourselves must show up and be in balance and in alignment.

Life is spiritual and is lived one minute, one experience, and one interaction at a time. I know of a man who had difficulty playing golf this way. For example, he focused so intently on playing par golf on a par five hole that when he hit a bad drive he told himself he could still make par by hitting a great second shot—and then a good drop onto the green. Then he could putt in with two strokes for par. He was so preoccupied with the outcome of the hole that when he would hit his second shot from 350 yards out, he was really thinking about putting in and not of the shot he was making. He was disconnected.

When we lie, attempt to control others, operate with too much fear, or get into our compulsions and addictions, the first part we disconnect from is the spiritual. We disconnect most easily from what we cannot see. Connecting to something we can see, such as ice cream, coffee, cigarettes, sex, money, exercise, or any other activity can lead to excess and compulsivity. When we push spirituality away—when we push it away with our egos and compulsions—the second part of us to go is the intellectual. The brain says, "Do not look at the porn site," or "It doesn't make sense to say those mean things about your neighbor," or "Purging your food again will someday create a medical problem." But the emotional and behavioral parts do not listen to reason, and they push the spiritual and intellectual aside. We do today what we did yesterday out of habit and without reason, and we often operate out of fear. My patient June sobbed and said: "I know I have a pear-shaped body and I'm fat. I'm afraid to not purge because then I'll get fatter." She continued to purge at home. And so one more time she performed the behavior or compulsion out of fear. One more time she practiced it, and it kept getting stronger. We become good at what we practice.

When I am doing couples therapy, I often find that at least one of the partners is significantly disconnected—not just from his or her spouse, but also from God and from him- or herself. One spouse may be having an affair and want out of a marriage. If she does not want to be the one who initiates the divorce, she may—even unconsciously—act more abusively toward her husband so that he will become angry enough to leave her. The spouse who is manipulating and hedging her bets is disconnected from her spiritual compass. She is probably practicing old patterns of abuse and is fueled by fear—in this case, of how filing first for divorce might appear to others. Her body is disconnected from her spirit because she is living a lie and telling lies. She disengaged her mind and body from her emotions to escape her guilt and fear. She worked long hours, drank too much, and exercised too much. That is, she engaged in some compulsive behavior to avoid her feelings.

All four parts of us fit together like a puzzle. If one or two parts are missing or misplaced through disconnection, then there is only the semblance of a person. We have identity and peace only when all four parts are assembled, one connecting to the other and all in alignment. The four parts are interconnected and each contributes uniquely to make up who we are. When all four are connected, we—and many others—see who we truly are.

FEAR AND AFFECTION

Some men are afraid to show affection to their spouses, parents, or siblings. These men may be very affectionate with their young children but only hug their spouses for a second or two, usually accompanied with three pats on the back signifying "that's enough" or "it's over." Spiritually and mentally they may want to be more demonstrative, but they fear doing so, and their habits show avoidance rather than approach. Unlike children, who can have fun with affection, these men are too deeply immersed in their fears. Their emotions and behaviors are disconnected from their intellects and spirit.

Some people detach from society, family, and friends by isolating themselves physically. Others disconnect by isolating themselves emotionally and mentally. One of my patients has difficulty remaining connected to herself when there is conflict at home. She says, "I just shut down or I leave." Either way, she is not present for her family at those times.

We heal our bodies of division, disconnection, and conflict first by being aware of the disconnection and then by accepting it. If we do not accept what it is, then we perpetuate the division. A man I know primarily uses his intellect to cope with life and his fear. His mind is well developed, but the other parts of him are underdeveloped and unconnected. He plays to his brain. This creates problems because he does not show affection to his wife and kids. It is as if he were a tennis player who hits only with his forehand. Most of his opponents learn that to gain a point they simply need to play to his backhand. The remedy for him would be to strengthen his backhand until it is solid. Then his game would be more balanced. The same would be true of him practicing all four parts of himself to create more balance.

RESOLVING CONFLICT WITHIN OURSELVES

Conflict within ourselves often occurs when we are not doing what we *know* deep inside at the spiritual level—at the God-within-us level—that we ought to be doing. In order to have peace, conflict must be resolved. We perpetuate conflict when we do not accept what is within us—in our thoughts, our emotions, and our memories of what we have done. These are ours: we create them, we embellish and nurture them, and we are responsible for them. No one but God and us can change them. No one else can accept them for us or do the work for us. No one else is at fault and there are no excuses. Responsibility for the quality of the life you have and want to have is what remains.

With conflict, a part of you builds and a part of you burns what is built. If you have too much conflict or if your focus is outside of yourself (that is, taking too many cues from others) you will have difficulty hearing God, who speaks to us in a quiet voice. God wants us to pay attention and be willing to hear. Unlike a loud commercial, God whispers to us. If you are distracted, you will not hear the message.

Claim all four parts of yourself. They are uniquely yours. Regarding your emotional part, claim all your emotions. Claim your anger; it is part of your power. Claim your sadness; it is part of your sensitivity. Claim your fear; it is part of your awareness. Each has value. Do not deny them. Accept them. But recognize that they, as any asset, can become a liability. For example, some fear is motivating, but too much fear is paralyzing.

Other people can only make informed guesses about our spiritual lives, our thoughts, and our emotions. They notice our behavior: what we say and what we do. You may know what you intend to show, but they do not. They do not have access to your thoughts, feelings, and spiritual life unless you share with them. By sharing, people know better who you are. By sharing, *you* know better who you are.

It is the connection or disconnection of our four parts that has brought us to where we are at this time. Continued practice of disconnection will take us in a nongrowing, fear-based direction. Practicing the connection between the four parts will lead us in a growth-oriented and fulfilling direction. We have two arms and two legs. Would you tie one arm and one leg behind yourself and attempt to go through your life handicapped this way? These limbs are part of you—use them. Your spiritual, intellectual, emotional, and behavioral parts also comprise you. Use them as well.

What Runs the Four-Part Show?

Of our four parts, it is emotion and habit that will often override the mental reasoning skills in us. It is the fear that will often push aside faith in the spiritual life. We can talk with a person about a green, twelve-inch garter snake, or talk about a frog or even a worm. Most people will agree the little creatures cannot harm them. But if we toss a small snake at them, nine out of ten people might scream and jump out of the way—in spite of what their brain just acknowledged. In this situation, fear and habit regarding snakes (this was not the first time they recoiled) overwhelmed the intellectual and spiritual parts of themselves. Our emotions and our habits can run the show until we claim the emotions, particularly fear, make them our own, and become comfortable with them, and then the mind and the spirit can be in conscious charge of our lives. It is healthier to live in *choice* rather than in *habit*.

If you do not use your brain to discern the next good course of action or to have awareness, if you are not willing to move ahead into your unknown future with faith, then you will remain in fear and in habit. My patient Bill has a business that has been growing rapidly, and he now has a fear that his staff will not ramp up fast enough to meet the production goals. He does what he has done for years in the face of fear—he switches to his habit of yelling at others, being in their faces, and taking back the responsibility he has given them. Bill can be gentle with his grandchildren but then chew out his staff, even though his staff is very competent. His brain knows they are competent. He also knows his staff works better with compliments than with yelling. His brain may be talking to his emotions and to his habits, but they are not listening.

I know a woman who deflects, ignores, minimizes, or discounts any compliment that she receives. Now, is there a sound logical, reasonable, or spiritual way to explain this? We know she can hear. We know she can comprehend because she does so when provided other information. We know she can say thank you because she says this when a waiter brings her food in a restaurant. If there is not a sound intellectual explanation for her difficulty with compliments, then the explanation probably lies with two of the other four parts of her. She does not accept compliments because she is afraid, and she has a long habit of not accepting compliments. If we do not take the opportunities to grow, then we stay in the old patterns. Moving from the familiar to the unfamiliar involves psychology and a spiritual plan based on faith.

I was talking once with a young woman who was in medical school. She believed she might like to become a surgeon and thought it would be helpful not to be able to feel emotions while "cutting on someone." It can be useful, maybe even necessary, to do some compartmentalization of our emotions. I explained that some surgeons do that in the hospital with patients, in their outpatient practices with their staff, and at home with their families. At that point, they are then compartmentalizing out of habit and no longer by choice. Of course, it is not necessary to be a surgeon to practice this type of disassociation from yourself. These people become victims of their own habits, and in the process they victimize many others near them.

Another young man I knew had social anxiety and fear of being rejected by others and of not being good enough. His belief in his inadequacy kept him from changing. He would date a girl for a while and then drop her because he could not see why she would be attracted to him. And he would not talk with her about his reason for not dating her. However, he did find the strength to pledge a social fraternity in college. After being accepted as a pledge, he learned he was expected to call all the active members and meet one-on-one with all eighty of them. He found this very difficult at first, but "after calling and asking about twenty of them to meet with me and finding that they all would, I was no longer very afraid of calling the rest." He had desensitized himself to his fear situation and had brought the four parts of himself in closer alignment.

The idea is to have all four parts of ourselves existing in the same plane. However, not even the Dalai Lama or the pope may be able to remain connected all the time. Maybe they can achieve this 95 percent or more most of the time. The rest of us just need to be making progress. A woman I know remained in an emotionally abusive relationship for nine years. The problem was not with God, the spiritual part, and it was not with her intellectual part—she was more intelligent than most. The problem was with her emotional part, particularly her fear, and with her habits, the unconscious in her. After nine years, she left the abuse. Her percentage of disconnection inside of herself went down, and the percentage of connection went up. How far can she grow? We do not know. That will be determined by the amount of faith she utilizes to overcome her fears and habits.

Life is like a buffet, one with salads, entrees, vegetables, and desserts on it. That is, there are four parts of the buffet. The buffet will taste best when we sample from all four groups. A little from each group enhances the flavor and enjoyment of the other groups.

I find it interesting how many of my patients attempt to predict the future, and they usually predict something negative happening. They might say a relationship partner is "going to be hard to talk with." Now, I cannot predict the future. Doing that talking may be hard. On the other hand, it could be easy or something in between. Saying it will be hard is their fear and their habit talking. With fear and a habit of avoidance, they will not test to see if the talking was indeed hard or if it was easy. The emotion of fear will run their lives.

I am reminded of the story in chapter fourteen of the gospel of Matthew when Peter sees Jesus walking on the water and asks if he can walk on the water to Jesus. With faith, he stepped out of the boat and walked toward Jesus. Then he began to concentrate on the wind, lose faith, and slide into the water. He asked Jesus to grab him. We can think about Peter losing faith, or we can focus on him walking on water for some time and for some distance. We can focus on getting wet or upon walking on water. And Matthew does not tell us how Peter made it back to the boat. I like to believe he returned to having faith so he and Jesus could walk side by side and reenter the boat.

Our lives do not work well and we are not in peace when we do not allow all four parts of ourselves to be in alignment or in harmony—that is, not in conflict with each other. I know a man who had a bird he loved, and he was devastated when the bird died. "I had a little bird that would run up and down my arm when I would read," he said. He started crying softly at this point and then said, "I'll never get another bird." He would deny himself the pleasure of another bird because of his fear of the bird's death. "I don't want to go through that again. I don't know if I want to love another bird again." He was mismanaging his fear and attempting to overcontrol the emotional part of himself. By connecting with his bird, he was connecting with himself. Denying this connection would be like attempting to disconnect from one of his legs.

CHAPTER 5

FEAR AND THE ROLES WE PLAY

Be yourself, everybody else is already taken.
—OSCAR WILDE

WE HUMANS, ESPECIALLY AS CHILDREN, are good at copying others, mimicking, and learning to play a role. When we are born—and for the following few years—we do not know who we are. Slowly, we learn about ourselves. We learn our names, our nicknames, if crying is okay, if we are supposed to be tough, if we can hit other children, and what we are not supposed to touch. We also attempt to make sense of our lives and of our place within our families. We might be taught that we are "the troublemaker" in the family. Or maybe we are labeled "the smart one," "the athletic one," or "the quiet one." We are not aware that we are assuming these roles and styles. And we don't know if the people who teach us are playing roles themselves, such as "the inadequate parent," "the angry father," or "the teasing brother." These teachers may not even know how they learned their roles. Perhaps they

51

did not understand how to change or move beyond their roles so that they could teach us to move beyond ours.

This is not to say that roles are bad. However, it is important to see that they are just one step on the ladder of psychological and spiritual development. We do not expect a four-year-old to throw a ball with fluid motion. Instead, we believe that he or she will develop beyond the current stage and learn to throw the ball with style and accuracy. Having roles and playing them are just stages of growth. Playing the part of "the good son" or "the one who is easily embarrassed" is not detrimental. However, the role may not fit well in the current time period. It may be part of a stage that can be left behind, updated, or simply used occasionally instead of most of the time.

Roles

"When I was ten my father died, and my mother became very depressed," she told me. "I guess that put me in the role of taking care of my younger brothers and sisters. I was the caretaker." My patient Linda learned to take care of people who needed her. That is what she did with her first husband and then her boyfriend. She had (1) learned her role early in life, (2) had it well rehearsed by the time she became an adult, and (3) transferred that learning style to adults around her so that she was able to continue in the familiar role. In order to prolong playing her part, Linda had to unconsciously find people who behaved like those who needed caretaking. She probably encountered people who were independent and self-sufficient, but they were not the types she spent much time with because they were too unfamiliar.

We take on roles and find facades to hide behind. But just like the building fronts in cowboy movies, our facades fall apart and lose effectiveness. That is, they no longer produce the effect we want. Roles— unless we are aware of them and choose to show them—may be based in fear. They keep us stuck in a previous time period, often with outdated behaviors. The parts we play are usually about the past or the future, not the present. And they are usually shallow. Roles for some people seem like chocolate Easter rabbits, because they are all about appearance. The chocolate comes in bright packages and looks good, but then we learn it is hollow inside.

Fear can make us very resistant to changing our familiar roles. Those around us may also find change threatening. So they stay the same, and at some conscious or unconscious level, they want us to remain the same as well. If we change, it puts pressure on others to think and behave differently. And doing something different or unfamiliar can be frightening. Moreover, many people do not know they are playing roles. If there is no awareness, there will probably be no change.

THE FIRST ROLES—WITH PARENTS AND FAMILY

My patient Phil was afraid of being sincere or showing who he really was to his mother because of his fear of her becoming stressed or overwhelmed. As a child, he saw his mother cry often and become easily hurt. He came to believe that he was responsible for much of her pain and also that he would be responsible for relieving her pain. Phil performed his role so well that as a middle-aged adult, when he talked with his mother and she became a bit upset, he would quickly change the subject. Phil excluded his mother from the banquet of his emotions. He banned her from having emotional intimacy with him. My patient might not have obtained closeness with his mother, but he never even tried. He can continue to deal with his mother using his childhood habits or make new ones as an adult.

This patient went on to tell me that he was angry with his father. Phil said, "He was a crappy father, and now he is a crappy grandfather to my children even though he is no longer so angry." He was afraid of telling his father his thoughts and feelings because he did not want his father to be disappointed in him. Phil continued to play a role with his father that he had learned as a boy. He did not update to the current time period and did not utilize skills that were more appropriate. It was as if he were still driving a Ford Model T. There is nothing wrong with the eighty-year-old car. It just does not fit well into the present time unless you want to drive less than forty miles an hour and stay off the freeways because it would be dangerous for you and your passengers.

Phil said that he might be willing to talk with his father, but he had a lot of fear. He said, "I guess I could ignore the fear, or I could just plow through it." I asked him to remember these fears were his; he created them and had been nurturing them for many years. His fears were like a dozen dogs he had raised from puppies. When the dogs would see him coming, they would all turn and run up to him. They knew him well, and he knew them well. They had all been together for years. So if he were to talk with his father, he would not need to ignore the fears he knew so well. They would not go away just because he was ignoring them. He could walk through them as he worked to get to the other side. These were Phil's fears, so I asked him to claim them. If he wanted to write a letter, he would not ignore the fingers of his writing hand. He would use them, claim them as his, and move on. His fears, like his fingers, were his. Ignoring would not work.

Business, Family, and Roles

We are raised in close relationships with others, primarily with family members. This is where we learn the roles that are the strongest and the most familiar. These roles are the earliest and thus the ones that are practiced the most. They are the most intimate—physically and emotionally—because they were with people who knew us before we knew ourselves.

When we leave home to go to college or begin a job, we can start over with new behaviors and new views of ourselves. The *new us* may be more assertive, humorous, or outgoing. We change ourselves to try new behaviors. And these new behaviors may work well until we are once again in an intimate situation, such as when we return to our families for a visit or become engaged to marry. During these times we are also in intimate relationships. The actions around close connections trigger old habits. We unconsciously return to what we learned years ago. So now we might be mature and kind in our jobs or at parties but immature and nasty when we are at home. It is the ones we love the most who suffer the most because of our behavior. We might drive our car as an adult but drive our intimate relationships as a child.

We can fly or drive back to our parents' home for a holiday and be our age as we leave in the car or plane. But after five minutes being back, we may feel, think, and behave as if we were children or teenagers again. The triggers are strong—both in the home and in us.

Jobs are different from intimate relationships in numerous ways. Jobs involve an organizational chart, a clear hierarchy, specific responsibilities, and very little, if any, emphasis upon emotionality and vulnerability. However, when you return home, there is focus on equality instead of hierarchy. There is also more of a focus on sharing emotions and discussions of personal matters. In many ways, the eight to ten hours on the job are much simpler and easier than the few hours in the evening spent with a spouse and children.

Some people in business work extremely long hours to make a name for themselves: to try and achieve what they believe is important. They may be described as hardworking, independent, or go-getters. Many of these individuals are driven by the fear of losing their jobs or being found out for what they believe is their incompetence. Many are not team players because of this anxiety. They could surround themselves with people who excel at what they do not do well. They could share information and cooperate. Instead they hoard information like it is the only food they have to live on.

FUNCTION OF ROLES—TO PROTECT OURSELVES

The purpose of many of our roles is to protect us from the source of our fear—to provide some safety and predictability. This often leads to behaviors that are controlling. Yet people make their own choices, even if they are unconscious. Sometimes their choices are in line with what we want them to do, but this does not mean we can control or change them. However, we may still attempt to control, and we live in fear of them doing something that we do not want them to do. Another role might be to not let yourself be too open, so you play "the conservative one." There was a joke in my home state of Wisconsin—a state full of people of Swedish heritages—that the height of praise from someone was "that's not too bad." It really meant *wow*. But the role did not allow that behavior. Being too emotional was frightening and not safe.

We assume roles that protect the real person inside. In our recovery, it is important to identify, discover, and love that inside person. A new patient of mine, a man, was experiencing intense stress when he came to my office. As he talked, he began to let go of some of his anxiety. He told me later in the session that it had taken him years to learn to cry. The truth is that he knew how to cry as an infant. But he taught himself not to cry—probably because of his fear. His father was an angry and critical man who sometimes hit him.

FROM ROLE TO ROLE

Marilyn was stuck in an old developmental stage. She no longer played the role she had learned as a child. Instead she acted in an opposite manner. When she was a little girl, she was very dependent on her older sister, Lucy. Marilyn would sleep with her, wear her clothes, and became afraid when she was not around. Even in high school, she let Lucy do all the driving. Marilyn says that she was very shy then.

Now Marilyn calls herself "a competitive person." She explains that sometimes the ladies she golfs with don't want to play with her because of the way she behaves. These days, she works very hard to show that she is not shy but very independent. However, this conduct is artificial—just like her blonde hair. The blonde hides her true hair color, and her independence and competitiveness hide her fears. Marilyn is still afraid of not fitting in, being rejected, and feeling different. She still is not at ease inside her own skin.

Fear is behind many of the roles we play. There may be very specific fears, such as that of making a mistake in a certain situation. Or much bigger fears may exist—ones a person rarely voices or is not even aware of—such as the fear of being found out or vulnerable.

A man I knew was afraid of making a mistake, so he often avoided making decisions—especially with his wife. He would ask her opinion about a course of action. She would give it, and then he would argue with her, drawing her into a problem she wanted no part of. He behaved this way when they bought a washing machine. When it was delivered, the appliance had some corrosion on it, so the couple refused it and requested another. When it arrived it was better but not by much. This man asked his wife if they should just accept the washing machine or request another. He argued with her no matter what she told him. He was playing the role of a little boy, and he was setting up his wife to play the mother role. However, she would not do it. And he was frustrated.

PRISONERS TO OUR ROLES

Not all prisons are made of concrete and steel bars. If you are in a dysfunctional role, you are a prisoner to the role, to the past, and probably to a fear of change. Some of us are prisoners to our thoughts of inadequacy, and we are just as locked up as if we were in a concrete cell. Some of us are prisoners to alcohol, pills, or food. The prison serves a purpose: the third principle of learning. Its purpose is to keep us safe. It may accomplish that—but at a price. Prisons also keep others out, and they do not provide us the freedom of movement to change. Our responsibility is to be willing to recognize our own prisons and then be willing to change them. Our duty is also to recognize the prisons of others and to treat them with compassion. If we do not move out of our (usually self-constructed) prisons, we cannot have freedom.

My patient Henry said, "My mother moans and groans about my

father, her sisters, and her friends. But she never does anything about the problems. She puts herself in maximum security in her dealings with others." Henry was an adult son who learned how to avoid playing this game with his mother. He knew that the game had negative consequences because his mother does not have healthy relationships—she takes prisoners.

UPDATING—DO SOMETHING DIFFERENT!

If the role does not work well, if it is falling apart, do something different. If you typically do not stand up for yourself—because of your learned fear pattern of being rejected or hurting others—keep this in mind: You can say, "June Cleaver does not live at this house anymore, and neither does Beaver." It is no longer the 1950s. Learn some behaviors that are more appropriate and effective.

It is important that we work to uncover who we are inside. We must let go of the old roles that worked better in the past. A patient told me, "My Dad was a doctor, and I figured I should be a doctor. So I studied to be one, and then one day I realized, 'Hey, guy, you don't like to get up really early in the morning.' I changed for other reasons too, but, you see, being a doctor is not who I am." Being a doctor is what the little boy wanted. But now the man can find out who he really needs to be.

Another man I knew said, "I was always who I thought I should be, not who I was." He also described the ways he attempted to please others and the roles he played. These roles worked poorly for him for many years. He explained, "I've been so concerned about other people believing that I'm doing well that they can't see how poorly I'm actually doing. The problem has to do with my pride and my ego. I see myself in the water after a shipwreck. My face looks calm, but I'm paddling frantically under the water. And then others don't think I need much help. Then I get angry at them for not seeing me the way I really am: someone who needs help and attention." This is a man who worked hard to say "just the right thing" instead of learning to be at ease with others.

He was afraid of saying the wrong thing instead of having faith that he would recover no matter what he said.

Evan was very hard on himself and self-critical. I asked him how long it would take for him to be proud of his sobriety from drugs. He told me that it would take two years. But in the meantime, Evan could be proud of his thirty-five days, or one day, or just the past minute. We are only in the minute, so it is important to be here—now. This is where you live.

One of the values of psychotherapy or of talking with a religious leader is that these relationships allow us to practice emotional vulnerability and intimacy in a safe situation. We learn to address our feelings as adults, to share who we are, and to explore other parts of ourselves in ways that we might not have learned as children.

CHAPTER 6

FEAR AND CLOSE RELATIONSHIPS

> What you leave behind is not what is engraved in stone
> monuments, but what is woven into the lives of others.
> —PERICLES

FEAR AND CONTROL STRATEGIES DO not work to create healthy relationships. They do not promote intimacy and trust. They do, however, promote power games and secrets. Too many of us, because of our fears, try to change the *other* person rather than ourselves. There is a mistaken belief that if the other person changes our lives will be fine— even if we do not adjust. That is not communication and compromise; it is control.

Some fears have obvious and significant consequences for our lives. Fears of elevators, flying, and heights are obvious. With some inconvenience, we can avoid these situations so that they do not significantly interfere with our lives. However, other fears are subtler and can have substantial impact—even though we are unaware of them. We may have a fear of being honest with someone. So we keep secrets or tell lies. When the other person finds out, he or she is hurt and mistrustful of us. Then we have a damaged relationship.

As children, we have magical belief systems, such as beliefs about Santa Claus' gift giving or even changes in the weather. We chant, "Rain, rain, go away, come again another day." Many of us, including me, may have actually believed we could control the rain. But we grow out of that belief. However, some people maintain the belief or illusion that they can control others such as their spouses. They continue to use styles and attitudes that they used as children. If as an adult you are still sleeping with the blanket from your childhood bed, it is not difficult to determine why you are cold at night! The blanket is thin, faded, and full of holes and does not offer healthy and appropriate protection. The same is true of many of our behaviors.

THREE ON THE COUCH

With couples there are some problems that are his, some that are hers, and some that are theirs. In therapy, if there are two people on the sofa, there are actually three relationships to address: her relationship with herself, his relationship with himself, and the relationship they have with each other. The bond between the two is only as healthy as the least healthy person in the relationship. If the man is 75 percent healthy and the woman is at 50 percent, then the relationship is only 50 percent healthy. If they are both unhealthy, the relationship is unhealthy. Similarly, if a man is abusive and controlling and a woman is kind and gentle, the resulting relationship is abusive and controlling. The relationship can only be healthy if both partners are healthy. If both individuals make progress, then the relationship makes progress.

The Relationship Rowboat

When we consider the connection between two people, each person can do only 50 percent to move or "make" the relationship. Neither one can do 100 percent. It is like two survivors of a shipwreck when they crawl into a lifeboat and look at each other. There are two oars in the oarlocks, but the lifeboat is so wide that one person cannot row the boat by himself. He is unable to grab both oars or to dip them in the water. So both people decide to sit together on the seat between the oars. Next each has the choice to row, be passive, sabotage the other, or team up to move forward to the safety of an island. If they both say they want to go forward but neither one rows (because they fear to trust, perhaps) then they drift farther away from their goal of the island. If one rows and the other does not (because they fear the other will not continue), then they go in a circle. If the other one rows but the first stops rowing (because he or she is hurt), then they go in a circle in the opposite direction. Either one can sabotage the move forward. There is only one way they can advance. The solution is that both of them agree to row, do their part, and continue doing their part until they reach the goal. One person will not carry a relationship to the goal line.

Fear, Control, and Habit

Sometimes the tactics we use in our relationships do not work. They do not help us or other people. Even so, we continue to use them. Why? We may continue using them because of momentum, habit, or fear instead of awareness, choice, or faith.

Natalie's first husband had an affair and left her. Before that, she grew up in a family with much conflict. Now she calls her second husband often, sometimes twice an hour, because she is afraid he may be having an affair instead of doing his job. Her fear has led to the controlling behavior of calling frequently. By doing so she is able, temporarily, to reduce her fear about her husband's fidelity. But just like alcohol, the fix does not last very long, and the outer reality remains. In order to find peace, she will need to resolve her painful inner reality.

In his frustration with her frequent phone calls, Natalie's husband told me that he was going to tell her that he was planning to separate. Then he hoped that she would try to get better. So, the wife practices control tactics, while the husband considers countering with his own. This type of control does not lend itself to intimacy or problem solving. For the relationship to improve, they each need to heal themselves by resolving old issues, addressing fears, and learning new behaviors such as trust.

The husband in another couple I worked with was sensitive but turned his sensitivity into avoidance. The wife mismanaged her sensitivity into independence and rapid problem solving. She said, "He just avoids. He doesn't do anything to change." The truth is, he did change. It just wasn't according to her time schedule. He took a lot of time to address problems because of his role as the "hard worker" and "fixer." He did not want anyone to be upset with him. On the other hand, she zeroed in on problems and came up with quick and objective solutions. She had been doing this for years, even prior to meeting him. He may have unconsciously chosen to marry her because of his habits. Marriage to another passive person like himself would have resulted in very little getting done. If she had married another person like herself, there would have been constant conflict. They were both victims of the dysfunctional habits that characterized their relationship.

If the wife were to build a three-thousand-square-foot house, she would want it done in three months—if not sooner. If the husband were to do the building, he would still be talking with the architect after three months. His house would take so long to build that the wooden studs would rot from exposure to the elements. Her house would be built so quickly that the kitchen sink would be in the counter before there was any plumbing underneath. These two individuals needed to move out of their old, individual habit roles and learn new skills.

In therapy, they eventually agreed to the following: (1) neither would bring problems home from work, (2) she would listen to him for two minutes without offering immediate solutions, and (3) he would get to the point within two minutes instead of taking a great deal of time trying to avoid conflict. They also agreed to take thirty-minute time-outs when they were in obvious, nonproductive conflict and things were getting heated. Another agreement was to have potentially conflicting talks on Tuesday and Thursday evenings between eight and nine o'clock. If an issue could not reasonably be resolved in an hour, it probably was not going to get solved that evening.

Justin's wife, Claire, had ADHD and was a painkiller abuser. She was often gone from home and her kids to be with her mother. Their son may also have had ADHD, but she had not had him evaluated even though she had promised to do so for over six months. Claire disappointed the kids by making and then breaking promises, whether about where they could go or what time she would return home. Justin asked her to go for treatment for her addiction. She had agreed numerous times but never went. He finally told her to move out. When she refused, he said he would move out as soon as she went to treatment. If she could have done what he was asking, he would not be thinking of moving out. He was actually very afraid to leave. He feared her driving the kids around in the car. So he stayed even though he knew she drove the children while he was at work. He behaved as if he believed staying would prevent her from driving. Claire was still driving, and Justin was still hanging on to his control strategy. I did not know the answer to this situation, but I did point out that what Justin had been doing for years was not working very well. The proof to me was that he was in my office feeling extremely fearful and depressed.

The wife of another couple said, "He never gets things done that need to get done." His response was "I never get credit for what I do." She focused only on problems and counting solutions, so she took what he accomplished for granted. He focused on doing things and hoped she would notice. He would not tell her what he was doing. She was just "supposed to know." On Saturdays she had a list of errands to get accomplished. He believed that Saturdays were supposed to be more relaxed and less focused than the rest of the week. With a compulsion to accomplish, she said, "I'm not trying to get a pat on the back for doing things like the laundry." He stated, "I guess I've always done stuff for people and then if I get thanked it takes away from why I did it." At least the idea of not giving compliments was something they had in common. But even this commonality resulted in the minimization of communication. She wanted the relationship to be her way, and he wanted it to be his way. Both operated from fear, utilized control tactics to address the fear, and were very ego-involved in being *right*.

I had a patient whose husband had been an only child, and when his parents died he inherited quite a lot of money. He was also a professional and earned a high salary. He did not slow down in his retirement but continued to work to make money. Even so, he had a fear of not having enough money. However, this couple would have had difficulty spending all they had even if they traveled around the world and bought a new luxury car every year. When the wife needed an MRI because she had experienced some disorientation, he did not go with her. He was busy working. And when she went to meet with the medical doctor to review the results, he said he could not go with her because he had two *important* meetings. His god was money. He could never get enough of it. His most intimate connection was with his god, money. "Welcome to my world," the wife told me as she cried.

Control and Roles—Not Present for the Present

A previous patient, Amanda, was an elementary school teacher considering retirement. But when asked if she would teach adults in church she said, "No, I'm too afraid to teach anyone but children. I'm not good at working with adults." Amanda was also afraid to fly and had problems with her adult children. She was stuck in her fears partly because her husband was critical of her—and of others—and he was not a cheerleader for her. He teased and ignored her. His verbal abuse reduced growth for her. When she talked with him, you could substitute the word *Daddy* for her use of his proper name. She related to him like she would to a loud and verbally abusive father.

The roles that people play can have several consequences in a relationship. If two people both play the role of "the dictator," they will have much conflict and upset. If two "avoiders" or "victims" get together, they will not have blowups but may not get much done. If a "dictator" connects with a "victim," the roles are complementary. Not healthy, but complementary. So the controller needs the controlee and vice versa.

Many couples practice poor communication while using control techniques such as manipulation, pouting, and yelling. One of my patients from years ago had a leaky toilet. She wrote a note to her husband about it and left it on the toilet. She waited two weeks and then asked him about the note. He said, "I don't do plumbing." Unfortunately, the wife communicated like an adolescent by not talking directly with her husband. And he communicated like a boy with his avoidance and focus only on his priorities. They both played the role of "the avoider." The more they practiced the behaviors of adolescents, the better they became at them. Using childlike ways will keep anyone from practicing adult behaviors. To do the latter, we must interrupt the former. In order to accomplish that, we must have awareness and a healthy amount of anxiety—fear—to motivate us to *do* something different so we will *get* something different.

She grew up with exclusion, secrets, and power plays. Consequently, that is what she does with her husband. The decade, the home, the person, and the situation are different. But she has not changed herself. She is not present for the present she is in. "When I talk with her," he said, "I have that old tendency to withdraw, to go away." That behavior is his old childhood/adolescent habit. It is not a behavior that is carefully and consciously chosen by a man or marriage partner.

CONTROL AND COMMUNICATION

My patient Patricia told me the following about her husband: "He goes into his home office every evening, and I'm afraid to tell him I want to talk because he'll be upset." So she busies herself by talking on the phone and then avoids her husband. He sees her on the phone, figures she will be occupied for a while, and stays in his office. They do not communicate about their wants.

In another case, a husband said, "Just to keep the conflict down, I surrender more and more of myself to her. She handles the money, vacations, plane tickets, everything. She is controlling. I have sacrificed what I want for what she wants."

One of my male patients complained, "She speaks to me in code. She will not say, 'Will you please deposit this check for me?' Instead she asks me, 'Are you going downtown or are you busy tomorrow?' I like to think before I open my mouth, but this is like thinking in a chess game and anticipating moves way in the future." This is another person looking for the *Sherlock Holmes moment*—finding a simple answer to a complex problem. However, it would not be necessary if their communication was clear and simple.

"I won't say anything until I have the right answer," Lawrence says to me as we talk about his style of communication with his wife. He plays the relationship too safe, and his actions keep him stuck. Avoidance rarely helps us grow. We usually grow by taking small risks from the familiar. He talks easily with me, but he shuts down with his wife. He explains that his wife is demanding of him just as his father was. Lawrence is stuck in a time thirty years past.

He does not share his feelings with his wife because he is afraid she will be hurt. He behaves as if he wants to buy his wife a car, but will not allow her to drive it until he has some kind of divine assurance she will never be in an accident. Accidents happen sometimes with cars, and we learn to deal with it. Hurt happens sometimes in relationships, and it is important we learn to deal with it in some way besides avoidance.

At one point, Lawrence had pain in his hip intense enough that occasionally when he got in or out of his car he groaned. When his wife asked what was hurting he said that it was nothing. She told him she could hear him groan and wanted to know what was wrong. So he asserted that he knew his own body and nothing was wrong. He was not willing to share, which led her not to trust what he was saying.

COMPROMISE

If you have a conversation with someone but it is only in your head and not face-to-face, the other person *says* what you want to hear. You do not change because you win every time. In our own heads, we are omnipotent. Talking out loud with the other allows for saying the wrong thing or for making mistakes, but it also creates positive change. Change requires a give-and-take, a comparison and a contrast, and oftentimes a compromise.

There are different types of communication: verbal, emotional, and behavioral. I worked with a husband and wife who experienced the same emotions—including fear. However, they handled them differently. The husband had feelings, but he would go to his head first to address his wife and to solve problems. His style made him seem uncaring and cold. The wife had feelings, but she discharged them first—particularly at her husband—and then she would go to her head. Her style made her seem impulsive and hotheaded. His compromises could easily be called *surrenders*, and her compromises would be more appropriately called *controls*. A true compromise is when you give a little to get a little. Neither party gets all that he or she wants but can live well with what is agreed to.

RELATIONSHIP SABOTAGE

Control tactics and the damage they can cause to a relationship are demonstrated in the following quote: "She would say things to our friends that would make me radioactive in their eyes. She would say I stared at women or I used to drink heavily or I was fined once by the police. And then she would leave her comment hanging like a large, black balloon in the room."

In another relationship, the wife was threatened by and fearful of her boyfriend's one-night-per-week dart playing with his friends. The other evenings and weekends were spent with her. She tried to make him feel guilty about his game night by saying, "If you really loved me, you would stay here with me," or "Is there something wrong with me that you leave me?" or "Am I ugly? Is that why you leave?" She attempted to get her attachment needs met by having her boyfriend with her all the time. She had done this before when she forced him to give up a fishing boat he occasionally used. Later, he gave up bowling as well. He stopped these rewarding activities to please her.

Marriages in which there are stepchildren are rife for fear-based control strategies. A father gave his biological daughter a one-hundred-dollar advance on her budget in high school because of his fears: sparking conflict, not being liked, and being abandoned. He did not tell his second wife about the financial advance because he was afraid she would not understand and might be angry (his fear of conflict). As it turned out, she was less angry about the advance than about his secret, which she learned about the following month. Fear and control tactics sabotage relationships.

Another man I counseled always introduced the X factor into his relationships with new girlfriends. That is, with the current girlfriend he frequently discussed his ex-girlfriend, the one he still carried a torch for, and who was now married. Therefore, the new girlfriend was in the position of watching this man carry on an imaginary affair.

A single man I worked with, named Ray, had a problem seeing women for their sexual parts and not for their personalities. A therapeutic task for him was to not have sex with a woman for the first ten dates. The following week Ray said, "I put that goal on a piece of paper, folded it up, stuck it in my back pocket, and hoped I'd lose it. I'm scared to death of not having sex with my dates." But what he set in motion, what was triggered by the sex, was his fear of commitment and of vulnerability. His old habits and his old fears took over. Ray continued to see women merely as sexual parts, became bored, and then left them. He sabotaged numerous relationships. By not having sex, he would have confronted his fears and have had the opportunity to integrate all four parts of himself and to learn to see all four parts of a woman.

Change is part of life. Therefore, if you are not changing, you are not living. The young man above was not living in the current time period. Even though he was in his late twenties, he was just reliving age sixteen over and over again. He explained, "I'm never wondering what it would be like to talk with her in a restaurant. No, I keep thinking of what it would be like to be in bed with her." Because of his control (manipulation, secret keeping) he avoided sharing what was deep inside of him with a woman. So he did not get the love, happy marriage, and family that his brain said he wanted. His brain and his emotions were in conflict. They canceled each other out so no change occurred.

CREATING OUR FEAR—AGAIN

A patient of mine had divorced before she began working with me. She said that she started going out with men who were "below" her in terms of salary or education. They are the only men she felt comfortable being with. She was afraid that "the good ones" wouldn't like her and would leave her, and she would get hurt. She explained, "This way it doesn't hurt if they leave me or I leave them." Her fear was running her dating life. The intellectual part of her knew that the worst that could happen was that a man might say no or not want to continue to date her. No one would die; no blood would flow. She would go on. But she was not listening to her brain. She had a poor relationship with herself. She would stare in the mirror and tell the person looking back at her that she did not deserve someone on her level. All four parts of her were not strongly connected together. They were not in the same place at the same time.

Jason calls himself "arrogant" and has a fear of being hurt and abandoned. He does not talk much with his wife because he is afraid to. He spends a lot of time buying big-boy toys such as boats, cars, and four-wheelers. He says, "I have a fear of my wife leaving me. So I act like a boy so she will take care of me and won't leave me." The girlfriend he had before he met his wife left him after two years because she was tired of taking care of him. By playing his game of attempting to control his wife, he was able to distract himself from his fear. He was afraid to claim his fears, and he hid behind facades until his current wife said she was separating from him. This got his attention, and he scheduled an appointment with me.

Lisa told me that she had a variety of fears. Her father died when she was a child. She said the family mourned and had a funeral. Four days later her mother told Lisa that she needed to go back to school. Lisa explained, "We never talked about the death again." Thirty years later, her childhood fear of being left is still running her life. "It's very difficult for me to confront people, so I confront them on the phone," she told me. She is afraid to make a decision and is afraid of the consequences as well. Lisa added, "If I don't have my boyfriend, I'll be all alone. I won't have a date on a Saturday night. When I think this way, I go back into my teenage years. I fear being deserted."

Another woman said the following about her husband: "He is so controlling. He has his own business with a partner and employees, but he won't let anybody else write checks. He does them by hand! I've told him I could set up the checks to be paid on the computer as I did for my boss. He rejected the idea and doesn't even want me to write the checks at home. I know he's not hiding money from me or spending it strangely, but I'm concerned that he has so much fear of making a mistake or of someone else making a mistake. It's taking a toll on his health—and he won't let me in." This man was working to create *safety*, but the consequences were significant for him and for his relationship with his wife.

ADDICTED TO AVOIDANCE

One of my patients, Sheila, had been divorced for two years and started dating again after fourteen years of marriage. Her ex-husband was controlling and had also had an affair. Sheila was afraid of being hurt again. She did not want to get close—except on her terms. So she played it very safe. She avoided the possibility of being close to a man and of being rejected and hurt again. Sheila explained, "I don't want them to know much about me. I don't talk about my past. I keep it superficial. I even bought a small loft so that guys could pick me up there for a date instead of coming to my house and learning about me."

Sheila is addicted to avoidance just as some are addicted to alcohol. Alcoholics hide their use and keep secrets. So did Sheila. She did not follow common sense: If alcohol causes problems, stop drinking. If avoidance and fear are causing problems, stop avoiding and deal with the fear. Unfortunately, her life was run by her fear. She was not in balance inside of herself, so she could not be in balance with others.

Another woman had tremendous fear of being rejected by a man. "My brother was one year older than me, and we were best friends until he went into first grade. Then he dumped me, as strange as that sounds. His friends teased me, and he would not stand up for me. But I could not get away. I had to live with him, and I think that is why I stay in relationships that are not good for me. My husband had multiple affairs, and I not only stayed with him but also had another child with him." It is true she had much fear. It is also true she stayed with the familiar—what she knew. She behaved in a very controlling way, but her avoidance continued year after year.

Mary said, "I was unable to tell him he was a jerk when he said he wanted to have sex. My ex-boyfriend dumped me two years ago and never told me why." Then I made a point. She was not *unable* to tell him. That was another word for *afraid*. "I can't tell him because I'm afraid, just like I was afraid of my mother leaving me when I was a girl. And now my mother has had four marriages. She does not do relationships well with men or with me," she explained.

Bob complained to me about his wife's fear of him working with other women. He said, "I had to work on committees with women sometimes, and my wife would ask me what the women looked like. I think she wanted them all to be ninety-five years old, four hundred pounds, and ugly. Then she would be safe."

Francine had a powerful fear related to rejection. She recounted, "I was dating Jim. If I did not get pregnant by him I was afraid I would never find a man to marry. My mother had told me that once you have sex without marriage no man will want to marry you. I had sex with another man, and now I am afraid that if I am not pregnant with his baby, Jim will not marry me. We were naked and rubbed together and it felt good. We didn't have sex. Then Jim said that we should not do that anymore. I felt rejected, afraid, and not pretty, so I pushed him to have sex with me."

I had a patient who very much wanted and needed what she did not have with her boyfriend. She wanted friendship, courtship, and love. She became angry when she tried to turn what she did have into what she did not have. The square peg does not fit into the round hole. "I do have this Cinderella thing, and I do want someone to take care of me," she shared with me one session. But her fantasy was not working in the real world. She explained, "I do okay when I reject men, but not when they reject me." So she attempted control by rejecting first.

APPROACH—DON'T AVOID

Conflict in a relationship is often related to issues with egos and control strategies. Healthy people recognize and admit to this. They work to move the egos aside and to open up instead of trying to control. Some conflict in a relationship simply means you are normal and that you are two people attempting to communicate and compromise. When you buy a car it will get dirty or rained on or get a small ding in the door. If you don't want these things to happen, don't buy a car. Instead, just look at them in the showroom or in a magazine. If you don't want—or fear—conflict in a relationship, don't get into a relationship. Otherwise, learn to handle it as an adult, fear and all.

You do not have to learn to like fighting or arguing. Just learn to fight and argue well enough so that you have this skill as a tool. Do not always work to avoid conflict because there is bound to be some in any healthy, growing relationship. The conflict itself is often not the problem. The problem is caused by not addressing and resolving the difficulty well and maturely. This is one way that you protect yourself in the current time period—instead of avoiding, which you learned to do in a previous time period. You would protect your car from a hailstorm. Learn to protect yourself; you are worth much more than a car.

CONTROL AND UNAWARENESS

"My Dad sent me an article on controlling spouses. My wife read it first and said she did not agree with it. And now she will not let me see the article. So my Dad is sending me another copy." The wife was unaware that she was controlling, but her behavior showed it. Awareness is the first step toward change. If a person is not aware that what she says does not match what she does, there is no incentive for change.

Another woman told her boyfriend, when they were in my office, that he did not have to change. She did not want him to change. However, later she said that her boyfriend isolated himself too much and that she needed a deeper connection. She said she was not controlling him, just getting him to connect with her. But the look on her face and her tone of voice showed that it was control on her part. She did not accept him as he was, and she did not ask him to change in an adult manner. She used guilt induction and victim behavior to get him to change, and she did not realize it.

Fred's wife asked him numerous questions in her attempts to reduce her fear, which was based on not knowing. These control tactics resulted in him going away emotionally and sometimes behaviorally. When he did not answer a question the way she wanted him to, she would ask, "You're selfish, aren't you? Isn't this important to you? You just don't love me, do you?" She was unaware that her behavior triggered his old habit of emotional and communication avoidance. It was possible for both of them to change. She could have not overreacted and stated clearly what she needed without being threatening. Instead of avoiding, Fred could have said that he would answer her questions—just not all at once. He could have proposed some type of compromise so that they could have learned to talk more respectfully and maturely.

FEAR AND STUBBORNNESS

Jim's mother, sisters, and friends said that his girlfriend was not good for him. Jim was stubborn, ran on fear, and did not listen to them. He said, "I don't want to be alone. I'm almost forty-two years old. I miss having company, someone around me. I don't know if I can find someone else if I do not have her." So Jim's "stubbornness" is driven by fear. He can temporarily reduce his fear by staying with the girlfriend. In a similar manner, a person can temporarily reduce his fear by drinking alcohol, eating, or exercising.

Jim was a man practicing avoidance of what he believed to be painful and punishing: being alone. He was able to reward himself by reducing his physiological and psychological pain through this avoidance. Like cats, dogs, and chickens, we avoid what causes us pain and move toward things that provide pleasure or relief—even if what we do is not healthy in the long term.

During one session Jim asked, "Where did I learn stubbornness? Maybe it was because I was an only child for a while. I was the oldest. I was given a lot of what I wanted, and now I still want things my way." He was not prepared to have a healthy relationship with someone else because he did not have a healthy relationship with himself and with God. The problem was that he was coming from stubbornness and fear. It was difficult for him to have a strong relationship with God because he behaved as if he was God. It was difficult for Jim to have a good relationship with himself because he did not face his fears.

STUCK IN THE PAST WITH THE FAMILIAR

The wife of a patient of mine was angry with him because she caught him using the Internet to look at soft-core pornography. Now, at what stage of life are people most interested in sexual matters? For many it is adolescence, and some people do not grow out of it. This was a man in his forties who was taking care of himself and his sexual needs with the style of a sixteen-year-old. He was not compromising with his wife and was depriving her of attention, affection, and sex. For her part, she practiced the self-care of a child or adolescent. When she went on a three-day spiritual retreat, she refused to tell her husband where the retreat was! Her disconnection within herself was gaping because she was attending a spiritual retreat while practicing revenge and resentment. Her self-care, like his, involved too much ego and outdated styles of relationships. Both were out of touch with God, with themselves, and with each other. They were married adults having a childlike or adolescent relationship. Unfortunately, parts of them became stuck in those previous developmental years. They could raise children, have jobs, and pay bills as adults. But they did not relate well as adults.

The wife used control strategies rather than providing love and forgiveness or establishing boundaries and new agreements with her husband. Her fear was the fear of a child. Maybe she was playing a childhood game of "If you won't let me play, I'll take my ball and go home." Maybe she wanted her husband to pursue her or show he cared. In any event, she did not communicate in clear terms what she felt. Unfortunately, she did not begin therapy with me, or anyone else, to examine the usefulness of her behaviors and to learn new, appropriate ones.

Chapter 7

Compulsions

People occasionally stumble over the truth, but most of
them pick themselves up as if nothing had happened.
—Churchill

THIS IS THE BASIC TRUTH about compulsions and addictions: they
become your god. When you act out your compulsion, you have
no great need or awareness of a god you cannot touch. This is because
your god *can* be touched: it is food, sex, exercise, work, money, control,
power, cleaning, or any of many other possibilities. Whatever you are
preoccupied with, whatever you obsess about, whatever you want to get
close to, whatever you are passionate about—even though it brings you
negative consequences—becomes your god.

With a compulsion, the individual is focused on the object of the
compulsion and on the next use. He is like a Labrador dog focused on
retrieving a ball his owner has thrown into the water. All the dog may

79

have in his mind is "ball, ball, ball," and the focus is so strong that he might even ignore the hamburger sitting at the edge of the water.

ADDICTIONS AND COMPULSIONS

The line between addictions and compulsions can become fuzzy. At times, people have called any or all of the following behaviors an addiction or a compulsion: working, eating, having sex, using tobacco, people pleasing, avoiding conflict, shopping, volunteering, exercising, viewing pornography, watching TV, Internet gambling, using of the Internet, and buying lottery tickets. Some of these involve chemical substances that are taken into the body, but some do not. Whatever you call them, they do share numerous characteristics that keep us disconnected within ourselves and keep us from growing psychologically, socially, and spiritually. Common characteristics include the following:

1. Temporary escape from emotions
2. Mood change
3. Adrenaline rush
4. Fantasy bonding rather than reality bonding
5. Increased tolerance
6. Preoccupation with the next episode of acting out
7. Withdrawal symptoms
8. Protection of the supply
9. Selecting friends who do the same
10. Diminishing returns
11. Increasing negative consequences to self, family, and job
12. Lying and secret keeping
13. Rationalization and minimization
14. Poor boundaries

15. Breaking of values

16. Strengthening erroneous beliefs

17. Increasing feelings of guilt and shame

18. Increasing losses and grief

19. Increasing defensiveness

The Compulsive Cycle

Most compulsions are habits that have been repeatedly rehearsed, often for years or decades. While a person may no longer know the origin of the compulsion, it is usually to distract the individual from some fearful experience or image. No matter what the compulsion is, the cycle remains the same: (1) we feel fear, (2) we distract ourselves from the fear with the compulsion (some activity outside of ourselves), (3) we get temporary relief, (4) the fear slowly builds up again (it is inside of ourselves), (5) we feel fear, and (6) we distract ourselves again.

Developmentally Stuck

With any addiction or compulsion, we become developmentally arrested at the age we were traumatized or when that activity became the most important priority in our lives. For example, a twelve-year-old girl may become compulsive about not going outside unless her hair and clothes look a certain way. Twenty years later, she may still have the fears of the twelve-year-old regarding how others will judge her.

If at age twenty-one you become compulsive and stuck with a need to keep the kitchen floor super clean—to the point of mopping it several times each day—and decades later you want to become healthy, you will need to address the fear you had as the twenty-one-year-old. The fear does not go away just because you were busy and distracted by mopping.

With an addictive or compulsive set of behaviors and symptoms, we drag our baggage of yesterday into today. We do not have balance in our lives because our bodies show up for the addiction or compulsion but the spiritual part is on hold (it is the first to go). Our emotions are what we want to hide from, and our minds are working to justify our behavior. We have difficulty dealing with our emotions without a compulsion. We have not learned new and functional coping skills, but rather continue to use what we learned as children and adolescents. Our minds can temporarily deny, explain away, or otherwise cover up our activities. People are very creative and are rarely as creative as when they want to get away from something. Change through psychological and spiritual means is all around us, but we may not use those means often. If we did we would be doing something different from our compulsion, and that would put us on unfamiliar and fearful ground. Fear is often the primary emotion we want to escape from—so we return to the wheel called the compulsive cycle.

We search for activities, chemicals, and people to bring us the connection we desire and need. We will even choose a pseudo connection because it, temporary though it may be, is still better than no connection at all. We may try to connect with what can be seen and touched because it is concrete and measurable. And we have seen many other people utilize concrete material for their connections. We have watched parents, relatives, friends, TV and sports personalities, and politicians use alcohol, drugs, sex, money, power, food, tobacco, and shopping to alter their moods. They obtain a transitory connection with something or someone outside of themselves. The role models for healthiness are fewer. That makes it more difficult. And the problem with the spiritual is that it is unseen and difficult to explain and does not play well on TV or in the headlines. We cannot touch it, and to achieve it is not as easy as simply eating sugar, drinking caffeine, or working long hours.

CONNECTION WITH OBJECTS AND DISCONNECTION WITH OURSELVES

The material world is composed of objects—objects we use and abuse to obtain the results, although short-lived, that we need and want. Some people see food as an object that will change their mood and help them to cope with their problems. Others see sex as a way to connect through fantasy, so people become objects to them. Cigarettes, slot machines, and shopping malls are all objects that we use to stimulate some senses and to dull others. In the process of relating to objects, we may begin to see ourselves as objects as well. As we struggle, we become further disconnected from the four parts of ourselves. It is a slippery slope, and we usually end up sliding downhill for a great distance. We experience many negative consequences of our behavior and remain in our habits, in our fear, and in our unawareness.

CLEANING COMPULSION

A woman I knew was very fastidious about keeping her home clean. The day after she and her husband had hired workers to update their kitchen with granite countertops and new appliances, she was up at midnight cleaning the kitchen of the dust and mess the workers had made. The workmen returned the next morning to continue the process, but this woman had fear in her strong enough to push her into fatigue. She had a vision in mind that required midnight cleaning. Now, this is the same woman who had a fear of small lizards. When she was a girl, neighbor boys used to chase her with lizards and even say they had put them in the toilet. She said, "They told me the lizards would come up and bite me in the rear." The fear of lizards had its origin in her past just as the beginnings of her cleaning compulsion were in her past. Over the years, she continued to practice the same fears rather than learn new and more adaptive behaviors.

My patient Agatha would vacuum the carpets in her house when she was anxious. Her cleaning compulsion cost her greatly in many ways, including financially. In fact, during one session she admitted, "I usually go through a vacuum a year."

TV Compulsion

If you spend much time watching TV as a means of avoiding socializing, growth, or spiritual change, then someone—including an alien from space—might wonder if maybe you believe your god is a TV or resides in the TV.

Germ Avoidance Compulsion

I have had patients come into the office using small plastic bags to cover their hands when they open doors. They will not shake hands because of their fear of germs. Before sitting down, they take a large garbage bag from their pocket or purse and place it over the seat. The behavior is excessive and out of the range of appropriateness for the situation.

Eating Compulsion

One of my patients could not figure out why she was not losing weight. "It doesn't make sense that I'm not losing weight." She wanted to lose the weight, but cried about feeling sad and lonely and not wanting to be a grown-up. Contrary to what she said, her difficulty with losing weight did make sense. She had a fear of adult responsibilities. It was her fear and habit of eating that was not in line with her intellectual choice and spiritual desire. The emotions and habits were blocking her growth. In order to lose the weight, she would have to face her fears.

WEIGHT CONTROL COMPULSION

A patient told me, "Weight has always been an issue for me. I didn't have a great childhood. I used my weight as a control mechanism. It was something I could control. I couldn't control Mom and Dad and their yelling and fighting."

ANTI-TOUCHING COMPULSION

One of my patients did not realize he had an aversion to touching others and to being touched until one of his neighbors said the following to him: "I've been watching you when you go outside. You have cats. I see you feed them when they are hungry, and you take them inside when it's hot or cold outside. But I have never seen you touch them." My patient and I talked about that for a while, and he came to the conclusion that his parents gave him money and things to play with, but they did not touch him or his sister. And now he does not touch others even when he is in a relationship with them.

CLEAN YARD COMPULSION

The husband of a woman I knew had a particularly bad type of cancer reoccur. Even though he was receiving chemotherapy, his prognosis was poor. The wife coped by becoming compulsive. "My yard has been my therapy," she said. "I could get yard of the month if we had a competition. There is not a weed in my yard. But I went overboard. This is not good when you're picking up leaves as they fall from the trees."

SHOPPING COMPULSION

Some people practice "retail therapy." That is, they go shopping to change their moods or to give them nurturance and support. By itself, shopping can create problems. However, when it is paired with buying, even bigger problems can occur.

Shoplifting Compulsion

Compulsions can become stronger or have more urgency as we exercise or practice them. I met a woman who was a shoplifter. She started with the occasional theft of small items and then graduated, with practice, to more frequent shoplifting of bigger items. She said she knew that the compulsion was running her—and not the other way around—when she was in a specialty kitchen store and planned to push a big butcher-block table out of the front door. She worked so hard to fight the compulsion that she broke out in a sweat and tensed her hands and arms because she knew she would get caught if she did what the compulsion part of her was telling her to do.

Compulsion for Affairs

A man had five marriages and five wives. There was a time when he was paying for three expensive watches simultaneously on a time payment plan with a jeweler. One was for his ex, one was for the current wife, and one was for the woman he was having an affair with.

Activity Compulsion

Jim's parents drink excessively. His mother is now obese and has fallen several times. The parents' financial situation is declining due to their spending and drinking. The more problems Jim's parents have, the more he becomes involved with activities such as hunting, coaching kids' sports, and his job. He comes home, eats, uses the computer or TV, and goes to bed. Jim is avoiding his fears—fears learned years ago when he lived with his parents.

Work Compulsion

"When I really get into my work, I stop doing other things," Timothy said. He doesn't spend enough time with his family, won't take a break to exercise, and often works from 4:00 a.m. to 10:00 p.m. His life is then out of balance, and he is leaning severely in the direction of his work compulsion.

Computer Games Compulsion

"It's just like a drug to him," the wife said. "God help someone trying to take his games away. It's like Jekyll and Hyde. His personality changes that much when he plays."

Recovery Process

You are the one who carries around the pain, and you will continue until you deal well with it. Just as with the stuffed hallway closet that has been closed for years, we have forgotten what is in it. And we fear opening it because we believe the contents will fall on us and injure us. Recovery from a compulsion or addiction is not only about stopping the compulsive or addictive behavior. It is also about resolving old pains, learning new behaviors, and reintegrating all four parts of ourselves into a whole again. Stopping the compulsive behavior is necessary but not sufficient. Stopping sets the stage so we can clean ourselves out just as we clean out a closet before we put more in. We create ourselves anew from the inside.

Some alcoholics or problem drinkers stop drinking by slamming a door on their drinking. The have white-knuckle sobriety because they remain tense, physically and emotionally, even though they are not drinking. Spiritually they remain shallow because they hang onto secrets. The context for this person is tension. Some alcoholics sober up and eventually become relaxed because their context is openness—with no secrets and with reliance upon God. Sobriety, from any addiction or compulsion, is not simply the absence of the toxic substance or action. Healthy sobriety is the presence of all four parts of you connected together.

Compulsions create distraction and pleasure, but there is no peace. Joy said to me, "With the compulsion, when I did it, I wasn't happy. It just covered up the pain and fear. Now I've learned to have joy and peace without the compulsion."

No matter what culture you examine or what age of person you look at, most people are searching for love—or even starving for it. We want the connection with others, we want to be comforted, and we want to be significant for someone else. This type of connection is not easy to find. When we fear we may not find it, we can end up seeking a love connection or comfort connection with a compulsion. Compulsions can give us a rush, like a hug, or they can distract us from pain or help us feel significant.

PART 2

PSYCHOLOGICAL TOOLS
FOR RECOVERY

CHAPTER 8

DEALING WELL WITH FEAR AND
HEALING THE WOUNDS

Before I can live with anyone else, I've got to live with myself.
—ATTICUS FINCH IN *TO KILL A MOCKINGBIRD*

My UNCLE GAVE A SERMON once in theological seminary on Psalm 63, and this was the comment given to him by his professor: "There is an old saying among hunters, 'Never scare up more rabbits than you can shoot.'" My uncle later said, "I guess he thought I brought up a lot of points and did not tie them together." In the next two sections of the book, "Psychological Tools for Recovery" and "Spiritual Tools for Recovery and Growth," I will attempt to tie together the information introduced in section one.

When I was a senior in high school, I enrolled in a composition course taught by Mr. Joseph Fisher, a favorite teacher of mine. One of his requirements was that each of us give a thirty-minute, oral book report, something I dreaded all year. I chose *Madame Bovary* by Gustav

Flaubert, probably because I heard it had some steamy narrative and I was a normal, male adolescent. I practiced my report with three-by-five cards, looking into the bathroom mirror for days. It was typically in the range of twenty-nine to thirty-one minutes long. I clearly remember the day I was scheduled to give my report. It was a beautiful day in May in northern Wisconsin. The sun was shining, and the classroom windows were open. I walked up to the tan-colored metal podium, arranged my note cards, and then looked out at the thirty students and friends staring back at me. I saw sixty large eyes! I began to talk and very quickly became aware of the amount of sweat that was gathering in my armpits and on my forehead. The room seemed very, very hot. I checked to see if the windows were still open. They were. I was feeling a little weak, so I decided to hang onto the podium with both hands and to lean on my elbows, fearful all the time that would cost me points on my talk. Then I noticed a gray curtain beginning to drop down seemingly from my forehead, and it was blocking some of my vision. The gray curtain continued to drop lower, forcing me to raise my chin up so I could see. I have no idea what I said from then on.

The next thing I recall was waking up on the floor in the boys' restroom with two of my friends leaning over me and Mr. Fisher fanning my face with a sheet of paper. My mind was still focused on fear, because my second thought, after determining I was still alive and on the bathroom floor, was to think that I would not have to finish the book report! After fainting, no sane teacher would insist I return to the cause of my fainting. I was wrong. Mr. Fisher must have grown up around horses, because he believed in getting right back on after being thrown off. So I trudged down the hall like a prisoner on death row, returned to the lectern, and gave the rest of my oral book report. And I did not faint.

I have several points to share about this experience: the classroom had not changed, my classmates had not changed, and the weather had not changed. I had changed! I clearly recall thinking that "people just don't faint twice in the same half hour" and "it can't get any worse than this." So I reasoned I would not faint and that I would finish. I might not get a very good grade, but I would finish the report. I still had some fear and anxiety, but it was not as strong as it had been. Something had changed inside my brain and inside the rest of me.

Different sections of the brain have different functions, and the brain is connected through various intermediaries to our body functions. The average adult's brain weighs only about three pounds. The part of the brain that reacts to danger and manages a relaxation response when the danger is gone lies where the spine and skull meet. The weight of this area is measured in ounces, not pounds, but it is powerful for its size.

The higher order lobes of the brain, such as the prefrontal cortex, are located above the midbrain and the hindbrain, which came before the executive functioning of the cerebral cortex in our evolutionary development. These older lobes operate at the basic, unthinking, and automatic level. This is where body functions such as heart rate, blood pressure, gastric secretions, and temperature in our extremities are managed. This is also where the fight-or-flight response originates.

When we perceive danger or when we are afraid—as I was in Mr. Fisher's class—the autonomic nervous system is activated. *Autonomic* refers to an automatic functioning. The autonomic nervous system is composed of the sympathetic system and the parasympathetic system. The sympathetic activates us for action partly through the release of adrenaline. The parasympathetic does the opposite. It relaxes us as it helps with the reuptake and storage of adrenaline and the release of feel-good chemicals such as serotonin.

We would not be here as a species if we did not have this sympathetic system functioning to help us flee from danger or decide to fight. At these decisive times, we need to automatically switch to an increased pulse rate, shallow breathing, tension in the large muscle groups, constriction of the blood supply to the extremities, and concentration of blood in the chest and large muscles. This was an adaptive response and facilitated our survival.

There are times when we are in danger, but they may be less frequent than they appear to be. Many of us live in a perpetual state of vigilance, hyperawareness, and readiness—as if we were airports on high alert because of a bomb threat. Most of the time, throughout the majority of our days, we could be more in touch with the parasympathetic system and allow ourselves to relax. Too much fear in the form of stress will cause heart attacks, cancer, and premature aging. Too often we are stressed, defending what does not need to be defended and fighting what does not need to be fought. However, there are ways we can "reset" the needle on the gauge so that it points more frequently to the parasympathetic, or relaxation, side of ourselves.

This approach is very important because it is about managing ourselves well. As discussed in previous chapters, we cannot control others, and there are very few events that can be controlled. While we interact with others, it is important to manage well the one person we can actually manage well: ourselves. If you want to communicate effectively with others, if you want to have intimate relationships with others, if you want to be less defensive, less critical, and less judgmental, you will need to exercise the *calm/relaxed* side of your nervous system instead of continuing to use the fight-or-flight side. When the sympathetic is activated it is difficult to forgive, let go, stop being resentful, and not want to hurt back. This primitive part of the brain is about survival often through self-centeredness, attack, or avoidance. The cortex, however, is about sharing, forgiving, and socializing. The higher-order cerebral functioning has logical processing; the lower order has win-or-lose functioning. Sadly, we learned many of the fight-or-flight reactions as children. We have carried them forward, often unchanged, into our adulthoods. So we have become prisoners of our past—a past that we drag into the future.

We can use the principles of psychology to help us uncover, recover, and release the compassionate human and spiritual beings that we are. We are spiritual beings in physical bodies, and we are subject to physical and psychological principles. However, we strive to be more than the physical, and we can feel deep within ourselves that there is more than this. So we are not entirely physical or entirely spiritual. It is important we find balance while in our bodies. We must learn to let go of useless fear and anxiety and live more in faith.

In order to see how the process of recovery operates, imagine a pyramid with three levels. The first level is the foundation. It is on the ground, and the other two levels are built on top of this base. The first level is the learning we receive in the first ten to twenty years of our lives. Some was good and some was not so good. We learned as children when our worlds were small, our experiences few, and our choices very limited. Much of this learning was adaptive, such as walking and talking, but there are also experiences that were maladaptive and damaging: abuse we suffered or loss we experienced.

The second level of the pyramid represents the psychological recovery and the updating of the first ten to twenty years. In this recovery, we learn the names of our fears and techniques for reducing them. For example, it is here that we discover that comments from others *trigger* our emotions and overreactions. Removing all fear is not the goal. Denying fear is not a goal. Feeding an addiction or a compulsion is not a goal. Admitting to fears and managing them well *is* the goal.

In the third level, that of spiritual recovery, we move our focus beyond this world to the spiritual world. This level can occur without addressing the issues in the first two levels, but that would be very rare. It can happen when someone has a horrendous car accident—and walks away from it. He or she may be transformed from that day forward, knowing they live in grace and seeking ways to be of service and giving love freely. Usually, however, spiritual recovery comes as we address the learning and psychological blocks, such as fears, that keep us from a life of faith and joy. In the spiritual world, we know we are loved—not just by others, but also by God. At the spiritual level, we are triggered less often. We understand how to care deeply about others. We also know, deeply know, that we are not in charge of the world. There is much we can do, much we ought to do, but the outcomes are not up to us. It is here that we have spiritual peace and not just relief from our previous psychological problems.

In our recovery, it is important to recognize that we are responsible for addressing our problems. We have been nurturing and fertilizing the problems for many years. To get out of the problem, we will need help, because we may not be aware enough of the problem, and we may not know what to do next. Recovery is usually more complete and effective when we begin to rely on a power greater than ourselves.

AWARENESS AND PERSONAL RESPONSIBILITY— NOT BLAMING OR MAKING EXCUSES

Self-care is what we do in therapy or any other time we share ourselves honestly and openly with others. Sharing changes us, but it may not change anyone else. A patient told me, "When I was fifteen, I went to my father's apartment and begged him to come back home. But he was an alcoholic and he didn't." And then my patient added that you couldn't teach an old dog new tricks. I disagreed and said old dogs can learn new tricks, but there are limits on their bodies. They can learn to sit, for example. But an old dog may no longer be physically capable of jumping through a hoop. We humans can learn much more than dogs because of our increased mental abilities. Telling yourself you cannot change because of your age is an excuse based on fear.

We do not need to repress or deny our fears, or deny our attempts at control. To grow we will need to identify the fears: be in touch with them, claim them as our own, and then do something different. Awareness of our fears can lead us to more faith. Awareness of our control attempts can lead us to freedom. Awareness of our egos can lead us to humility. Claiming our humanity and our mistakes can lead us to demonstrate our divinity.

Responsibility is necessary for psychological recovery and is a better word than the words *fault* and *blame*. Responsibility leads more easily to a course of action than the other two do. Responsibility leads to updating, and the others do not. Psychological recovery is partly based on the following:

» Making no excuses for your behavior

» Not blaming others for your behavior

» Admitting to mistakes

» Taking responsibility for your actions

» Being content with progress

» Knowing life is about relationships with people—not with things and possessions

CONFIRMATION BIAS

Once you have established a habit of viewing yourself as a *victim* or as the *quiet one* or any other role, you unconsciously work to confirm what you know and have been led to believe. Psychologists call this *confirmation bias*. Research has shown many people do not seek new experiences and information that challenge their beliefs about themselves and their worldviews. On the contrary, many people seek information that confirms what they already know and believe. So if you believe another race is inferior, that a different make of car is superior, or that you have a fear that you know cannot be overcome, then you will search out sources of information that confirm those points of view. You will stay stuck, unchanging, deteriorating, and not recovering. Seeking new information that does not fit with what you know can put you in frightening territory. Therefore, many people do not seek divergent points of view and are not open to investigating them.

LEARNING TO LIVE, NOT JUST TO EXIST

Animals have a survival instinct, a mechanism that protects them from danger and death. They have fear, but it is in an immediate situation, such as when they are faced with a larger animal or find themselves in unfamiliar circumstances. When they are not in those situations, they can relax completely. A cat might be afraid when it sees a dog and may run. That same cat might not have any fear when it is lying on the hood of a warm car later in the afternoon. It is not thinking about the next encounter with a dog! Now, we humans have fear in specific situations, and we can also relax. But we have the cognitive ability to anticipate future events, recall previous experiences, and prepare for possibilities. Unlike animals, we humans create fear, anxiety, and worry even when they are not necessary for survival. Even when they are not present, we can react as if they were present. We can generate fear about some presumed inadequacy, financial problem, or weight gain even when that issue does not actually exist.

Existence is like a black-and-white movie while living is a 3-D color movie. We can recover from cigarette use, overeating, undereating, and habits such as swearing and resentments. As we interrupt old habits, we are still toxic, and the likelihood of relapse is high. We must put in place new habits. As we practice these, we learn to live. There is a big difference between white-knuckle sobriety when you force yourself not to do certain things and healthy sobriety when you practice new behaviors. We must get rid of the toxic chemicals in our bodies, the toxic thinking in our brains, and the toxic behaviors in our lives, so that we can make room for new thoughts and behaviors.

REINTEGRATING THE FOUR PARTS OF PEOPLE

If you change one of the four parts of yourself, the other three will also change. They are separate only conceptually. In reality, they are all connected one to the other. In dysfunction, one can drag the others down. In recovery, one can raise the others up. For example, as you engage in fewer controlling behaviors, your mind acknowledges the change, and you can praise yourself. You become more satisfied and joyful and have less to fear.

Psychological recovery recognizes the role of the spiritual in our lives (we did not create the universe, and we do not have the power to control others). Psychological recovery also involves a new way of thinking (Who am I when I do not play my roles and games?), a new way of dealing with emotions (What am I feeling? What is my fear? What is a good way to manage these feelings?), and a new way of behaving (What different behaviors can I practice?).

It is a truism in therapy that if an individual overreacts in the present it is because some emotion or memory from the past has been triggered or activated. The memory is not lacking in energy. In fact, it has enough energy to drive fear and to cause a person to overreact as if he or she is still ten or fifteen years of age rather than an adult. Recovering the four parts of ourselves often requires a close examination of old triggers.

Sometimes we are too busy. We take on too much, just as some people buy a house that is too big of an economic stretch for them. So when problems such as unusual maintenance needs or increased taxes occur, there is no money in reserve. The same is true with some of our activity levels. We may not have time and energy in reserve so that we will have the resources to deal with unexpected issues such as funerals or illnesses.

I believe we came from the spiritual realm and will return to it when we die on earth. We borrow this material body for a few years. We know we exist; we have a sense of ourselves and of our thoughts, emotions, and behaviors. We are part of the material world, but we are more than that. We do have an awareness of ourselves, of being here, and of being different from others. We live at the juncture of the spiritual and the material. But if we are not aware, we are likely to become too materialistic. We are usually not at much risk of becoming too spiritual.

Awareness Is Necessary for Change

I was talking one day in my office with a man about his obsessive-compulsive functioning. "When I go grocery shopping," he said, "I go up and down all the aisles with my list, and I buy everything in order from my list. I have it all organized beforehand. It's not fear; it's efficiency." "All right, I hear that," I said. "But do you think you have a fear of making a mistake?" "Well, yeah, that goes without saying," he answered with some irritation. But just a few seconds earlier he had denied having fear. He was unaware of fear. We continued talking about his shopping habits and he said later, "Last Saturday, I forgot to buy the butter. I looked at my list three times and I missed it. That worries me. But worry is fear, isn't it?" He was now more likely to make progress because he was becoming aware of what he did and why he did it.

As long as you are alive, you have a pulse, a breathing rate, and a body temperature. You also have thoughts and feelings. The feelings and the thoughts we have do not come from nowhere. They do not exist in a vacuum, but in a relationship with other people, situations, and yourself. These are all part of being alive. So if someone asks you, "What are you feeling?" and you say, "Nothing," it is as foolish as saying no if someone asks if you have a pulse. You do not need to tell everyone what you are thinking and feeling, but it is good if you know what is happening inside of yourself. So ask yourself, "What feelings do I have when he says that?" Or ask yourself, "Where does that memory come from?" You need to ask yourself those questions if you do not plan to stay the same today as you were yesterday and the day before.

Awareness is necessary in relationships. Otherwise, we might say or do something that does not make much sense. For example, if you say that golfing is important to you and then you admit you haven't played in six months, it is reasonable to surmise golf is not as important as you made it out to be. If you say a relationship with your spouse is important and then admit you haven't been on a date together in months, it reasonable to theorize the relationship is not as important as you said—or as important as other people and activities in your life. These are messages about your priorities.

A patient of mine, Julie, often had difficulties with her mother. After an argument, Julie recounted, "My mother said I did not support her. I said I did by my daily phone calls and my visits. Then she got really angry and hung up. I called her right back because I wanted …" "You wanted what?" I asked her. She explained, "I don't know what I wanted, but all I was going to get from her was more abuse. It's been that way for years." My patient was becoming aware of the habits that she and her mother had developed.

She and her mother had been in this habit pattern for a long time. Fear was strong in their relationship. Julie called her mother often to attempt to avoid having her mother call her while angry. I did not know her mother, but maybe she called because she was afraid of being left alone or of dying alone. Because of their fears, each attempted to control the other, to maneuver so that certain consequences would occur and others would not.

To make changes, she would need to have more awareness, such as knowing this: she was not born with difficulties with her mother; she learned them. She can also change them. She learned the old habits by practicing them, and she can learn new behaviors by practicing them. She could learn to behave differently toward her mother. She could do this with vulnerability and with love. The process would benefit her even if her mother did not change. This is similar to talking with someone about religion—not attempting to convert, just sharing. He or she may not listen to what you are sharing, but the act of sharing will most likely strengthen your faith.

When we deal with others we tend to believe people act *on purpose*, as if they are fully and consciously aware of what they are doing and why they are doing it—and of the possible consequences. But this is not necessarily true. It is important to recognize that others may operate from unawareness also—as we do. By the time we reach adulthood, we are in well-rehearsed patterns of behaviors and habits that were practiced to reduce fear.

We will not change if we continue with dysfunctional and maladaptive habits. Psychology indicates that what we are unaware of will still influence—or even run—our lives. Reflexes such as blinking do not require conscious thought or decision to occur. Our habits that have been practiced for years, and for maybe thousands of repetitions, do not require a conscious decision. We do them without thinking, even if they are decades old, do not make sense, and do not fit into the current time period of our lives.

DEVELOPING AN IDENTITY

The developmental path from role playing to identity involves awareness and experience. It is difficult for a twenty- or thirty-year-old to have identity because she has not experienced enough to be able to make numerous comparisons about who she is, who others are, and available options. People who have identity are much more at ease with themselves. They are not so full of self-doubt, roles, and fear. They also have learned that fault finding and excuse making will keep them stuck in some less mature developmental stage. It is when we take responsibility for who we are, how we think, and how we behave that we move forward toward greater identity. As we take responsibility, we may also find we have less fear and more faith.

People of identity recognize there are many negative emotions—possibly more than there are positive ones. Negative emotions can be useful in small doses, but they can also keep us stuck. Fear, loneliness, guilt, hurt, and anger have their places in our emotional toolbox. But they can also cause problems. Love and joy are emotions. They have their place in our toolboxes but do not cause many problems. We may want less fear or hurt in our lives, but who would want less love or joy?

As we develop an identity, we may find that we are less dependent upon who and what is on the outside to fulfill us and give our lives meaning. We look more to what is inside of us, including God, to help us find meaning and peace. If love or peace are where you are coming from, then you do not have to be on a desperate search to find them outside of yourself in others, cars, clothes, or careers. What we have inside, including faith, cannot be taken away. Identity assists us in moving into a life of relative calmness, stability, and safety—a type of safety that originates from within ourselves.

Some people behave as if they believe the sign that is sometimes posted in a restaurant window: Free Food Tomorrow. They neglect the present and focus on tomorrow's possible reward. However, that "tomorrow" is always twenty-four hours in the future, no matter what day of the week it is. While you are waiting for the free food, your today is now. And you will have identity and find more peace when all four parts of you are connected. You can think about the future, but you cannot be in the future. You will have more peace if you accept yourself as you are today: warts, fears, and all. Live in today, but keep yourself open to change.

If we care to be free to discover who we are, we must individuate from our compulsions and addictions just as we individuated or separated emotionally from our parents. We could maintain many of our parents' values, but, to be an individual, we had to stand up for ourselves, even with our parents. In the process of letting them know what we believed and who we were, we strengthened the process of becoming us, of becoming unique, and of being comfortable with that. We are not our parents, and we are not the compulsion or the addiction that we practice.

THE VALUE OF PRACTICE

There are individuals in my practice who resist practicing healthy behaviors to become more psychologically healthy because they say it is not "natural." Apparently, they believe they can become good at some activity without practicing it. If I could play the piano like a concert pianist just by taking a pill, I would most likely quickly tire of playing. If we could have peace and acceptance without doing anything to earn them, we would probably discount and not value the peace. There is a learning curve involved in the acquisition of any new skill. Those who practice often and for the longest period of time learn new skills well. They move from the "unnatural" to the "natural."

It is action—doing something, practicing something—that begets progress. A myth we have in our culture, right along with "forgive and forget," is "time will take care of it." This is not true. If you enter a coma and regain consciousness six months later, you will not have improved your knowledge of world history, will not be an improved public speaker, and will not have learned how to talk yourself into patience. You will be, six months later, where you were six months earlier. Practice, not time, is the major variable in the acquisition of new skills. It is what you practice thinking, seeing, and doing that will make the difference. If you like the results you achieve, then continue to practice in that manner. If you desire different consequences, you must practice something different.

By the time we become adults, we have been negatively sensitized to a variety of issues, people, and situations. These may be emotion and fear triggers for us. We are sensitized to small places, to being criticized, to people not liking us, to big men, or to women who sound like our mothers. We can also be positively sensitized to such things as rainbows, puppies, and gentle touches. The positives do not cause us problems; the negatives do. It is important that we desensitize ourselves to negative triggers, release ourselves from their grasp, and not continue to spend energy running from these concerns or attempting to bind them with denial and repression.

Usually, a new behavior must be practiced for a significant period of time—measured in months—for the old habit to be appreciably interrupted and the new to become strong and reliable. Many people who have worked to lose weight complain that they have lost the same ten pounds about ten times. Almost every alcoholic or drug abuser can stop drinking or drugging long enough to look good for their court date. Smokers can quit for a few hours or days. They can interrupt the habit, but if they do not practice the new behavior long enough or are not truly willing to change, they return to the old habits in just hours or days.

Phil Mickelson, the professional golfer, practiced putting by placing golf balls around the hole and then putting until he had successfully placed one hundred in a row into the hole. Through this type of repetition he became mentally and neurologically changed. He gained physical skill and mental confidence.

My friend Ralph hired a professional golf instructor for two days of lessons. The instructor asked him how many balls he usually hit in a session. My friend answered, "Well, a few on the practice range before a game." The pro said, "Ralph, if you are not willing to hit hundreds or maybe thousands of balls, you are not going to improve." It is in the practice that we make the progress. Good intentions are not enough. They are similar to flying chickens. They are good for about thirty yards, and then they hit the ground. Completing a recovery plan ought to be for the long term—like a soaring eagle. We tend to get what we practice. Many people practice being hurried and harried—being anxious and worried. If you say you would rather be healthy than wealthy, you will probably have more gratitude and peace. It is better to be prayerful than fearful.

OLD HABITS FADE BUT DO NOT DIE

Society has numerous statements that make sense and some that do not. Some are simply false. One false saying is "Old habits die hard." The truth is that old habits do not die. They just become weaker as we practice new habits. The fears of our childhood, such as shyness and inadequacy, never go away completely until we physically die. They are in our neurological pathways, hardwired into our thinking. A recovering alcoholic will return quickly to drinking if he begins to taste alcohol again—it is in his neurology and habits. That is why the term is "recovering" and not "recovered." As we change our habits, we do not "unlearn" old behaviors. We learn new behaviors that largely replace the old as we continue to assimilate the new.

A man I worked with off and on for several years came to a session and said he had been doing fine at interrupting his controlling ways and his hostility. Then he described a recent event in his company where his supervisors made changes in procedure that had been discussed for about a year. Yet he became very angry (fearful of change and mistakes?) and said, "I could have yelled at them. I was so angry I could have hit them. I probably would have years ago." But this time he went home, talked with his wife, walked the block, and then watched a comedy DVD. And the next day he handled his supervisors well. Then he looked at me and asked, "It never goes away, does it?" "You're right," I said. "It's always just a trigger away. So stay aware and practice the way you want to be—not the way you were. You will keep on making progress, but you are not going to do it perfectly in this lifetime."

REACT OR RESPOND: IS THIS LIFE THREATENING?

Some things are more important or urgent than others. Everything cannot be number one, or there would never be priority. Now, the problem with many of our fears is that we react, or overreact, to them. Not all cuts require sutures, a flat tire is not the same as an engine blowing up, and a bad hair day is not the end of the world. In fact, on your bad hair day only you and a very small number of people know about it. It is not in the headlines, and it is not on the TV news. Responding involves all four parts of us, while reacting involves primarily the emotional (fear) and the behavioral (habits).

Do not exaggerate the appropriate intensity of your fear. I knew a woman who was afraid to have any conflict in her relationships. "I'm afraid of being hurt," she said. "If you are hurt, what will happen?" I asked. "I'll be sad and afraid they may break up with me," she explained. So I asked, "Well, how many times in your life have you felt hurt, sad, and had people break up with you?" When she answered, "Many, many times," I said she was obviously not dead and so could handle rejection. It was sad and painful, but not death producing.

We can teach ourselves to respond appropriately to most situations. We can respond intensely and quickly to extreme situations, and we can respond more slowly and lightly to normal and frequent situations. However, this does require us to assess a situation accurately. Most situations in life fall into one of the following four categories.

Emergency situations are dramatic and intense. They require urgency because there is often blood flowing or a life-or-death situation. These are very infrequent, but when they happen fast action is necessary. Here is an example. A woman took her husband to the hospital with a 104-degree fever. He was diagnosed with pneumonia and could have died the following day without treatment. This type of situation requires immediate and focused attention. Fortunately, they are uncommon or we would age very quickly.

Critical situations are not at the same level as emergencies because they do not involve immediate life-or-death circumstances. However, they could in the near future. Preparation for fast action is required. A critical situation might include listening to newscasts tracking the path of a hurricane. If you learn that the storm will make landfall near you, it becomes critical. These also are intense situations and involve activation of the fight-or-flight response. A patient of mine had inherited a medical condition that affected his kidney functioning. One of his sisters had the same condition and died from it. This man had been on a dialysis machine for several years and had been told by numerous doctors that he would need a kidney transplant soon if he wanted to live. Even so, he did not sign up to be on the transplant list because he was afraid of the surgery and recovery. This rapidly became a life-or-death situation for him.

Important situations are more frequent than emergency and critical situations, but there is no blood flowing, and no one is likely to die. So urgency and fast action are not necessary. If you have not paid your federal income taxes in three years, that is important. You do not need to have a fight-or-flight response to the situation, but you do need a plan to take care of your responsibilities. Arranging funeral preparations is important. Not having chosen the piano music by 9:00 a.m. for a 10:00 a.m. worship service would also be included in the important category. The majority of situations that you encounter within a year probably are not of the emergency, critical, or important type. The majority is reserved for the following category.

Normal and usual situations define most of our daily and weekly lives and do not require activation of the fight-or-flight response. Without them we would have huge gaps of time in which nothing would happen.

These include signing children up for after school activities. Scheduling visits with professionals falls into this category. Waiting in line for your car at the dealership is another example. Being fired is neither normal nor usual, but dealing with most coworkers is. Misplacing car keys, losing socks, and forgetting to pay a bill are all part of this category.

Recently, in a four-month period my wife and I had the following occur: my wife's cousin died of pancreatic cancer eight months after being diagnosed, another cousin had cardiac surgery, my wife tore her ACL and had surgery on her knee, I performed the wedding ceremony for our niece, water leaked from the upstairs toilet into the ceiling of the living room, the water heater leaked water into the ceiling of the master bedroom, the water heater died and was replaced, the drain in our backyard deck clogged and water backed up close to our doors, my brother-in-law had a colonoscopy, and many, many other things happened—thank God. How many of these experiences were life-and-death emergencies? Probably none. Which were critical? Maybe one. The rest were mostly normal. The majority of time, my fight-or-flight response, my adrenaline activation, was turned to *low* or *off*.

I chose to focus on all that I had to be grateful for. Having a house with water damage on two ceilings was better than not having a house. My wife tore a ligament. She did not break her neck. Recognizing that most experiences in life are normal or usual or can be handled without extreme fear allowed me to continue to hold life gently as if I were holding ten eggs in my hands—gently holding them and breaking none.

Imagine you are floating on a river and have been floating at the same speed for days. But then you convince yourself it cannot last and that there must be a waterfall around the next bend. So you yell and scream for help, paddle for the sides, and grab desperately for anything that may slow you down. But the river, as life, is strong, and you are pushed around the bend. You open your eyes and see more miles of water much like what you had been floating through. You prepared for a crisis when it was not imminent. You prepared for a waterfall, and most rivers do not have them. In life, for most of us, there are relatively few emergencies and crises.

CHAPTER 9

SELFISH, SELFLESS, AND
HEALTHY SELF-CARE

*While you are waiting for someone or
something to change, change yourself.*
—DR. RICHARD KRUMMEL

I T IS THROUGH THE PRACTICE of healthy self-care that we effectively
address the learned patterns of mismanaging our fears. Through self-
care we can reintegrate all four parts of ourselves into a healthy whole.
Healthy self-care allows us to move beyond old roles into a current
identity—to move beyond compulsions into being and balance.

When I was a child, I was taught not to do anything selfish. I wasn't
quite certain what selfish was, but I learned fairly quickly from the looks
and words my mother, grandmother, and aunt used. In my young mind,
being selfish was bad, so I learned not to be that way. In fact, in my effort
not to be selfish I went to the opposite extreme. I began to give away
the bigger piece of pie to my sisters. I stopped speaking up for what I

wanted for dinner because asking seemed selfish. I began to function as if I were less important than others—as if my needs and wants were less important. I learned to make decisions about myself only after carefully considering the consequences for others. I did not want them to be hurt by or upset with what I did. Not only had I learned how to be socialized, but I had also become "oversocialized."

As we move through the early developmental stages of childhood and adolescence, we learn to take care of ourselves by interacting with others. Unfortunately, these styles of protecting ourselves are often learned without much conscious awareness. We acquired these skills according to the four principles of learning. Some styles of self-care simply work to reduce our fear or get something we want, such as attention, food, or time with someone. The style serves a purpose but may no longer be the most functional, growth-producing, or mature approach we could use.

For example, we may have learned a style of self-care that involved whining to get what we wanted when we were children. Whining to get a cookie from Mommy may have worked. So we whined to get more cookies and then learned that whining to stay up later or go to a friend's house worked. Thirty years later we whine to get our spouse to go to a certain vacation spot. We learned the role of "whiner" early in life without consciously choosing to do so. We whined because we feared not getting what we wanted. Other children learned different styles. Some other children who feared disappointing others learned the art of perfectionism. Still others feared being alone and learned to cling onto others.

A pattern of self-care is often not consciously chosen and may not be updated to the present time. Moreover, self-care may not be God connected. If it is not God connected it may have too much ego and fear. Consequently, there may not be enough compassion or caring for ourselves as well as for others. The relationship patterns that we learned in our childhoods may prevent us, in our adulthoods, from having healthy relationships with God, ourselves, and others. Updating requires a conscious decision to practice different behaviors in order to achieve different goals.

If you do not want your children or others you love to take care of themselves in the same way that you take care of yourself, then your style is probably unhealthy. This unhealthiness can look like self-centeredness, selfishness, or self-enhancement. It can look like selflessness or self-denial on another extreme. But none of these may be genuine because they could just be old roles being acted out.

Healthy self-care is not selfishness. It is also not giving all of yourself away so there is nothing left. Healthy self-care does not mean you will operate in a self-centered or selfish way. Care of yourself involves an awareness of yourself and your needs and, simultaneously, an awareness of the needs of others. It is not selfish, because self-care recognizes that you are no better or more important than any other person in God's eyes.

Two Learned Roles or Styles: Selfish and Selfless

As we develop, we are likely to learn two behavioral styles: to do what others do or to do the opposite. The easiest path is to copy others. If mom argues with nearly everyone, we learn to argue with nearly everyone. The second easiest is to do the opposite of what other people do. So we decide to not argue much at all. It is easiest to imitate or to reject the extremes and more difficult to live the gray area or the balanced area between the extremes. Just because we move 180 degrees from unhealthiness does not mean that we will find ourselves in the middle of healthiness. The in-between is often where the balance is found.

We learn by copying and reacting, and we also learn what we are taught by others. Others may teach us that we are worth little. So we behave that way. Some parents are afraid to discipline their children and may give them too much of what they want. These parents rescue their children from problems, thereby teaching them not to be responsible for the consequences of their actions. Children may then learn to behave as if they are entitled; they are entitled to much in life simply because they are alive, and they behave in a self-centered way. They may be afraid to change.

My patient Joshua painfully and tearfully said, "I'm still trying to please my mother even though I'm fifty-two. I have a distant cousin here in Houston I haven't talked with in decades. She had surgery last week, and my mother told me that I needed to go see her. I explained that I really didn't even know her. Next my mother asked how far I was from the hospital, and I told her I did not know the name of the hospital. She said she did not know either but that I should look in the phone book and find out." Joshua feared displeasing his mother. The relationship consisted of his mother, the boy he was years ago, and the man he had become. "Of those three, who are we working to help grow up?" I asked him. Through his tears, he said, "Me, the little boy part of me." I told him that we were attempting to update all parts of him to the current time. There are no disconnections when we take care of ourselves so that all four parts of us are in the current time period simultaneously. The mother also had fears and was controlling. She behaved in a selfish manner. Joshua was tired of giving himself away to his mother in a selfless way.

I talked with Joshua about the definition of priority—to have only one number one. I said, "If you have three or four number ones (pleasing your mother, wrestling with fear, juggling your self-esteem, and wanting to get off the phone to her) you no longer have a priority system, just confusion. Figure out as best you can what is the most important or pressing issue for you to work on at this time."

Apparently Joshua's mother felt guilty about not seeing the cousin in the hospital, and she attempted to control her son rather than communicate with him. The reality was that he did not have to eat liver and onions just because his mother did and wanted him to. Joshua actually had numerous choices regarding his cousin and his mother. The best choice is always the one that involves a conscious contact with God, balance, and the alignment of all four parts of ourselves.

By focusing on his mother's emotions and wanting her to have peace, Joshua did not work on his own emotions, and he had no peace. He could directly manage his peace—but not his mother's. Self-care involved changing his insides, not his mother's insides. If Joshua waited for his mother to change before finding peace, he would probably be waiting a very long time. By changing his thinking, Joshua would not have ignored or minimized his relationship with his mother. He would have acknowledged the reality that peace comes from working with and listening to God. As Joshua finds peace inside of himself, he can then share it with his mother. He would be working to change what he could change.

Many of us learned two extremes: selfishness (self-enhancement) and selflessness (self-denial). We may not have learned or been taught enough healthy self-care. Characteristics of all three ways of thinking and interacting are listed in the chart below. Our behavior usually is a combination of these three. But we also have one as our primary style—a basic part of our personality. Still, with willingness and practice we can become a person who embraces healthy self-care most of the time.

Selfish (Self-Enhancement)	Healthy Self-Care	Selfless (Self-Denial)
Plays roles: Dictator, General, Victimizer	Has an identity	Plays roles: Victim, Martyr
Operates from habit	Operates from choice	Operates from habit
Abuses power	Uses power well	Gives away power
Is grandiose about himself	Is realistic about herself	Discounts himself or herself
Blames, excuses	Accepts responsibility	Blames, excuses

Selfish (Self-Enhancement)	Healthy Self-Care	Selfless (Self-Denial)
Sees no reason to change	Accepts change	Waits for others to change
Has problems with intimacy	Wants connection with others	Is enmeshed with others
Pushes for conflict	Resolves conflict	Avoids conflict
Has fear of being found out	Is at peace	Has fear of being found out
Has poor and rigid boundaries	Has healthy boundaries	Has poor and weak boundaries
Manipulates others	Accepts others	Manipulates others
Focuses outside	Focuses inside	Focuses outside
Is hypocritical about God	Is sincere about God	Is hypocritical about God
Controls	Manages him or herself	Controls
Exists in fear	Lives in faith	Exists in fear
Represses many emotions	Shares emotions	Represses many emotions
Blames others for her feelings	Accepts own feelings	Takes responsibility for others' feelings
Is stuck in the past	Updates him or herself	Is stuck in the past
Works to induce guilt in others	Accepts others	Accepts too much guilt

People who grow up with *victimizers* are often the *victims*. When you have seen one extreme, such as an abuser, and seen or experienced the other extreme, such as the one being abused, you learn two styles instead of one. You learn to victimize, and you do that most of the time. Or you learn to behave as a victim, and you do that most of the time. With either role, you occasionally swing back and forth because you know both. A victimizer feels guilty sometimes. He or she might apologize or make some type of compensation but then returns to victimizing. And people who usually behave as victims are sometimes good at victimizing. We will never forget how to behave as victims and victimizers—or to be selfish or selfless. But if we practice self-care and acceptance, we will become good at them, and the old roles will weaken. They do not die; they become weaker. These three approaches are on a continuum. They are not separated by neat and obvious dividers. Because self-centeredness and selflessness do not ever go away completely, we will have occasional opportunities to forgive ourselves and to ask others and God to forgive us.

SELFISH CHARACTERISTICS

The definition of selfish includes a self-concern to the exclusion of others. It means regarding yourself as better than others. The emphasis is upon "I'll win and you'll lose" and upon "I'm right and you're wrong." There is a primary concern for your advantage over others. Selfishness involves a focus on controlling people and events. It implies a willingness to use unfair means to get what you want. Unfair means include victimizing, gossiping, spreading rumors, manipulating, justifying, blaming others, and making excuses. Selfish behavior is evidenced when a person's focus is directed first at himself or herself and not upon God, in spite of what they say. This makes these people hypocritical.

Daniel's story provides a good example of self-centeredness. Daniel was developmentally arrested in both his childhood and adolescence. He was stuck in childhood because he had learned to always expect to be taken care of by others. At family gatherings he did not bring food, help set the table, or even clean up. He was stuck in adolescence, and he continued to fight against authority. He was undiplomatic, demanding, and rude.

When Daniel's mother fell ill and had major surgery, he was unfit to take good care of her because he had never had to focus on anyone but himself. He talked about his mother being on major painkillers because of her hysterectomy and described how unstable she was using a walker. Even so, he did not remain beside his mother as she inched toward the restroom just days out of the hospital. She fell, and Daniel was not able to get her up because of her weight and her pain from the incision. Later that evening Daniel said to other relatives, "Well, I was just a few feet behind her. She just started leaning and she went down. There was nothing I could do. I don't feel any guilt, man, because it would have happened to anyone." He was taking no responsibility. Of course Daniel could have remained beside his mother, steadying her as she walked to correct any leaning. But he did not, and when asked what he could do differently next time, he answered, "Well, these things happen, so I'll just call 911." Daniel had no intention whatsoever of walking alongside his mother through her recuperation. In fact, he left her alone in the house while he walked outside to smoke cigarettes or go to the grocery store to buy more cigarettes.

Daniel's mother was near retirement age but did not have enough money on her own to retire. He had assured his mother and other relatives that he would financially contribute so that she could retire. He even specified how much he could afford to give each month. However, later, when his mother was ill, Daniel told the relatives that he had other obligations and could not give much to his mother after all. He was self-centered, controlling, and fearful of his mother knowing the truth about him. What he did not know was that his mother was well aware of his self-centeredness and that she could not depend on him for support. Daniel was a disappointment to his mother, but she continued to play the game of "Let's pretend everything is okay." This young man belonged to the church of self-centeredness. He was the only parishioner in the pews, the preacher, and the god.

Some people seem not to hear us when we talk. They interrupt us, talk more loudly than we do, talk over us, and switch topics from the ones we are discussing. Some people who seem "self-centered" have a mental health diagnosis. They could have ADHD, which would explain their behavior of interrupting and being impulsive. Others are very anxious and may have obsessive/compulsive disorder. They interrupt or do not track with us because they feel an internal pressure to stay with a certain thought they have. They may change topics because they fear forgetting a thought. Be careful of criticizing or judging others and calling them inconsiderate or lazy. Some of them have anxiety-based disorders that have a biochemical basis.

SELF-DENYING CHARACTERISTICS

Selflessness is often viewed as a positive characteristic, but that is not necessarily true. We are taught to let the other child have the big piece, or to let them play with our toys. We are told to learn to share and to play nicely. Many of us learn behaviors that are the opposite of self-centered.

One of my patients took care of himself in an unhealthy way, but he followed the path of selflessness—specifically, victim behavior. During one of our sessions, he said, "I'm having an angry day, but I don't want to show it. I've been afraid that people will see me as hotheaded because I come from a hotheaded family." So he allowed himself to be victimized by others, and he chose a wife who was hotheaded, because that was familiar to him.

One day Danielle talked with me about her relationship with her husband and what she had asked him to change. "Maybe I should just be selfish," she stated. Then she went on to discuss how she "bends and bends and takes care of others." I suggested the possibility that she had a fear of appearing selfish, so she did the opposite. The problem was that she often reached a point of *not* bending. She would become angry at and then demanding of her husband. She victimized him with yelling and criticisms. Danielle's pattern was the following: (1) she overcompensated for bending by showing anger, then (2) would feel very guilty about the anger, and (3) would return to bending and giving away too much of herself. In spite of her fear of appearing selfish, she was in no real danger of behaving that way very long. She was sensitive and not selfish or self-centered. She was likely to continue to have an unhealthy and selfless role as her default position.

I asked Danielle to imagine that she and her neighbor both had five-hundred-acre farms with cattle. One day the fence separating the two ranches is pushed down by a strong wind, and the neighbor's cattle move over to her field and begin eating her cattle's grass. She does nothing and continues bending over and over until the neighbor's cattle are on her porch making cow pies. Next, she finally overreacts and warns her neighbor that she is going to shoot all of his cattle. If she had quickly moved the neighbor's cattle back to his pasture and then fixed the fence, she would have been practicing healthy care of her ranch and herself.

Selflessness and self-denial are often the result of not truly accepting that we cannot control others and that they cannot control us. For example, a father used control, manipulation, and maneuvering with his adult son. He said, "I thought it looked like a reflection on me that my son, my thirty-year-old son, quit a job, again." He took responsibility for his son's choices and habits. The father felt guilt and a fear of being found out that his son did not feel. I told him that if we had one hundred people in the room with us that the majority would say that he was not responsible for his adult son's decisions. He could not make his son be different. The father did not believe this and did not do anything differently with his son. What he had been doing did not work well, but he continued to do it. It did not make sense for this father to behave as if his son were more important or more valuable than he was. But he seemed to think so, and that is why he kept sacrificing himself to his son. He made himself sick with worry and worked extra hours to cover his son's rent because his son was unemployed and could not pay. This man's appearance of *selflessness* was actually a control maneuver to get his son to grow up and get a job. "I could write a book about pawn shops," the father told me one day. "I went into so many getting the items my son pawned. I could work for the police because I went to seedy parts of the city, putting myself in danger, paying off his drug debts to dealers."

He came to admit that he could not control his son—could not change his son. If he could have, he would have done so years earlier. His son would have finished college instead of dropping out, would have had a career instead of a few skills, and would have stayed with one job instead of having ten in six years. He could talk with his son, he could cry with him, he could beg, he could lend money—but he could not control him or make him change. That was up to his son and to God. As my patient learned to let go of the *illusion of control of others,* he correspondingly became more in control of himself. As he let go of fear and control, more patience and peace came into his life.

A man I knew was the executive director of a nonprofit organization. He wanted to be of service to others. He was caring, compassionate, and worked long hours. He said, "That's what I like to do. I want to help people." It sounded very noble. However, part of his motivation was also to avoid conflict. Because of this fear he took on too many tasks and even did the work of people he had hired. His self-sacrifice and his service to others were often in the service of his fear.

A patient of mine had fears that resulted in him choosing poorly in business relationships. His father had been angry and physically abusive. "I got my butt kicked by Dad until I was fourteen years old. I went to the doctor a lot and told him I had fights with friends. I was afraid my Dad would lose his career if I told the truth. I would take a beating from him so my sister and my brother would not get beat," my patient disclosed. Now he gets into business deals with people who lie to him and take his money, and then he repeats it again. He said, "I'm like Old Yeller. I'll die for you." He was still taking the beatings, three decades later.

THE VICTIM'S TWENTY-THIRD PSALM

The Twenty-third Psalm in the King James Bible Version reads, "The Lord is my shepherd, I shall not want. He maketh me …" It is a prayer of hope but also one where faith is the requisite ingredient. But some people seem to follow a different prayer. It sounds like this: "The Lord is my shepherd. I shall want very little. He maketh me to lie down on stones of pain. He leads me beside overwhelming waters. He drains my soul. He leads me in the paths of hurt for His name's sake. Even though I walk through the Valley of the Blood of Pain I will be ever-super-alert, for I really trust only myself. Your rod and your staff inflict pain upon me. Thou preparest an empty table before me while my enemies have much food. Thou anointest my head with dirty cooking oil. My cup is full of it also. Surely, my old and outdated habits will be with me all the days of my miserable life, and I will be unhappy on this earth until I die. Amen."

Now, that would be a ridiculous prayer, a ridiculous theology, and a sad way to live. Even so, some people run their lives this way. Most of us know people like this. Maybe we are one of them. As Pogo said in the cartoon strip by Walt Kelly, "We have met the enemy and he is us."

HEALTHY SELF-CARE

Healthy self-care is not selfish. It is not a role. It is not greedy. It is not exclusionary. It does not have undue fear. It does not have envy or jealousy. It is an awareness of our strengths and weaknesses—with an acceptance of all of oneself. It does not reject the self. It is love of oneself. It is reasonable and responsible and does not make excuses or assign blame. It is a recognition that joy comes from within, not from outside. It is letting go of what we cannot control and turning that over to God. Self-care involves the forgiveness of self and of others. Selfish people often blame others. People who operate with self-denial often blame themselves. But those who utilize self-care recognize that they are not perfect, that others are not perfect, and that we can forgive ourselves and them.

We are always busy attempting to take care of ourselves in the best way we know how, but our unhealthy self-care often leads to poor consequences or keeps us stuck. The reason for poor self-care is usually related to fear. "Two weeks ago my father-in-law was in the hospital and he was very ill, possibly dying, and he told me he loved me and I did not say it back," the man said. He was afraid of emotional vulnerability.

If we hide behind a wall of fear of our own creation, we talk and listen only to ourselves—not to God, not to others. Fix yourself with the healthy psychological tools you have and with God's help. If you have a fear of elevators, the problem is not the elevators. They did not cause the problem. You caused the problem with your negative thoughts, negative self-talk, and mismanagement of your emotions.

People who practice self-care know that they can learn much from others if they are open to receiving. We are like pianos. As a piano is played it can get out of tune. If we know how we can tune the piano and ourselves. However, sometimes it is too complicated for us to do. Sometimes it is good to have our pianos and our lives tuned by others. Keep in mind that God is a great piano tuner.

I knew a man who gambled on his ex-wife and sons. That is, he gave them money, energy, and time for many years and expected a big payoff. He continued to give money to his drug-abusing sons, each time hoping it would be different. But he had not landed on his number yet. He could have stood in front of his two thirty-year-old sons and his rescuing ex-wife with signs that said Grow Up, Don't Do Drugs, and Stop Enabling. But they probably would not have changed. During a session he told me that his ex-wife had called him, again, and said the sons were living with her, again, and were fighting each other and threatening to kill each other, again. So he called the police, again. The other numerous times he had intervened, his sons had not changed. While he was waiting for them to change he could have tried taking good care of himself. His job was to feel his feelings, including fear, to think his thoughts, and to learn such things as problem-solving strategies. His job was to do this without using the old rescuing habit and to do it with faith in God instead of his own way. Most of the time, moving toward healthy self-care will require changing habits that have been relied upon for years—habits that do not work.

Do not give up on prayer, compassion, and helping others even if their behavior does not change. Just give up those unhealthy behaviors that do not get you what you want for them and for yourself. You can decide whether or not you go to Las Vegas. If you go there, you can choose whether to gamble or not. But you probably cannot change the casino owners or the gamblers who choose to be in the casinos. Being of service to others can be very healthy and is necessary if a society is to have cohesiveness and compassion. But, as with any good thing, it can be taken to an extreme where it is no longer healthy: when you abuse yourself and allow yourself to be abused by others.

Jeanine was a patient of mine who struggled in her relationship with her boyfriend, who was emotionally aloof and verbally abusive. She also had one daughter who abused cocaine, another that was using cocaine after her divorce, and another whose controlling husband had sex with the wife's girlfriend. Jeanine said, "I am so overwhelmed by all that is going on with my daughters and then I still have this relationship problem with my husband. I have all this chaos in my life." She could not control her daughters' lives even though she had tried for years to get them sober and happy. The daughters will become sober and happy when they are ready, and they were not ready when I talked that day with my patient.

She could directly control and change herself. She could not directly control and change her daughters. They might eventually change if they decide they want the kind of peace that Jeanine has now. They might change if they learn how her new church involvement has helped her find peace. Christianity is a religion of love, and it is also one of attraction. If you have from your religion what others want, then they may do what you are doing. They may change because of the way that you are, but they are changing themselves. You are not directly changing them.

A man I know planned to drive to Disney World during an Easter vacation with his extended family—all eleven of them. He and I discussed what healthy self-care might look like during that week. To take care of himself intellectually he took along two good books to read. To take care of himself emotionally he decided to open up and share with his family rather than "buy something like I often do to change my mood or just tune them out." Behaviorally, he planned to interrupt his habit of disciplining the grandchildren and instead "learn to discipline myself. I will talk with my children and ask them to discipline their children." Instead of going into Disney World three days from very early in the morning until late at night, he and his wife decided to take a day off to lounge around the pool. To take care of his body he did not plan to drive an entire day and then go into Disney World the next day. Spiritually, he intended to go to a church on Sunday while in Orlando. All of this was healthy self-care.

Poor self-care for him would have been the following.

1. Spiritually, he would have avoided church and then been angry.

2. Intellectually, he would have known how to do some healthy behaviors and then not done them.

3. Emotionally, he would have been angry at others and at himself when he was actually fearful or sad.

4. Physically, he would have continued walking a great deal when he knew his feet would hurt after about two hours.

Martha was a patient who was very confused about the issue of self-care and selfishness. She behaved and talked as if any attempt to take care of herself was an act of selfishness. She had an adult son who not only had ADHD but also bipolar spectrum disorder. He had a long history of not taking his medications, stealing from his parents, using his parents' credit cards to buy alcohol, and taking his mother's car without permission. After his last accident with her car, she bought a metal bar that could be locked on the steering wheel, preventing unauthorized use. "I bought the club for my car," she told me, "but I feel so guilty. How could I do this to my son? What is wrong with me?" I reminded her that her son was different than she was. He had a different set of values. He abided by a different set of social rules than she did. He was also highly impulsive and had an impaired ability to consider consequences. I explained that there was nothing wrong with her. Moreover, protecting her property was not a selfish act. It was an appropriate act of healthy self-care. Martha was not at risk of being selfish. She was more at risk of returning to her default of practicing unhealthy selflessness.

Healthy self-care does not mean we stop caring for others. It does, however, mean that we care for others in an adult, mature, and God-centered manner. It signifies responding out of choice rather than simply reacting out of habit. It means our insides do not have to match the intensity of problems happening on the outside. If your spouse is anxious or controlling, you do not have to be. You are not him or her. You can be you—the kind, caring, and God-focused you. You can care for someone in a spiritual fashion even if he or she tells you that you are uncaring and emotionally dead. You are not dead, but simply behaving like an adult in a world where a crisis-oriented response is not needed very often. You do not have to participate in someone else's drama.

As I wrote in the previous chapter, in a recent four-month period several significant events happened around me: my wife tore her right ACL and had surgery to repair it, a toilet upstairs had a leak which resulted in two large holes in our living room ceiling, the water heater leaked and damaged our bedroom ceiling, and our cousin had open heart surgery to replace her aortic valve. All of this occurred during the time just prior to our niece's wedding: a wedding for which I performed the ceremony, and my wife and I organized a shower and other get-togethers. My wife and I both knew God was in charge of all of these events. We knew we had our responsibilities but were not in control of consequences such as infections from surgery or the weather on the wedding day. We worked to stay in the present, to respond rather than react, and to thank God for the opportunities given us—whether we truly liked them or not. Our self-care did not involve dragging out our egos and wondering why all this was happening to us. We talked about being typical people, and we focused upon God. We made it through all that and more. Praise God.

Many of my patients report that at the end of a session they are calmer than they were when they walked in and sat down. The problems with their spouses, families, or bosses remained and were probably unchanged outside of the office. If they are calmer it is not because of the coffee I give them, because I perform brain surgery on them, or because I call their spouses and pay them to start being kinder. My patients are calmer because they change themselves. The words and concepts I used may have made sense to them, and they believed them. I did not change them. They changed themselves. They could have given themselves the credit—not so that they can become arrogant, but so they become realistic about the mechanism of change. They could give God the credit because they were willing to let go of some fears and to practice patience and faith. If what you are doing is working well, keep doing it. If it is not working, begin to look around to see what you might do differently. Have faith that the something different, with its different consequences, might have positive results.

There are some days when you are upset, when your friends, family, and colleagues are troubled and troublesome. And the next day you can be feeling good even though those same people are just as troubled. The other people are obviously not in charge of you, your emotions, or your well-being. If you hold life with tension, attempts at control, and fear, you will be tired, frustrated, and fearful. If you hold life gently and live in faith, you will learn to be relaxed and peaceful most, but not all, of the time.

A patient of mine broke his leg while on a skiing vacation. When I saw him he was wearing a brace on the leg to take care of it, to support it. After calling his sister to share the problem with her—and after receiving many "too bads" from her—she began to tell him how he *should* be raising his daughter: she should study more, write longer thank-you cards, and have more chores around the house. My patient took care of himself by telling his sister that he did not care to hear that type of information that day. He said he would speak with her at another time about those issues. As we talked, I pointed out the obvious to him: his leg and psyche are both parts of him. He can take care of or neglect them. His leg was not ready for full use, so a cast and crutches were helpful. His psyche was not ready to hear criticism from his sister, so stopping the conversation was helpful.

With healthy self-care the idea is not to create crises. Life will certainly give you some of those occasionally. The goal is to have balance—a normal life—and then to maintain it. It is good to go to your physician sometimes even when you don't have a specific problem. It is good to be assessed to help prevent future problems. The idea is to maintain a normal life. You can wait to meet with a psychologist until you have a crisis. Or you can proactively go to maintain peace and a healthy adjustment. You can wait to pray until someone you love is dying. Or you can pray with gratitude on a regular basis for the health your loved ones do have.

CHAPTER 10

AFFIRMATIONS

The question is not what you look at, but what you see.
—HENRY DAVID THOREAU

SELF-TALK IS STRONG

WE ALL TALK TO OURSELVES. When we think, we actually are talking to ourselves. "Okay, now what was I going to do today? Why did I come into this room? What was that woman's name and how do I know her? Uh-oh, looks like rain again." These are all examples of how we talk to ourselves—and answer ourselves. We talk to ourselves about whom and what we see outside of ourselves, and we talk to ourselves about what we imagine inside of ourselves. This is all normal. Unfortunately, when we talk to ourselves about ourselves, the tone is often negative, critical, and judgmental. "I made another mistake. I'm fat. I wish I was smarter. They probably won't like me." These are examples of negative self-talk.

We humans are innovative, and we create stories about our worth, ability, and skills. Many of them are negative and outdated. We would not want our children or friends to hear those negative stories, yet we may hold on to them for decades. We were not born with the stories; we learn them. We also learn to apply negative words and concepts to ourselves. We acquire the words according to the four principles of learning, and we can use the four principles, along with our creativity, to develop and rehearse different, positive words and stories.

Negative self-talk is like a prison. We run the risk of building a prison with bars of fear that keep us confined and stuck in our narrow and familiar surroundings. Alternatively, positive self-talk—affirmations—is like a set of bar cutters that release us and allow us to grow.

We can learn to say appropriate and positive statements to ourselves about ourselves in the same way we learned to use negative self-talk. The learning principles are the same, but as adults we can choose what we want to practice. If you want to feel poorly about yourself, practice negative comments. If you want to feel good about yourself, practice positive self-talk. Practice is necessary to make progress. Not practicing and expecting a change in your self-talk is like standing in your garage and expecting your wheelbarrow to turn into a new car. It won't happen!

Sometimes in my office I emphasize this point about the strength and frequency of negative self-talk by challenging my patient. For instance, I may tell her that I will begin by saying a positive statement about her and then ask her to say one about herself. Then we continue alternating until one of us runs out of positive self-statements. Most patients have only two or three positive things to say about themselves. I usually go on to provide another five or so about them. Next, I write them all down on paper for my patient to take home to practice.

As we work to change ourselves, it is important to recognize that we do not unlearn old habits, and we do not usually forget what happened to us. Rather than unlearn, we learn new habits. They are the result of practice. New habits can have stronger neurological pathways than the old ones did, but the old ones do not die away. That is why you can return to riding a bike at age forty even if you have not ridden one since age sixteen. You still remember how to balance and to brake.

WRITING POSITIVE SELF-STATEMENTS

Many people can quickly make numerous critical comments about themselves, their bodies, and their abilities. However, when asked to write complimentary statements about themselves, their bodies, and their abilities they slow down to a crawl. That is because they have practiced the negative for years—and they are good at it.

To make progress in reducing the frequency of negative self-talk and increasing that of positive self-talk there are two main strategies to follow.

1. Get a sheet of paper and write down all the negative and critical comments you can think of about yourself. You do not need to do this all at once. You can add to the list from day to day. Plan to complete this task just once and not to reread it.

2. Get a sheet of paper and begin to write down positive statements that are the opposite of each of the negative statements you wrote. These are the sentences you will plan to practice often enough that they become second nature to you. These are the statements you will read and reread.

When I ask my patients to do the above, I tell them to practice positive affirmations until they are memorized. I often say, "When you bring in your list of positive statements to show me, have them memorized so if I ask you what number eighteen is you can tell me." The value of this technique is that by the time they have them memorized, they will have begun to believe what they are saying. If you do this, you will come to believe about yourself what those people who love you believe about you. In terms of the four parts of people, you interrupt the old behaviors, have less fear, and update your thinking to the current time period, and your spirit shines through.

Read the examples below and use them to do the two-part exercise. Your negative self-comments may be like the following:

1. I'm not very smart.
2. My hair is stringy.
3. My nose is too big.
4. My breasts are too small.
5. I don't know how to talk with people.
6. I make more mistakes than most people do.
7. I should have stayed in school.
8. I don't have any artistic (musical, athletic, etc.) talent.
9. I'll never get any better.
10. I don't make enough money.
11. Etc.

Your positive self-comments would then be the opposite of the ones above:

1. I am smart enough to get a diploma (get a degree, get a job, own a car).
2. I know some hairstyles that work well with my hair.
3. I like the size and shape of my nose. It's all part of me.
4. My breasts are big enough. I like my breasts.
5. I can talk with other people, and I can learn to talk even better.
6. I make more good decisions than poor ones.
7. I have choices. I can still take more courses if I want to.
8. I am good at baking (gardening, changing oil, etc.).
9. I can make progress if I practice.

10. I can think of more ways to make money, and money is not everything.

11. Etc.

When I ask my patients to do this assignment many of them resist and say, "Well, that would be just doing a snow job on me. Those affirmations aren't true about me. They're just lies." My answer to them is this: "The negative statements you've been rehearsing all these years were a snow job you did on yourself. They weren't true; they were lies. You practiced them, and now you believe they are true, but they're not." If you believe that you are good at something, whether it be golf, baking, swimming, or building, it is because you practiced that activity and have the affirmation that you are good at it. You were not born telling yourself positive statements about your skills in that activity.

To help yourself memorize affirmations you also might do any or all of the following:

1. Write down affirmations on a three-by-five card. Number each one and highlight them with different-colored highlighter pens to help with visual memorization.

2. Tape the three-by-five cards to your bathroom mirror or to the dashboard of your car so that you see them often.

3. Tape a different affirmation statement each day to the face of your watch. When you look at the time you will also be rehearsing an affirmation!

4. Make a new habit of rehearsing some of your affirmations each time you use the restroom. This will guarantee that you practice several times each day for at least a minute or two at a time.

As you practice the above and make progress saying and believing the positive about yourself, you can move onto more abstract comments about yourself and your world. These might include the following:

1. I cannot control others, but I can manage myself well.

2. I can practice and make progress—perfection does not happen on this planet.

3. Life is a big circle. If I give away peace, I receive peace.

4. There are many unconscious triggers in me. I am becoming more aware of them.

5. Most people are basically good.

6. I can see the good in anybody.

7. I can learn something from everyone—if I am willing.

8. I can share my opinions and do it with respect for others and their opinions.

9. Most of the time, most of us are behaving okay.

10. I am learning to be at ease with all parts of me. All the parts are connected.

11. Etc.

If you practice your affirmations twenty times per day when you look at your watch, six times each day when you look in the mirror, two times a day when you drink a glass of water, and two to five times per day when you use the restroom, then you will have rehearsed various positive statements approximately thirty times per day. That is thirty times each day you can compliment yourself! And that is 10,950 times each year you can be supportive of yourself. If you said these that often to a child, at the end of the year, her self-esteem would probably be higher and her inadequacy would be lower. You are also worthy of compliments and praise, just as a child is.

CHAPTER 11

FEAR, RECOVERY, AND
INTIMATE RELATIONSHIPS

*In this world of overrated pleasures and underrated
treasures, I'm glad there is you.*
—"I'm Glad There Is You" by Jimmy Dorsey and Paul Madeira

WHAT TO DO WHEN THE NEWNESS WEARS OFF

THE FIRST STAGE IN A love relationship may "just happen" between two people, or it may be the result of some strong physical and emotional connection—a connection that is special. But the newness of a relationship is temporary, like the newness of a car when you first buy it. Eventually, the newness wears off, and then we must keep working to update the relationship—help it move along as circumstances and life move along. Otherwise, we may stay stuck because of fear. To maintain a love relationship and successfully move through its stages takes work. It does not "just happen."

A man and a woman may fall in love, and that may be good for several months or even several years. Things may change if a couple has children. Kids can detract from the time it takes to maintain the relationship. The couple's attitude toward the union may change as well. Careers and volunteer activities will also detract time from a marriage. After the children leave for college, the couple may find they have little in common because they had not been working at maintaining an intimate, vulnerable, and loving relationship. I often find in marriage therapy that the woman wants to talk, to be heard, and to have emotional closeness. However, many husbands are not good at this, largely because they do not practice it. Sadly, numerous couples divorce without making substantial changes in themselves and in their relationship. Many husbands fearing vulnerability with their wives may divorce and find another, younger woman who may not require closeness. Or a man may be searching for the honeymoon phase again. They remain stuck in the "just happen" stage of love, and they do not work to update the relationship.

A woman I know believed she was not being acknowledged by her stepchildren for all she did for them, including making their birthday celebrations special. She was raised by an angry and controlling father. The other dysfunctions in her family of origin resulted in a belief that she was always "on the outside"—being too different and often excluded. When the stepchildren did not call her immediately to say thank you, her unresolved issues of fear of exclusion were triggered. At her house she yelled at her husband, slammed doors to get attention, made a point of not eating much—just some cereal—for dinner, and avoided speaking with her husband. She was, unconsciously, attempting to engage him in the old pattern of abuse she knew so well from her childhood. Except this time, instead of behaving as the victim, she behaved as the victimizer of her husband and of herself. As soon as this behavior started, the husband told me, "This is ridiculous. It has to stop. She needs to fix this problem she has!" I asked him to consider talking with her from openness and love. He could say, "I am sad when I see you not eating. When you hurt, I feel hurt. I am your partner, and I want us to work together. Will you team up with me?" He then said, "Oh, I should handle her with kid gloves?" indicating he was still thinking of being something other than open. "No," I said, "handle her with gloves of love." Those would not only be new words for her to hear from him but also a new attitude.

A patient of mine, Jonathon, behaved with assertiveness at work but was meek and conflict avoidant at home with his wife and children. I told him there seemed to be two sides to him: the assertive side and the other side that showed up when he crossed the threshold at home. It was easier for Jonathon to be confident at work because it was the newest part of his life, and it was usually not emotional. It was more difficult for him to be assertive with his wife because that relationship was based on intimacy and was often emotional. His relationships with his parents and siblings were the most difficult for him to function in as an adult because they were the oldest. They began at his birth and involved much unconscious, often emotional material. Jonathon avoided conflict only in situations of emotional intimacy. He could be an updated adult with strangers, but he did not do that with his wife and family of origin.

What to Do to Reduce Fear

It's called *free* will. It is not called *control-others* will. So you are left communicating and compromising—if you want to use your free will to do that. We are given free will at birth. As we age, we become bound by our fears and habits. Then we are no longer free. Our fear reactions often lead us to develop defenses to protect ourselves just as people in medieval Europe built castles to protect themselves. Castles can keep us safe behind ten-feet-thick and thirty-feet-high walls. Inside we are safe, but it is a very small world. The walls keep others out, but they also keep us in. Our fear-based habits are like those walls, preventing us from growing and compromising.

Healthy relationships involve several components. One is responsibility—to God, to yourself, and to the other person. Another component is honesty. Another is vulnerability. And another is reciprocity. Not in the sense of "you hurt me, so I'll hurt you back," but in the sense of working to be fifty-fifty in the relationship so that there is balance. A healthy relationship attitude would be the following: "I will be responsible for sharing my thoughts and feelings honestly with you. Please do the same for me. I will be responsible for helping you get your needs filled. Please do the same for me."

Developing a healthy, satisfying, and rewarding relationship with another person requires you to develop a healthy and rewarding relationship with yourself. You need to be mindful of the opportunities for growth. This awareness helps you reassess your fears and their place in your relationships. For example, if you have a fear of rejection in intimate relationships, a four-point approach to effectively addressing it might look like the following:

1. Emotionally, identify the fear by writing down where it came from, who you learned it from, who else in your life may have the fear, who first and most significantly rejected you, or who you feared would reject you. Remember, the "wolves of fear" from our childhood may have weakened or died years ago, but we did not know it because we did not stop running and turn around to check reality.

2. Intellectually, admit you learned this fear. You were not born with it. Talk to yourself and reassure yourself you can change. You learned the fear by interacting with significant others in your young life, and now you carry it with you. You can learn an interpersonal skill that is more mature and adaptive to your current time and life. Tell yourself you do not need to continue to have a pattern you learned in your childhood or adolescence.

3. Behaviorally, remember that what you practice is what you become good at. Put together a list of positive statements about yourself you can memorize, and then practice saying them several times every day. You have spent years practicing negative self-talk about yourself and your fear of rejection. Now assemble positive statements such as these: "I'm strong. Rejection hasn't killed me. I have been rejected, and I am doing well." Practice positive thinking and you will probably feel better. Practice negative thinking and you will probably feel worse. There is no magic to it—it is just common sense. There is no more artificiality to it than there is to fertilizing a rose bush. If you want the rose bush to bloom, then feed it. If you want to bloom, then feed yourself something nurturing.

4. Spiritually, do some *faith stretching* to increase your faith and simultaneously reduce your fear. We are not alone—God is always with us. Practice saying that to yourself. In spite of our mistakes—sometimes in spite of ourselves—we have made it this far in life. God and the angels are watching over us, doing for us what we are not doing for ourselves.

In therapy sessions with couples, I sometimes ask the wife what her opinion on any given subject is worth. She might say she does not understand. So I will restate the question and then give her the answer, which is "one unit." Next, I ask the husband what his opinion on any subject is worth and he usually asks hesitantly, "One unit?" Subsequently, I ask both of them whose opinion is worth more. Typically, each answers neither because they see that each of their opinions is worth one unit. Then I inquire how valuable each of them is, how much worth as a human each has, how important they are, etc. The answer to each of these questions is one unit. For many couples this is radical thinking! We are all equal on these dimensions. You can reduce your fear of being honest with others, especially with those you love, by seeing your worth as the same as theirs and your opinion having the same weight as theirs.

Two People Together Are Really Three Relationships

As I stated in chapter six, when I work with couples in therapy I often tell them that we are dealing with three entities: one individual, the other individual, and the relationship. The relationship is built with the tools the individuals bring to it. The relationship is a reflection of the combination of the individuals. The relationship is only as well adjusted or healthy as the least well-adjusted or healthy individual. If one individual is selfish or unhappy, then the relationship mirrors selfishness and unhappiness. If both individuals refuse to compromise or to respect each other, then the relationship is uncompromising and disrespectful. On the other hand, if both individuals are healthy, or moving toward healthiness, then the relationship is healthy or moving toward healthiness. If both individuals show care and compassion, then the relationship has care and compassion.

Similarly, each individual has the power to sabotage the relationship, usually because of fear. The relationship does not sabotage itself; only the partners have the power to do that. If the two individuals want the relationship to grow, they will both have to show growth. The two of them cannot grow the relationship except as a team.

The Three C's

The three C's of a relationship are:

1. Compassion
2. Communication
3. Compromise or conflict resolution

Compassion for Others

When I open the door to my office waiting room, I usually see one of my patients. The word *patient* comes from the Latin root *pati*, meaning "to suffer." So when I open the door, I am planning to talk to someone who is suffering. They are not in my office because they feel great but because they are in pain. When I sit down with him or her, I often ask, "What do you want healing from today?"

The word *compassion* also has Latin roots: *com* means *with* and *pati* means "to suffer." According to *Webster's New World Dictionary, Second College Edition*, compassion means "sorrow for the suffering or trouble of another or others, accompanied by an urge to help; deep sympathy; pity." Therefore, I can have sympathetic concern for my patients and their suffering. My compassion for them is an attitude that I have and that I can show them. My attitude is where I am coming from; it is inside of me. An attitude is something that I cultivate so that I can be of service to my patients—so I can hear them and be present for them. I call this an attitude of inclusion. Of course, I could do the opposite and practice an attitude of exclusion. That would probably create conflict and stress between us. The two concepts have characteristics such as the following:

Inclusion	Exclusion
I have also suffered.	You're just whining.
We have all suffered.	My suffering is greater than yours.
We are all similar.	You are very different than I am.
We are all Children of God.	You are alien.
God is in all of us.	God is not in you.
I want to help you.	Go away. Go help yourself.

When we want to accept and to work with another person on a relationship, it is important we develop an attitude of inclusion rather than exclusion. The latter sets the stage for judgment, friction, and conflict: a me-against-you approach. With inclusion we do not want to isolate someone. Rather, we want to involve them in our lives and to be involved in theirs. When using an inclusion approach, we recognize that other people are very much like us: they laugh, they hurt, they love, and they have fears. We share a common boat on this journey of life. If we search for connections with others we will have more compassion for them. We also position ourselves much better to communicate and to compromise.

I once spoke with a young mother who was describing her fatigue as a result of her four-month-old infant's feeding schedule. She told me she was angry, felt deprived, and didn't feel as if she had a life of her own any longer. "But then," she said, "one night at about two in the morning I looked down at my baby breastfeeding, and I realized she woke up because she was hungry. She was in pain. So there we were in the dark, both of us in pain. But I could help her with hers. I felt calmness, and my anger went away." This was a young mother who found compassion.

Janice, a patient of mine, was having difficulty with her husband, Gavin. In her opinion he was too afraid of change and too secretive. Janice was judging him and excluding him. She had pushed Gavin into the corner of her world where *wrong* people are. She noticed she did not often respond to him. Instead she reacted. Janice explained, "I get defensive often with him. I take our little disagreement to be on the level of him attacking me with a weapon. And it is not that important usually." After discussing acceptance of him, she grasped the concept and moved on to another. She asked, "What can Gavin *teach* me?" I suggested that question might be phrased more accurately by asking, "What can I *learn* from Gavin?" Gavin was not in charge of Janice's life, motivation, or attention. She would learn when she was ready to learn, not when he was ready to teach. And she could learn more if she saw that she and Gavin had much in common—including their fears.

Janice came back the following week and said she believed that she had made some progress in showing vulnerability and love. Her husband, she said, reminded her often not to leave food on the kitchen counter because it might attract ants. One evening Gavin left some food on the counter. She thought of leaving it there. She called that tactic "feeding the ants." She would point out his mistake and hypocrisy in the morning. However, compassion required a different approach from her. She admitted she also made mistakes and was sometimes hypocritical. So she went to Gavin and said, "Honey, you left a plate on the counter. Do you want me to put it in the dishwasher for you?" And she spoke in a loving voice. Because he could feel he was not being attacked or criticized, he was pleasant in return, which led to a breakthrough in their communication style.

Some basketball and volleyball coaches ask their young players to carry the ball with them everywhere they go for a week. In this way, their handling of the ball becomes habitual and unconscious—a desirable characteristic on the playing field when the action is fast. If each individual in a relationship were to carry the other's heart, pain, or sensitivity everywhere for a week, they would become very good at caring for that heart or pain or sensitivity. They would probably gain compassion for each other. Unfortunately, many couples do not have even a two- or three-hour "date night" every two weeks in which to practice caring for each other's heart. If you want to improve your relationship with your loved one, you have to be willing to make time with him or her a priority. You will also need to move your ego off to the side so you can show compassion instead of working to be right or to have things your way.

Think of your spouse when she was about three months old. Or look at a picture of her when she was about that age. What words would you use to describe her? Probably words like *sweet, cute, cuddly,* and *adorable* come to mind. Now look at her thirty, forty, or more years later. What words come to mind? If they are not the same words, what happened? She may have learned to defend herself with approaches that are not sweet, cute, cuddly, and adorable. But she learned the same way you learned. She was not born being mean, loud, and self-centered. And neither were you. She learned most of her styles just as you did. Moreover, she can learn some other styles—just as you can. Be patient with her and with yourself as you change.

Think of your partner at a time when he was very vulnerable. Seeing him this way will help you become less ego-involved and more compassionate with him. For example, I recall very clearly my wife on a hospital gurney after a surgery she had. As she was wheeled out past me her face was contorted in pain and she said, "Oh, it hurts. It hurts so badly." The love and compassion that I had for her at that moment is what I try to recall about our relationship when she does not do or say what *I* think she ought to. That image of her—kept fresh in my memory—helps me to hear her and to show compassion.

COMMUNICATION

Communication is the second of the three C's, and it can be either positive or negative. Either way, it is a major source of energy in a relationship. It is like electricity. It can be used to charge a battery, to light a lamp, or to create sparks and a fire. The way we communicate can help or harm a relationship. If we have an attitude of compassion, we are more likely to create positive communication—that is, to express ourselves effectively about who we are, what we need, and what we want. If you want to "recharge" your relationship, you will need to carefully examine your communication style.

Communication also has characteristics of inclusion and exclusion, and if we are aware of them we can communicate more effectively.

Inclusion	Exclusion
Disclosing	Controlling
Open	Closed
Let's talk	I'm right, you're wrong
Awareness	Unawareness
Sharing	Secrets

I once worked with a couple who, like many of us, had issues about money. They both were stubborn in their thinking and were running on fear. We agreed to examine their budget in detail. I thought they might learn to communicate better if we had some concrete material in front of us. The issue of unawareness was obvious one session when the wife—while pointing her finger at her husband and holding it about twelve inches from his face—said, "You can read any book on personal finances, and they will tell you that you have to remove the emotions from the equation when you are talking about money!" She was unaware that what she was doing was the opposite of what she was saying.

Many of us take better care of our cars than we do of ourselves. Imagine that you are a car. So, for example, this car is called Ryan. It is valuable and one of a kind, and only one person can drive it well. Now, you can let your wife or girlfriend get behind the wheel and drive it, but she is not the car, so she will not know it well. She will only know about the surface, but not about the deep insides of the engine. She can hear the engine, but she cannot see or experience what is moving inside of it. Only you can do that. Because of this she will sometimes turn the wheel too much or too little and may bump into things. She cannot run you. And you cannot run her. So you are left communicating with each other and talking about how you want to drive, where you want to go, and how fast you want to go.

A patient of mine made a comment to me about her husband. She explained, "I don't understand why these little things bother him so much. I tell him they are small, and I ask him not to focus on them." But when she thought and said these sentences, she practiced control and criticism, not vulnerability and love. There is no criticism in love. She could have said, "I can see these things bother you a great deal. And I am sad about that. Can I do anything to help you?"

The interplay and crossover between psychology and spirituality is evident in many of the handouts I give to individuals and couples as "homework" between sessions. One of the handouts is designed to improve communication. The task is to refrain from criticizing and judging by using a four-part technique called "Feeling Communication." The participant utilizes four sentence stems to make his or her feelings and desires known. The first sentence stem is "I feel ..." and the person is asked to choose a feeling from a list of nine. The next stem is "When you ..." and then the patient describes a concrete behavior. The third is "Because ..." and the person then lists the consequences. The fourth is "I want ..." followed by a brief description of the desired behaviors. This is a good strategy to interrupt old, critical statements. This is a technique; it is not natural initially but can result in more effective communication. However, these sentence stems can still be said with an edge to them, some sarcasm, or a certain disdainful look. This is where the spiritual side comes into play. For this technique to be effective in assisting change, the words must come from attitudes of vulnerability and love in the sender.

After saying "I feel," it is then important to choose an emotion. When people say, "I feel like ..." they will usually give an opinion or thought—not an emotion. You must make certain that you use a feeling word, possibly by choosing an emotion or feeling from the list of the nine basic feelings: sad, angry, glad, fearful, hurt, lonely, guilty, ashamed, and love. You will notice that seven of the nine are negative, while two are positive. It is the seven that cause problems. Therefore, it is best to practice dealing well with them. After all, most people do not complain about having too much gladness or too much love. But they do complain about too much anger or loneliness.

It is important to identify the seven negative emotions and learn to manage them well, because they are connected to the sympathetic nervous system. This is the side where the fight-or-flight response originates that is also associated with excitation, arousal, preparedness, and vigilance. It is the arousal of this nervous system that can create poor communication. Many times we feel fear along with this excitement. When we believe we are under attack or are being hurt, we often hurt back, and that attitude and defensiveness will injure good communication. This is why is it so important that we explore ourselves, resolve old issues, and learn to be responsible and compassionate adults in the here and now. Learning a potentially effective communication technique or techniques will not be of much help to you if it is built upon a weak foundation. It is not the part of the iceberg you can see that will sink the ship—it is what is below the surface that is dangerous.

There are more than seven billion people on this planet. Maybe only one or two hundred know you exist. Even these people have their own lives to live and their own concerns. They are not focused on you all of the time, just as you are not focused on them all of the time. They are not inside of your skin, and they do not know what you are thinking. If you want them to know, it is up to you to share with them and to tell them what you want and need. What is important to you may not be important to your partner. You will need to speak up for yourself. Your life and your relationship with your partner will be easier if you share what you see, hear, need, and want.

The truth is that a new behavior will seem contrived because it has not been practiced before. But instead of continuing to think of a new behavior or goal as contrived or unnatural, think of it as the initial stage in the process of acquiring a new skill. At first it will appear halting and jerky. With enough practice it becomes smoother. Six months after you begin a new skill those people who did not know you previously will say the behavior seems natural. The husband in a couple I worked with insightfully stated the value of practice. He said, "We're practicing some new communication and working to really hear each other, but it's so cardboard that it's comical. She was planning to tell me her thoughts and she said, 'I don't know how to tell you this, but ...' and we both started laughing because it was just what we had been practicing in your office."

COMPROMISE OR CONFLICT RESOLUTION

The word *compromise* also has Latin language roots. *Com* means *with* or *together* and *promittere* means "to promise." *Compromise* means a settlement of differences in which each side concedes to an agreement and then promises to keep it. To do what you said you would do develops trust.

A compromise occurs when each side gets some of what they want—but not all of what they want. Both sides are neither very happy nor very unhappy. However, the agreement is acceptable to both, partly because it does address and potentially resolve a conflict. There is a new balance that is achieved, and the compromise is better for both parties than the continued conflict. Compromise is not the same as surrender. Compromise is close to fifty-fifty, while surrender is closer to ninety-nine–one.

If you are willing to label and deal with your fears in a close relationship, you will have more energy to address the relationship in a healthy way. If you practice compassion and show effective communication, the chances of achieving a compromise are increased. As before, there are characteristics that fall under the labels of inclusion and exclusion.

Inclusion	Exclusion
We can compromise	I win and you lose
50/50	99/1
Consideration	Greed
Boundaries respected	Boundaries violated

An example of exclusion arose with a couple I used to work with. The husband traveled out of town several times a month and would be gone for two to four days at a time. His wife often asked him for a copy of his travel itinerary so she would know where he was in case of an emergency. He refused to give it to her. But sometimes he relented to her nagging while on the drive to the airport and would tell her, very rapidly, where he was going and how long he would be in each location. However, he recited the information so quickly that she could not understand it. In this case the husband did not compromise. He did not meet her halfway regarding the information she wanted, and he did not help her meet her needs.

There are numerous characteristics of compromise, including the following: being willing partners, listening, being fair, meeting halfway, practicing patience, being trustworthy, and understanding consequences. These can be grouped into five categories that show the progression required to reach a compromise:

1. Motivation on each side to change
2. Each side stating their positions
3. Bargaining to arrive at a middle ground
4. Establishing an agreement
5. Keeping the agreement

I frequently work with husbands who are having marital problems, and I am often impressed by what they seem to believe compromise is. Most think that a compromise is compliance with the wife and doing whatever she says. A patient who believed this told me that his wife requested that he read two books on marriage and to call her once a day when he was out of town on business trips. He made the agreement but thought it was ridiculous. He complied, but did so while hanging onto anger, resentment, and fear—fear of vulnerability, fear of giving in, and fear of change. If he had viewed the compromise as a fifty-fifty arrangement and viewed his wife's request with compassion, then he would not be resentful, and his fear would be minimal. This attitude might be one where he would take ownership for his 50 percent and do his part because he, as an adult, had agreed to do so. He would then not resist his wife or himself or his fear.

Compromise involves making and keeping agreements, agreements that benefit each party. If we do not make new agreements we will exercise the old agreements, stated or unstated, and those might be very dysfunctional. For example, a woman and her husband owned several rental homes. When they bought four more from a broker, they also inherited a custodian who had been taking care of the homes for renters. When the husband was on the phone with the man, the wife became fearful she was missing some important information. So she began to tell her husband what to say while he was on the phone. When we analyzed this incident in my office, I suggested applying the idea of inclusion to the situation. In the future they could use the speakerphone so all three parties could hear each other. This compromise allowed them all to be included in the communications.

CHAPTER 12

SPECIFIC BEHAVIORS TO PRACTICE

Courage is resistance to fear, master of fear, not absence of fear.
—MARK TWAIN

FOR MANY OF US, THE most rewarding journey is not in a plane or car to a geographic destination. Rather, the most rewarding journey occurs when we explore ourselves. It is an *inner journey* beginning with where we are now and continuing into our futures. Identifying our fears is part of this inner journey: discovering the real person inside. When you know this you can learn to manage your life with more joy, love, and peace. You will also come to realize what you have allowed to run your life. One of the first steps on this voyage is to explore your fears. This exploration falls into three categories.

1. **General fears** are numerous for most of us and number in the range of thirty to fifty.

2. **Fear themes** are categories into which general fears can be organized. There are usually four or five major themes. These

might also be called core fears because they have a strong impact on our lives for a long time.

3. **Triggers for our fears** are usually small events and occurrences that set off our fear reactions. Triggers include certain words or tones of voice used by other people, small mistakes you make, or particular social situations. It can also be a specific look by someone else, such as a roll of the eyes.

IDENTIFY GENERAL FEARS

There does not need to be any shame in having fears. We all have them; they are ours. They may be similar to the fears of others, but they are still ours to claim, to ignore, or to attempt to run from. If you do not change how you deal with your fears, they will probably not change either. Some of our fears and fear memories are very strong. They may be firmly imprinted upon our neurology and may even be considered trauma imprinted. Examples are rape, molestation, major accidents, medical emergencies, or someone's death. The memory of the shock or intensity of the event is always present, just as lighting hitting a tree will leave a permanent scar. Your fears can become the drivers in your life, pushing you in certain directions—toward something or away from it. A life run by fear and not by love and peace will be unsatisfying, bound up in tension and not focused on growth. You may have small, medium, or traumatic fears. Nonetheless, you must address enough of your fears to release yourself to move on with more peace in your life. Writing down your general fears is a beginning step in this direction.

I recommend that you write a one-sentence description of each fear you have. Do not write just a word or two—that makes it too easy to minimize or continue to avoid the fear. You do not need to write the list all at one time. Begin to compose your list and plan to add to it as you become more aware. It is typical for most of my patients to compile lists of thirty to fifty fears. Examples of sentences that describe fears include the following:

» I am afraid I am not as good as others.

» I have a fear that others do not like me.

» I have a fear of being rejected by people.

» I fear making mistakes.

» I am afraid of people knowing the real me.

» I fear not having enough money.

» I am afraid of my spouse's criticism.

» I am afraid I am not a good father/mother/son/daughter.

» I am afraid of death.

» I am afraid of being terminally ill and of being a burden to others.

» I am afraid of speaking in front of others.

» I am afraid I am not using my potential.

» I have fear that I will not be forgiven for what I've done.

» I have fear that I will not change much.

» I am afraid my son will have sex too early.

» I'm afraid my son will have his heart broken, again.

» I am afraid my daughter will not get into the college she wants.

» I am afraid my son will miss out on some worthwhile things because he is always so late and laid-back.

» I'm afraid my husband will die in a car wreck.

» I'm afraid my husband and I won't make it staying married.

» I'm afraid my parents will move to a new house that is too far from me so caring for them will be hard.

» I'm afraid my parents won't ever accept me for who I am.

» I'm afraid I will do or say something wrong at work and get reprimanded.

» I'm afraid people will find out how old I am.

» I fear I weigh too much.

» I'm afraid I do not forgive as I should.

» I am afraid people will gossip about me and my family.

After making your list of thirty to fifty fears, go over them, and put a number in front of each one using the scale of one, for "little fear," to one hundred, for "overwhelming fear." You may change your mind about the intensity of certain fears as you do this exercise. If so, just go back and change the numbers. Take a look at the overwhelming fears. Are they life-and-death issues? Have you overreacted?

Fear Themes in Our Lives

The inner journey continues with your willingness to read over the general fears and begin to see how some of them are related. That is, some will seem to be about the same topic or theme. For example, the fears of "I am afraid of making a mistake" and "I am afraid I don't fit into groups of people" might fall under a theme of inadequacy. And there might be others that fit under that theme also. The names of the categories, the larger concepts, are fear themes.

A patient once told me that he wanted to be married, but he was thirty-eight years old and still single. He dated often and had sex early on in his relationships. That may have prevented emotional intimacy, growth, and commitment. He did this so often and for so long with so many women that he was probably dealing with a central fear issue. The numerous fears he had included fear of commitment, fear of not being seen as sexual, fear of growing older, and fear of vulnerability with a woman. He and I labeled one of his fear themes as "fear of emotional intimacy with marriageable women."

We all have a small number of themes in our lives that began early, that may run our lives, and that we are unaware of. The person who has identified her or his themes is the person who can change, because awareness is the first step to change. We may have only three, four, or five such themes. The themes are not just occasional and temporary, but are frequent and have been present for years or decades. Other names for fear themes include:

- » Fear of rejection
- » Fear of inadequacy
- » Fear of conflict
- » Fear of authority figures
- » Fear of abandonment
- » Fear of intimacy or vulnerability
- » Fear of showing anger
- » Fear about money

There is no right or wrong way on this inner journey. So allow yourself to be open to exploration of your fears. You can always change the names of the themes you have chosen. As you change, how you view people and your themes will also change.

If you throw fifty different types of items on the floor it is useful to organize them into categories, such as marbles, buttons, bolts, and fears. Knowing how to deal with one item in a category can help us deal well with all other items in the same category. For example, if we begin to feel some fear around a coworker, neighbor, or sibling, knowing that one of our themes is inadequacy can help us chose an appropriate plan of action to address our feelings, thoughts, and behaviors. We can then run our lives instead of allowing fear to do it. These themes are not present at birth—we learn them. We never unlearn them. They just become weaker as we deal well with them and learn new coping skills.

Particularly as an adult, if your fear does not make sense in the current time period—given the current situation—then the issue is probably emotional and habitual. Your reaction has been practiced so many times that it has become a habit: a habit attached to some event you may not recall. Writing about your fears will help you become aware of *yourself.* We must resolve the core fears if we are to become good at self-care and to live in faith. Addressing the fears will help us find freedom.

It is important to take risks and be honest. One of my patients, Brad, was in charge of money from the family business. He had been disbursing money to his mother for years and continued to do it even though the business income was very low. He was at risk of losing the family business because he did not want his mother to know how bad the situation was and didn't want her standard of living to go down. Brad was a man who had been open with his wife and with his business partners for years. His fear of being honest with his mother was a fear theme. We could argue he was not treating his mother with respect and honoring her because he was secretive and assumed he knew what she wanted.

IDENTIFY YOUR TRIGGERS FOR FEAR REACTIONS

The experiences we encounter early in our lives can be wonderful, supportive, and growth producing. They can also be damaging and fear producing. Just as love does not cause problems, wonderful experiences do not cause problems either. But, like fear, negative experiences can keep us stuck and weigh us down like an anchor on a ship. With practice, we can make significant changes in ourselves to release us from the pain of the past. However, we can never erase it completely, because it is in our neurology: the physical makeup of our brains and bodies. Like an alcoholic who sobers up, we practice *recovering*—not *recovery*—from past experiences, actions, and memories. But they never go away completely. The alcoholic is just one drink away from a return to alcohol drinking, and we are always just a trigger event away from the habits of our past.

A trigger is any person, memory, activity, image, sound, or thing that cues or elicits a fear in us. The trigger, the latest event, is like the tip of the iceberg. It is not the entire fear or the fear theme. Keep in mind that fears may have been accumulating for years. When they are triggered the reaction is not appropriate to, or consistent with, the current situation.

My patient, Marcia, was a real estate agent. She did well in this career and usually had one or more contracts with individuals to sell their houses. She came into my office one day and was in a near panic. She said, "I don't have any contracts now. What's going to happen to me? If I don't get another contract, I might lose everything that I've worked for over the last twenty years. I don't know where I'd live. My children have their own lives with their children. I'll be poor and alone." I listened to Marcia and made some notes as she continued talking. She slowed down after a while, and I shared with her the names of some of the fears she seemed to have. She nodded her head, appearing bored and frustrated that I failed to see that money—and not fear—was the problem. I then asked her if she had ever known anyone else who had fears about not having work that brought in money or who had fears about being poor and a burden on their children. Marcia looked at me with wide and startled eyes as if I had just said there was a big bug climbing through her hair. She responded, "My mother. My mother had a huge fear of being poor. She had it all of her life. All she talked about was money and how she never had enough and how she did not want to have to live with us. She never did live with us, and she had money in the bank when she died."

Marcia was a woman who learned her mother's fears. She had learned them when she was young and had been practicing them for decades. The trigger event for Marcia's fears was not having another house contract. As expected, she soon obtained a contract to sell a house. To her credit, she also continued in therapy and did the work necessary to effectively address her fears about being poor and dependent.

STRATEGIES FOR DEALING WELL WITH FEAR: SPECIFIC POINTS TO PRACTICE

1. **Listen to your vocabulary!** Listen to the words you choose to describe your experiences. Listen carefully to them and for their possible impact upon you. The words you choose will strengthen or weaken the victim role in you; they will strengthen

or weaken your *personal power*. A patient of mine told me about her relationship with her verbally abusive husband. She spoke like a victim when she said, "I don't have a backbone, and I can't stand up for myself." Her own words victimized her because they indicated to her that she did not have the ability, power, or choice to change. She could have said, "I'm afraid to stand up for myself" or "I want to learn to stand up for myself." Both of these statements signify that she is in charge of herself and imply she can change. When you ask yourself, "Why am I so tense around men?" and "Why can't I be more confident?" you are still rehearsing the negative. Instead you could rehearse the positive and say, "I am becoming more relaxed around men" and "I am more confident now than last year."

2. **Watch what you think!** If you see the negative in your mind and then rehearse it, you increase the chance that you will get the negative. If in your mind you see the golf ball you're hitting going into the water, the odds are increased it will do so. Think about positive outcomes. We tend to get what we think we will get.

3. **Do not say "I have to …"** Consciously choose healthy and mature language to weaken the unconscious and old, habitual language. Many of us say "I can't …" or "I have to …" This is language we learned as children but that may no longer apply to us. Children are frequently very literal in their thinking. They actually believe there is a Santa Claus or that there are monsters under the bed. We all thought that way at one time and may still think that way sometimes even when we are older. When I do hypnosis with a patient and she is in a trance, she returns to thinking literally. When she is hypnotized and I ask, "Will you tell me your name?" She will say yes but not her name. Her unconscious, old thinking is very literal. As adults, we may say, "I can't ride elevators," "I can't work iPads," or "I can't talk chitchat with my wife." The unconscious grabs onto a thought and makes it literal and black-and-white. Then that person does not change. In order to change,

you must strengthen the conscious and weaken the unconscious. You make yourself free when you choose to do something. If you believe you *have* to do something, you do not see yourself as free. So say, "I can learn to ride elevators," "I can learn to work iPads," and "If I practice, I can learn to chitchat with my wife."

4. **Practice saying "I can ..."** It was Saint Paul who wrote in Romans 7:15 (NIV), "For what I want to do I do not do, but what I hate I do." It was the unconscious in him that often determined his actions. But when he was conscious, he was amazing. Similarly, some people say, "I just can't turn down someone's request of me." Sure you can ... but you may have a fear of the consequences so you choose to acquiesce.

5. **Learn the value in "paired practice."** Many of us can reduce our fears—such as those of inadequacy and of making mistakes—by developing and practicing a plan to associate positive statements about ourselves with other well-established habits or activities. The first step is to develop a list of positive statements about yourself, such as the following:

   a. I can change and grow.

   b. I am as worthwhile, no more and no less, than anyone else.

   c. I may make a mistake, but I am not a mistake.

The second step is to make a list of some activities that you do repetitively in your typical day. These may include looking at your watch, looking in a mirror, getting a drink of water, or using the restroom. The third step is to pair the positive statements with the repetitive behaviors. For example, tape one of the positive statements on your watch so that when you want to see the time you have to lift the piece of paper to do so. In the process, you will be saying the affirmative statement to yourself. Place a positive statement on your bathroom mirror at eye level. You will have to see it and look around it to comb your hair or brush your teeth.

Buy yourself a clear drinking glass and affix one of the statements to the bottom of it so that you see it as you drink. Tape a statement on your toothbrush. Wear a child's plastic bracelet on which you have written an encouraging statement. If you look at your watch twenty times per day, look in the mirror six times each day, drink a glass of water two times per day, and use the restroom two to five times per day, then you will have rehearsed various positive statements about thirty times per day. That is thirty times each day that you will have complimented yourself! And that is 10,950 times each year you will have been supportive of yourself.

6. **Involve another person and update.** Many, if not most, of our fears have their origin in our childhoods. One way to update is to talk with a therapist, a close friend, a sponsor, or a religious specialist. Hearing ourselves talk in detail about the fears in the presence of another person who does not recoil from us or ridicule us diminishes the energy in the fear. By hearing ourselves talk, we move the fear from a child's point of view to that of an adult; in the process, the fear is weakened.

7. **Desensitize.** If you have a fear of snakes, you will avoid them at your safe distance, whether that is ten feet, fifty feet, or behind glass. If you have a fear of flying, heights, inadequacy, achievement, or failure, you will avoid these at your safe distance. It is important to desensitize yourself. For example, if you are sensitized to a fear of elevators, the desensitization process might first involve talking about elevators or looking at pictures of them. Another step might be to look at an elevator from fifty feet in a hotel lobby. And then you might look at it from thirty or ten feet. Each experience of coming closer to the feared object—if done slowly—reduces the fear, because the feared horrible consequence does not happen. Eventually, you might just look inside an open elevator and then practice going in and out of it quickly. You might desensitize to the point of going up or down just one floor in an elevator. You might go farther.

The point is that you can change, and there are behaviors and programs you can practice to change yourself.

8. **Hold life gently.** My patient Trey asked, "How do I deal with the stress of my job, my boss, the home? I can't go away for two years and learn how to meditate." I asked him to practice holding life gently—while being in life and not escaping from it. I suggested that if he were a baseball player, Trey would be tense at the plate and fearful of striking out, view the pitcher as his enemy, be aware of the people in the stands, and grip the bat so tightly his knuckles would be white. Then he would probably strike out because that was what he was thinking about as the ball was pitched. The player batting after him could use the same bat, be in the same game, have the same pitcher, and also be aware of Trey's out. But he might hold the bat lightly without white knuckles. "You see," I said, "it's about the batter, and not about the bat." It's about how you hold issues in life. It is not the absence of issues that will bring you peace but how you embrace the issues. Imagine you are holding a crystal bowl with both hands. You can hold it with tension or with calmness and peace. Now, the contents of your bowl are all the people you know, everything you own, all your memories, all your fears, all your joys—everything in your life. You can learn to hold it with peace. Remember, peace is where you are coming from, not where you are going.

9. **Write to yourself.** On a piece of good stationary, write a letter to yourself describing how you would like to be two years from now. Write about how you would like to think, how you would like to handle your emotions, and what behaviors you would stop and start. Address the envelope to yourself, put a stamp on it, mail it, and wait for the letter from your good friend—you.

10. **Consider significant people.** Write what you have learned— particularly fears—from significant people in your life prior to age twenty. Beside each name write down the main characteristic that the individual had or has. Then put a check mark by the

characteristics that you share with that person. Ask yourself if that specific characteristic is still functional or makes sense in the current time period.

11. **Label emotions.** Make a small note to yourself on a Post-It and stick it on a mirror where you will see it several times during the day. On the note, write, "What emotions have I felt the past hour?" and "How did I deal with those emotions?" Remember, practice makes progress. So take the time to practice.

12. **Label the worst.** When you have fear, such as that of conflict, ask yourself what the worst thing that can happen is. One of my patients, James, had a father who would not leave New Orleans prior to the hurricane in 2005. He said he was angry with his father for endangering another adult son, his stepmother, and his wife and child. James would not leave if his father did not. Finally, the stepmother, wife, and child left the city and joined the lengthy caravan traveling to Houston. But the father and son stayed. James asked himself what the worst thing that could happen would be if he told his father what he thought about his attitude, actions, and choices. James imagined that his father would yell and stop talking to him. He decided he could live with that and told his father what he thought. The father said, "I hear you, but this is my house. It has been my house for years, and when I die I want to die here. But thank you for telling me, son."

13. **Write your roles.** Take the time to write down a description of your various roles. Then write down what you are attempting to protect with your roles.

14. **Think of an audience.** Do not say or do to yourself what you would not say or do to a child or what you would not be willing to repeat if you were on TV in front of a national audience. This will help you stay conscious and manage yourself well.

15. **Relax while waiting.** We do not know what the future will be, and there are usually too many variables to make any accurate

predictions. My crystal ball is good for only about one-half of a second into the future! So take care of yourself while you wait for the future. Learn to relax and enjoy the time you have while you are waiting for something else to come along.

16. **Be held accountable.** Find a person you trust, and then ask him or her to hold you accountable for the issues you want to change. For example, if you say that you will write down all of your fears within a week, the person will agree to check with you in a week. This is about accountability and responsibility, not abuse.

17. **Look at the rest of your life,** assuming you will live to be ninety. What activities and thoughts will have characterized the first half of your life? What do you want to characterize the second half? Writing these on paper will make them stronger in your mind.

18. **Observe and relax.** Instead of immediately reacting, we can facilitate calmness and interrupt the fear habit. For example, if you observe storm clouds on the horizon, you can immediately stop what you are doing and prepare for the storm, or you can observe it. You may notice it is weakening, blowing away, or coming closer. Too many times we prepare for problems that do not happen.

19. **Practice a goal of the year.** Write a sentence or even a paragraph that summarizes a goal you have. Say it once when you begin to brush your teeth in the morning and once when you comb your hair. Recite it as you have a cup of coffee or when you have lunch. Find ten opportunities per day to practice. Your sentence may read like the following: "I am working on being more compassionate and patient with others." Your paragraph may be similar to this one: "I am working on compassion for others because what I have been doing is not working. If I keep doing what I've been doing, I'll keep getting what I've been getting. I am choosing to have choice about my habits and how I express my emotions rather than to be the victim of my habits." Remember, awareness is the first step to change, and practicing the change is necessary.

20. **Embrace all four parts.** It was the connection, or disconnection, of the four parts that brought us to the point where we are at this time. Continued practice of disconnection will take us in a non-growing, fear-based direction. Practicing the connection between all of our parts will take us in a growth-oriented and faith-filling direction. If you have a fear of rejection, a four-position approach to resolving it might look like the following:

Emotionally, identify the fear by writing down times in your life you were rejected or felt rejected. Write down your ages at these various times. Write down the names of the people who did or seemed to have rejected you.

Intellectually, admit you learned this fear—you were not born with it. You learned it by interacting with significant others in your young life, and now you carry it with you. You learned it, and you can acquire an interpersonal skill that is more adaptive and up-to-date rather than continue a pattern you learned in your childhood or adolescence. Draw a picture of what you see happening and what you fear if you are rejected. Also draw a picture of someone accepting you, because that can happen too.

Behaviorally, what you practice is what you become good at. You will not change and become a person who is doing something different until you do something that is different. Your plan might be to approach thirty people in spite of your fear of rejection. After the trial, assess the results.

Spiritually, we humans seek meaning, calm, and peace. The wiser of us have learned we cannot do this on our own; we are not up to the task. There are too many variables to be aware of, too many contingencies, and we recognize we cannot control outcomes with other people. Just as we needed nurturing parents, so we need a nurturing divine figure who lets us know that somehow, someway, everything will turn out okay. The necessary ingredient for dealing well with fear is to develop a powerful faith life.

21. **Leave the pity party.** If you say, "I just don't know how to tell people no," you are displaying the attitude of a victim and are in the midst of a pity party. Now, if you choose not to say no out of fear of the consequences, then that is a different matter. You are an adult, in charge of yourself, with a fear, and you have made a decision. That is very different than pretending you are pitiful and lack the capacity to say no.

22. **Interrupt the habit chain.** When a particular habit is practiced, it connects to related habits into a chain of habits. In this way, fear of meeting someone new leads to an anticipated fear of rejection, negative thoughts, avoidance, physical relief when the avoidance is successful, and fear of meeting someone new—over and over again. To change our behavior, we must interrupt the chain at one of the links. Practicing positive thoughts rather than negative ones leads to change, which leads to continued positive thinking.

23. **Know your control strategies.** Be aware of your control strategies and the forms they take. Do you attempt to manipulate others by guilt—by what you say or do not say? Then work to identify your fears in the situation. Are you afraid of rejection or inadequacy? Identify the needs that are disguised by your fears and control maneuvers. Allow yourself to feel your fear. It is unlikely you will die from the feeling. After all, you have had fears for years and have not died yet from them. Are your control strategies worth the price you pay for them?

24. **Progress, not perfection, is the goal.** As we work to change ourselves, it is important to recognize that we do not unlearn old habits, and we do not usually forget what happened to us. Rather than unlearn, we learn new habits that create stronger neurological pathways than the old ones. But the old do not die away. That is why you can return to riding a bike at age forty even if you have not ridden on one since age sixteen. You still know how to balance and to brake. It is also why you will say or do

something once in a while that you had told yourself you never wanted to say or do again.

25. **Be willing to make a mistake.** Without the willingness to fall down and skin a knee, how can the child learn to ride a bike? Without our willingness to risk making a mistake—not *being* a mistake—how can we learn at any age?

26. **Identify your prisons.** Write down the names of your self-made prisons. Our prisons could be our compulsive behaviors. However, they are also the way we think about ourselves, our lives, and our potential. Saying "I can only relax when I'm alone" can be a prisoner statement.

27. **Examine painful memories.** Write down what you think is the appropriate and mature way to deal with a painful memory and the feelings attached to it. My grandmother had a diagnosis of pancreatic cancer that I was not told about by my parents when I left for my second year in seminary. It was very important that I addressed my fear, hurt, and anger with them.

28. **Make a gratitude list.** Write a gratitude list and practice it so that it becomes an unconscious motivator of your behavior. Be grateful that you can read this list: you can read, you have eyes, you can reason, and you can afford a book.

29. **Eat healthy.** Eat healthy so you have energy for change. Otherwise, you are going on a backpacking trip with nothing in your backpack.

30. **Do yoga.** Take a yoga class. It is a great way to learn how to relax, meditate, and breathe.

31. **Do not turn on your TV during the week**—or at least leave it off for a day or two per week. In that time, you can talk to your family without distractions. Another idea is to maintain a room in your house where you talk and TV is not allowed.

32. **Be realistic.** Teach yourself to count the positive. If ten people say that your hair looks good and one person says that he does

not like it, focus on the ten. This is not living in la-la land, but accepting reality.

33. **Look at pictures.** Look at old photos of yourself and write about what you see. What ages were you then? Where was the picture taken? What are people feeling? What had just happened in the picture, and what happened next? What else happened to you at that age?

34. **Be present for your present.** Sometimes we minimize the current time period; we focus too much on the memories and fears of our past or on fears about anticipated stories in our future. It is more important to learn to deal well with the fears in the present and simultaneously address the fears in the other two time zones. As we resolve them, we have more energy available for the present. When dealing with fear, it is critical to get past the past. Be present for the present. And have faith about the future.

35. **Learn the relaxing way to breathe.** There are two parts of the nervous system: the stress/activation part and the calm/relaxation part. It is the sympathetic nervous system that is activated when we are stressed. It is from here that the fight-or-flight response originates. It also results in tight shoulder and chest muscles and shallow breathing. It is the parasympathetic system that is associated with relaxation, calm thoughts, and deep sleep. Many people are shallow breathers. That means they breathe by using their chest and shoulder muscles to expand their chests. Shallow breathing is what we do when we are afraid and stressed. Good singers do not do shallow breathing. Good singers breathe by using their diaphragm and abdominal muscles. This results in more air in and more air out. You can learn to breathe the relaxing way by lying on the floor or a bed with your hands over your navel. Breathe in through your nose while pushing up with your abdominal muscles. You ought to feel your hands rise. If they do not, you are breathing by using your chest and shoulder muscles.

Breathe out through your mouth and notice your hands fall. Repeat this drill until you have a good idea of what abdominal breathing is. Next, stand up and place your hands over your navel again and breathe. If your hands are pushed out, you are breathing with your diaphragm, which is a much more efficient and relaxing way to breathe. It is deep and allows all the lobes in your lungs to fill with air and then to empty. Shallow breathing tightens shoulder and neck muscles and does not allow all of the air in the lungs to be exhaled. It is inefficient and makes us tired from lack of oxygen. Practice breathing from your diaphragm for fifteen to thirty minutes per day to reset your parasympathetic nervous system to calmness and relaxation. If you have been stressed or fearful for a long time, you may be out of balance and leaning strongly toward the sympathetic side. To bring yourself back into balance, and even to lean toward the parasympathetic side, you will need to practice breathing from your diaphragm and to make that a habit.

36. **Use biofeedback.** Biological changes occur in our bodies when we have fear and stress. Different devices can measure these biological shifts and give you feedback by means of scales and gauges. This is the origin of the word *biofeedback*. A thermometer under your tongue provides feedback on your core temperature. An electrocardiogram gives you information regarding the functioning of your heart. When you are anxious and stressed, the temperature of your extremities, such as the fingers, will decrease because of reduced blood flow to them. This change in temperature can be measured by the use of a small biofeedback device, often called a stress thermometer, taped to the inside of your middle finger. The feedback is a digital number. The goal is to learn the words, muscle sensations, and visual images that are associated with relaxation—that is, with the temperature rising in your finger. The devices are available for about twenty dollars online.

37. **Use active listening** techniques to connect with other people. Look at them, not away, repeat what they have said to you, and ask if you have heard correctly.

38. **Use I statements,** especially when you want to state your feelings. Saying "I feel sad (mad, glad, hurt, lonely, etc.) when you ..." is much more accurate than saying "You make me feel sad (mad, glad, etc.)."

39. **Write to others.** If you are fearful about communicating with someone, ask if she or he will communicate with you by e-mail or by writing messages in a notebook.

40. **Choose what you want to defend.** Make a list of what you truly want to protect and defend—possessions, people, thoughts, and opinions. This exercise will help you evaluate all of the rest that you may not need to defend. For example, an opinion may be too small to protect, or it may not be your job to shield someone. You may find that you have been fighting too many fights. The less you have to defend, the less you will be defensive.

41. **Have your blood analyzed.** No discussion of treatments for fear and anxiety would be complete without an examination of genetic and hormonal causes of fear and anxiety. Many individuals with these dynamics have a biochemical imbalance, and some have a genetic predisposition to anxiety. These diagnostic categories have a genetic correlation often similar to other medical issues such as diabetes, high blood pressure, and thyroid dysfunction. An individual's family history needs to be carefully examined for corresponding and predisposing conditions. I recommend a thorough and rigorous examination of blood composition to help determine if any hormonal imbalances exist. These are difficult to assess, and retesting, even with several specialists, may be necessary. Treatment of a thyroid imbalance can improve mood, memory, and cognition. Hyperthyroidism—too much thyroid hormone—can cause sweating, weight loss, and anxiety.

Hypothyroidism, which is too little thyroid hormone, can result in fatigue, weight gain, depression, and memory problems.

42. **Consider medication for anxiety.** If you are diabetic, treat the diabetes with insulin, and also consider psychotherapy. Psychological treatment of diabetes without medication will result in life-threatening problems, including a coma. Some anxiety is intense enough that it ought to be treated with medication as well as psychotherapy.

43. **Create a "reflective space"** for yourself—a physical space in your home where you can go to and reflect on yourself: who you are, what your values are, how you show your values, etc.

44. **Find a model.** When someone shows us how to perform a task, whether it is cooking a new recipe or painting a house, we often learn better and faster when we can see what we are supposed to do. Think of someone who has the characteristics and behaviors you want to have—and then copy them. I have been blessed with my wife and numerous other individuals who modeled behaviors and attitudes such as patience, relaxation, and acceptance. I even have had a literary model: Mr. Fezziweg in *A Christmas Carol*. He was a responsible businessman. However, unlike Scrooge, he balanced work and fun.

45. **Visualize an inner sanctuary.** Think of a place—preferably a safe place you went to in your childhood. Practice going there in your mind while you breathe from your diaphragm.

46. **Have a good-bye ritual.** After you have written down your fears, control strategies, or compulsions, take them outside and prepare to burn them. As you light them, say out loud, "I no longer need you. I am becoming healthier. I am becoming me. You are not me, and you do not define me. Good-bye."

47. **Memorize an introduction.** Write down a brief twenty to forty-word description of yourself. Memorize it so that when someone in a social situation asks you what you do, you can easily tell him

or her. My descriptor is the following: "I am a psychologist, and my wife is a psychotherapist. We work together providing therapy to adolescents, adults, and couples in West Houston. I treat anxiety, depression, ADHD, and other learning disabilities." Then I ask, "And what do you do? Tell me about yourself." This gives the person an opening for asking more questions. If she or he shares as much as I did, I will have much information to pursue.

48. **Establish an exercise routine.** Research shows that people who exercise not only get rid of excessive stress-related hormones and other chemicals, but also improve self-esteem and general mood because of the release of calming chemicals.

49. **Buy an amulet** that has an inspiring word or phrase on it— something you want to practice and keep for yourself. The word might be *peace* or *forgiveness*. Carry this in your pocket or purse or put it on a chain that you can wear around your neck.

50. **Place reminders** around your house and office about what you want to practice. My wife and I have placemats, candle holders, and floor mats with inspiring words on them to remind us of what we are working on.

51. **Before you go to bed,** write down on a piece of paper what you want to work on the next day as part of your psychological recovery. Put the paper by your bed or by your bathroom sink. The next morning read it out loud to yourself. This is a good way to prepare for the day.

52. **Write a letter to yourself** as if it is to you from your mother, father, or someone else you want to hear certain words from. Write the words you have long wanted to hear from that significant person. Write it on good stationery and then put it in an envelope, address it to yourself, and mail it. When it is delivered, go to a safe place and read it slowly out loud to yourself. Let the words and the power sink in to help heal you.

53. **Get a massage** and think of the emotions and memories that may

occur as various parts of your body are massaged. Just relax and let your mind drift. Be willing to pay attention to the emotions and images that may arise.

54. **Write a letter to your parents** and describe for them the fears you had as a child. Write these fears with a crayon or pencil, and write with your nondominant hand. You do not need to mail the letter. Writing with the instrument of a child—with the difficulty related to your nondominant hand—will help you recall the fears more easily.

55. **Make a good memories jar** where you put happy memories on small pieces of paper. Each morning reach into the jar and take out one slip of paper, read it, and reflect on it for one minute.

56. **Use the rule of two** when you are stressed. Ask yourself, "What impact will this have on my life in two seconds, in two minutes, in two days, in two weeks, or in two years?" Put the stressor into perspective.

57. **Remember that all of us have voices in our heads,** but we are not psychotic. Listen to the different voices, thank them for their input and opinions, and then make a wise, informed, and adult decision.

58. **Practice saying no** in an appropriate way. Disagree with someone without planning to be disagreeable. For example, if someone asks you to take care of his dog for a weekend while he is gone and that is not convenient for you, you could say, "That is not going to work for me this weekend, but thank you for trusting me with your dog."

PART 3

SPIRITUAL TOOLS FOR
RECOVERY AND GROWTH

Chapter 13

Spiritual Growth

Glorious indeed is the world of God around us but
more glorious the world of God within us.
—Henry Longfellow

My Cancer

I AM HERE TODAY WRITING THIS chapter because I heard a voice that saved my physical life. This is what happened. In our master bathroom the shower area is separated from two washbasins and a large mirror. In fact, there is a door between the two spaces. One weekend morning after showering and toweling myself dry I put my hand on the doorknob and opened that door. With the door wide open, I distinctly heard a voice seemingly about five feet behind me and over my right shoulder. The voice very clearly said, "Look at your back in the mirror." The voice, which I wasn't able to distinguish as female or male, spoke with authority, love, and gentleness. As if in a daze, I did not hesitate. I took two steps toward the mirror over my sink, dropped my towel, and looked at my back. Even without using a hand mirror, and by simply turning my head as far as it would go, I could see a large, dark spot in the area just over my spine in the small of my back. It looked bigger than a dime and smaller than a quarter. Pants or swimming trunks had always hidden its position. I never thought to look there.

I quickly called my wife to look at the spot. "You need to see the doctor right away," she said, and I agreed. The next day I was scheduled with a dermatologist. He numbed the tissue, cut out the colored area, and said he would have the lab results back in two days. When he called, he told me that the tissue was melanoma, and he referred me to MD Anderson, a cancer treatment and research hospital in Houston. One of the primary doctors at the Melanoma Clinic there scheduled me for surgery to have more tissue excised from the site of the cancer. Additional laboratory results confirmed the diagnosis, and all of the cancer was removed because of the early detection. The first year after the surgery, I met with the MD Anderson doctors every three months. The second year we met every six months. Now I go annually with a visit to a local dermatologist in between. I have had no cancer since.

If the voice had not spoken to me, or if I had not listened to the voice or had dismissed or denied what I heard, I would quite likely have died years ago. That voice did not come from this world. That voice did not come from a human body. I was open and ready enough to hear, listen, and follow. I trusted the medical doctors, but they had not spotted the melanoma. And it was not my training or the profession of psychology that saved me. I am convinced it was the spiritual that saved my life.

The four parts of people include the intellectual, emotional, and the behavioral—which are all parts of the self. And the fourth part, the spiritual, is another dimension; it is just not of this earth, and it is not just the self. This other dimension is in us and around us. It was there before us and will be there after us. This is a bigger dimension that we cannot see or touch, and we did not create it. The spiritual is not of this world as the psychological parts such as thinking, feeling, and doing are.

It involves a different kind of connection than that of seeing, touching, or talking. The spiritual is where we go in faith and where the small voice comes from that gives us direction. Like a rose plant that thrives when it is fed water, fertilizer, sun, and air, we also thrive when we are fed from all four parts of our lives.

We are spiritual beings in physical bodies, and we are subject to physical and psychological principles, such as how we learn. However, we also strive to be more than the physical. We can feel, deep within ourselves, that there is more than the physical. It is important we find a balance while in these bodies. It is important we learn to let go of useless fear and learn to live more in faith. Faith will release us and help us find freedom.

BEING

A reasonable expectation for psychological recovery is change from one set of unconscious habits to a different set of chosen behaviors. However, with spirituality we are talking not only about change, but also about transformation from "behaving-ness" into "being-ness." I know a man who was often in a rush when he visited his grandmother, a woman he loved. He did not visit her often, and when he did, his visit was not very long. There were many other things he wanted to do. Now, years later, he is sad that he did not spend more time with her. He said, "In my compulsion, I often behaved as if I wanted to be some place other than where I was and as if I wanted to be doing something other than what I was doing." Now he has learned *to be* with people and not just to be *with* people.

We are *human* beings, but we can attempt to behave as human *beings*—that is, to develop and show the spiritual part of ourselves. Spirituality is, in part, about stretching, growing, and moving into the unknown. We will not make much progress in that direction if we are held back by our fears. The spiritual dimension has no limit, but the body does. The spiritual dimension is like a bank account that is never diminished, no matter how many checks are written. When we commune with God, our capacity for love and all of its associated gifts, such as forgiveness and acceptance, are limitless. Sometimes we do not come to this change—this recognition of the Spiritual in our lives—very easily.

Saint Augustine did not come to Christianity quickly and easily. His mother was Christian, and she prayed for his conversion from paganism. But he fought the process. For a long time, he kept his soul confined and hidden under a covering of drinking and debauchery. It was after his conversion, after surrendering, that he wrote:

> Almighty God,
> you have made us for yourself,
> and our hearts are restless
> till they find their rest in you. (*The Confessions of St. Augustine*, Book 1, Chapter 1)

THE PROCESS OF SPIRITUAL TRANSFORMATION

The awareness that we can change and the motivation to do so usually happen because of (1) a miracle, (2) the slow accumulation of problems and the slow deterioration of out-of-date habits, or (3) a crisis or trauma, such as an accident, death, or disease that rocks the foundation of our lives and forces us to realize that life is precious and very short. Awareness is necessary for us to change. Without awareness there is no problem, nothing to give up or to acquire, and nothing to change.

With awareness we begin to accept that we are not in control of anything or anyone except ourselves. With awareness we can reduce the emphasis on I, me, and mine. We begin to be humble and appreciative for what we have; we recognize that it has been given to us. And this is how the process of spiritual recovery begins. For it to continue we must let ourselves be fed with spiritual food such as faith, love, and trust. And we must often practice new spiritual behaviors that are the opposite of the old, negative, nonspiritual behaviors. Eventually, when practiced enough, the new behaviors become new habits. Reaching a point where faith is stronger than fear and acceptance is stronger than attempts at control does not come without dedication, effort, and sweat. But the more you practice and move in the spiritual direction, the more you live rather than merely exist in this world.

Many people are afraid to try a new behavior, even a spiritual one such as praying on their knees, praying in public, or praying extemporaneously. This is because it does not seem "natural" or it appears "contrived" and "artificial." The new behavior appears to be contrived because it is contrived. You are choosing to do something that you do not know how to do well—something that is not natural to you. However, if you practice it enough, like a golf swing, it will come to look and feel natural. Someone who did not know the old you might believe you have shown the new behavior most of your life.

Life is a process, a journey, just like a drive in a car that has many years' worth of gas in it. Learn to relax and hold the steering wheel gently on a long drive. Gripping the wheel tightly with white knuckles will not speed up or slow down the journey. In life, learn the skills that help you hold it gently. Learn to wear life like a loose coat over your shoulders.

A patient of mine, Trina, had a mother-in-law who was critically ill. She had a fear of her mother-in-law dying, so she wanted the dying process finished quickly. She also had a fear of an upcoming job interview, so she wanted the company to make a quick decision. She was tense and did not deal well with her fears. After her mother-in-law dies, she may have a fear of sobbing uncontrollably at the funeral or of her own mother dying. And if she is chosen for the new job, she may have fears of keeping the job or of her relationships with coworkers. So when one problem is resolved and another is presented—also known as life—she may still have difficulty with her fears. An alcoholic who stops drinking or a cocaine abuser who stops snorting are not recovered just because he or she has stopped. They are recovering as they continue the process of not using alcohol and other drugs. We humans who try to stop focusing so much on the material world are also not recovered. The addiction is not in the past tense. As we continue our spiritual journey, we are in the process of recovering from our fears.

You learned your problems by interactions with others and the world outside of you. In recovery, the outside world and everyone and everything in it become opportunities for you to deal with your fears and to move toward spiritual growth. It is our job to look for what we can learn spiritually from every experience we have.

It is important to know and accept that as you move forward on your journey, you are not obligated to tell people about the progress you are making. Your focus ought to be upon God. It is enough for God to know and for you to know. You are not worshipping others, fame, pride, or ego—you are worshipping God.

In Matthew 6:16–18, Jesus said,

> When you fast, do not look somber as the hypocrites do, for they disfigure their faces to show men they are fasting. I tell you the truth; they have received their reward in full. But when you fast, put oil on your head and wash your face, so that it will not be obvious to men that you are fasting, but only to your Father who is unseen; and your Father, who sees what is done in secret, will reward you.

Wishing and hoping is not a good business—or spiritual—plan. Many patients have sadly told me something similar to the following: "I've wasted all this time" or "I've wasted all these years." Basically, they are saying that they wished they had made other decisions so that their lives would be easier or that they would be more mature or spiritual. Now, I could say that I wish I had traveled to a certain exotic location ten years ago. But because I did not, I "wasted" much of my time and money. But the truth is that ten years ago, like today, I could not predict the future. My crystal ball can "see" only about one-half second into my future. My patients cannot see the future either. Their time and money were not wasted. We made the decisions we did with the information we had at the time. Growth takes what it takes, and one experience builds upon another in an ongoing progression. The opportunities for visiting an exotic location are still present just as they were ten, twenty, and thirty years ago. The names and the scenery are just different now. The opportunities for personal and spiritual growth exist now as they did years ago. If you are ready to change, then change. If you are not, you can wait and time is not wasted. It just takes what it takes. Be patient, be gentle with yourself, and love yourself while this part of your life is unfolding. It is all part of you and of your world. Learn to love it—and smile.

"Why did it take me so long to see what I was doing wrong?" she asked me. "I went to my parents' fiftieth wedding anniversary. I left early because I wanted to get home so I could get some things done. I wasted precious time with my parents, and I feel so guilty." This woman was ignoring opportunities given to her. Was her time wasted? In one aspect, yes, it was, but in another, no. In life it takes what it takes, and she was not ready at the time of the anniversary to do something different. It was not wasted because she has now learned to cherish the time she has with her parents.

The process of change, when it is consciously chosen, involves some very simple rules for growth. These include the following:

1. Be aware that what you have been doing may no longer work as well as you want. That is, your behaviors may have been functional in a previous time in your life, but they may have outlived much of their usefulness. To change you must be aware of your actions and the consequences of them. You must be willing to take personal responsibility for those actions and consequences. If you do not take responsibility for your actions, then there is nothing for you to change.

2. Confront your fears of doing something different. Different behaviors will result in different consequences, some of which will be unforeseen and unfamiliar.

3. Put your energy for change where you can get the best results. That is, change what you can. Things that are external to you, such as the weather, the cosmos, and other people, may also change. However, they will change when they are ready or when God wants them to. They do not change on your schedule.

4. To change you will need to let go of what you have been doing. Many people say they want to turn over their problems or their lives to God. They may come to God with a problem in their hand, and they do turn over their hand but do not let go! You cannot change if you hold onto the ballast of your past. The ballast of our lives weighs us down and is usually made up of fears. We need to let go of it to make room for newness.

Having a Life of Purpose and Service

One of my patients was very successful in the material world. He had two houses, a golf club membership, happily married children, and a partnership in his business. However, he complained often of the pain and stress he had in his shoulders. Then a lady whom he and his wife met at a gym said she was a massage therapist. They agreed to meet with her for a session. The massage therapist said, "We moved here from Ukraine just two years ago. I was a massage therapist there, but I'm having difficulty getting my license here. We are living here in the small office of this warehouse because we can live rent-free while we guard the warehouse. We are saving our money so I can bring my eleven-year-old niece here to this country so that she can have the education and opportunity I did not have. We are also saving our money to build a small house. I don't want a big one to take care of." My patient told me, "I went for a massage and didn't know I was going to get a lesson on how to live life. I didn't tell her this, but I started thinking that I wanted to be in her place. She knew who she was and what was important. She had more purpose in her life than I did."

Another patient disclosed to me that she feared giving money to people on the side of the street or even doing charity work because it felt good. She thought feeling good was selfish. Giving to others is important in life, and being willing to receive is also part of the process. Feeling good or pleased might be negative only if others are injured in the process.

Being of service has a long history. It was a custom in the time of Jesus for the host of a dinner to provide a place for the guests to wash their feet or to have a servant wash them. At the Last Supper, Jesus washed the feet of his disciples. He was of service to them and then asked them all to love as he had loved and to do as he had shown them to do.

Service results in the reduction of our egos, the corresponding materialism, and competition. Service is necessary for the lessening of compulsions and addictions and for the demonstration of values and the development of identity and character. It moves us out of the material world and puts us more squarely into the spiritual world. Living a life of service minimizes the ego, increases our faith life, and keeps our focus on a power greater than ourselves. It was Mahatma Gandhi who addressed these issues when he discussed the Seven Blunders of the World. They were given to his grandson on a piece of paper a short time before his assassination. He wrote, "Wealth without work, pleasure without conscience, science without humanity, knowledge without character, politics without principle, commerce without morality, and worship without sacrifice."

With a spiritual orientation, we give service to others, knowing we may never see the benefits of our actions. We believe that some of those actions will be of benefit—somehow. A man I know helps facilitate AA meetings in the local county jail. Some of the inmates are hardened criminals. Even so, he firmly believes that his efforts will have a positive influence on many of the inmates.

Learn to be of service, but be wise about what and whom you serve. I am reminded of the story of Mary and Martha in the gospel of Luke. Jesus was in their home speaking to a handful of people, one of whom was Mary. Martha came out of the kitchen where she had been working and complained to Jesus that she needed help, and she wanted Mary's assistance. Jesus said, "Mary has chosen what is better…" (10:42, NIV). Mary was of service by listening to Jesus. Her priority was spiritual, and she was willing to be taught. Martha was of service by cooking. Her priority was food, and she was not learning anything new by being alone in the kitchen. Food is important, and sometimes spiritual food is more important than being in the kitchen cooking.

SIN

A definition of "to sin" may be to engage in those activities and attitudes that disconnect us from God and connect us only to what is in this world. In recovery, we work to reestablish our conscious connection with God. As we do so, we recover our conscious connection with ourselves. Then we can share what we have with those around us. We receive love from God, so love is what we can share. This is a process, so we do not fix one connection completely before moving on to the next. We work on all our relationships simultaneously while remaining very clear of the priorities—God, ourselves, and then others. This is similar to the process of grief, where we move from numbness to anger to bargaining to depression and to acceptance. However, we do not move from one step to another sequentially. We might move from anger back to numbness and from that to depression. But in the process of grief, we usually experience all the stages. The same is true with our spiritual recovery. It is important to be gentle with ourselves as we move forward—and sometimes even backward.

Sins are those things we do habitually that create barriers to close communion with God. So where is the sin in your life? Sin is usually attractive, appears good, and feels good, at least for the individual doing the thinking and feeling. What is the sin that is keeping you from knowing God more intimately? It may be your intense focus on food, your compulsive spending, exercise, or drinking. Your sin might be a preoccupation with sex or acting out with masturbation. When we are in conscious contact with God and go deep within ourselves to that spot where the divine is in us, then we *know* what to do and what is right. From that place we can ask ourselves if we are doing the best we can to live a God-focused life. If the answer is no, then why aren't we? What prevents you from converting your life? What is necessary for conversion? There is no need to be afraid. This is just about you and God. God is love and will not hurt you. You do not want to continue to hurt yourself, do you? A patient insightfully told me this: "I didn't tell lies. I just lived a lie because I was fooling around on my wife." Sex was his god.

It Is about Priority Relationships with God, Ourselves, and Others

Our personal journey on this planet involves three paths. One path is upward toward God. On this path we know or learn that we are loved unconditionally and are forgiven unconditionally. The second path is that which goes deep within us to uncover our God-given conscience, moral code, peace, and power. On this journey, we learn about our capacity to love God, ourselves, and others. The third path is to show that love and to give love in our relationships with others. We will not be able to complete the third journey with any success if we do not follow the first two. It is in relationships where there is love and service that we come closer to the presence of God. And by expressing love and acceptance in those relationships, we find a peace that may not be present in psychological recovery and healing.

If we do not make God our first priority, we are at risk of focusing on the material, and this focus will probably result in continued fear instead of an increase in faith and peace. Sometimes we seem to *worship* restaurants or even churches because we want to be seen in them. We want to be seen in the *right* restaurant or church, and we are afraid of being seen in the *wrong* ones. While we focus on these rights and wrongs, we do not focus on the love God has for us, just as we are.

In Matthew 22:36–40, Jesus was asked, "Teacher, which is the greatest commandment in the Law?" Jesus replied, "'Love the Lord your

God with all your heart and with all your soul and with your entire mind. This is the first and greatest commandment. And the second is like it: Love your neighbor as yourself. All the Law and the Prophets hang on these two commandments." I do not believe he was suggesting that we should love others with damaged and self-critical love that many have for themselves. I believe he was speaking of healthy and transcendent love. He was talking about the substance of love, not the shell of love. We have to love God first and have love in us before we can love others in the same way.

So the priority list is this. First, have a loving, open, and growing relationship with God. Next, have a loving, open, and growing relationship with yourself. And then, because you are receiving love from God, you increase the odds of having a loving, open, and growing relationship with others.

If you believe God exists, if you know God exists, or even if you want to believe God exists, put your thoughts and energy in the direction of God. If God is in the east, do not continue facing west (toward the material), south (toward control), or north (toward self-centeredness). Face the direction you want to go in, and go. You can either live spiritually or just exist materially.

Have you ever driven on a freeway and wondered why traffic slowed down in your lane? Then you see why. There is an accident, but it is on the other side of the road, and people are rubbernecking. I do not need to do what they do. I trust the police and emergency personnel to handle the accident. My job is to take care of me. Rubbernecking will not help the people on the other side. It will probably just distract me and may result in me having an accident. Don't get distracted from the goal and priorities on the journey.

It would be easy to practice self-care if not for our emotions—particularly fear—and our habits. I know a man whose mother said to him even when he was an adult, "Don't put your feet up on the sofa." Amazingly, she was referring to his sofa in his house. Then she says, "Shame on you." The mother was obviously exercising, one more time, an old habit of hers. Her son's (reactionary) habit had always been to become angry with her, resist, or be passive aggressive. But if he could operate with vulnerability and love, he could behave as an adult and not continue to practice the habits of his childhood. For instance, he could say, "Mom, I hear you, and I know what you want. I do not want you to be upset, but I am tired and I usually put my feet up on the sofa when I am tired. Let's not have conflict about this. I'd rather talk with you and enjoy your company."

It is easy to be led astray and to be distracted from a healthy and spiritual priority system. When one of my patients was dating a materialistic woman, she told him the following: "If you really loved me you'd buy me this diamond ring." He did buy it, and she kept on demanding and manipulating for more. He did not resist. His god wore lipstick—and a diamond ring.

Look carefully at your priorities as you work to be gentle, accepting, and loving toward yourself and others. I am reminded of a man I knew. He said to me, "At the end of the day, even if I have made mistakes but my son has done his homework, is washed, and has said his prayers, then I'm batting a thousand." This man had a healthy yardstick to use to measure his growth. Every day, every hour, every minute, and every second, you have the ability and support of God to start your day over. If you have been critical, you could practice accepting. If you have been judgmental, work to forgive. If you have been stressed, let go. If you have fear, let yourself receive faith from God.

Inside of your skin, there is only you and God. It is important to please God first and yourself second. This does not make you self-centered, and it does not give you permission to harm others. If you harm others, you are not pleasing God. If you want to please God, you will work through your psychological baggage and become practiced in spiritual concepts such as forgiveness. I told this to a patient, and he said, "That is easier said than done." Well, sure it is. And you can use that as an excuse. It may seem hard until you practice it enough that it becomes easier. It takes more gas to get a car going than it does to keep it going.

This is due to momentum, and momentum helps us as we practice. If you do not stand up for yourself enough, practice saying no two times a day for one year. Frequent practice will help you make progress. Of course, if you avoid saying no, then by the same psychological principle you will become more accomplished at avoidance after a year of practice.

A patient of mine once said, "I've been able to handle things I never thought that I could possibly handle. Now I know it is due to my spiritual life. That must be my priority. I have peace. My fear part is so much better now." She was willing to let faith take the place of fear. She now has the room to be fed more spiritual food.

Another patient, Marcela, told me, "Some things are the same or just about the same, but I am not the same. I am different. I used to believe I wasn't good enough to change, and now I know I am." She had finally realized that focusing on her husband, being preoccupied with pleasing him, and seemingly worshipping him was not working. In fact, it was so painful she was motivated to change. She arrived at the point of being willing to worship only God. She accepted that her husband's happiness was up to God and to her husband—not to her.

BATTERY-CHARGER PEOPLE

There are people in my life who help me restore and refresh myself. If I were a battery, I would receive a charge when I am with these individuals. They accept me, show their love of me, and show me respect, and I feel very safe with them. It is important to have these types of relationships with people in our lives. They revive us and help us grow. We can more wholly explore who we are with them. They demonstrate to us what God's attributes are. They also help prepare us for when we are not with them and are instead with people who drain our energy instead of charge our batteries.

I am fortunate to have my wife, some relatives, and other close friends who are battery-charger people to me. I also have people in my life who are more likely to drain my energy—because they do not easily show acceptance, love, and respect. They might be racially prejudiced, judgmental, egocentric, verbally abusive, or involved in unhealthy competition. These people provide a challenge and an opportunity for me to practice my spiritual principles. They require much awareness, and that requires energy. It is important that I seek out God and those others with whom I become charged. They help me to come from acceptance, love, and respect when I am with people who do not come from acceptance, love, and respect.

TWO DOZEN SPIRITUAL TOOLS

We may have had fifteen million experiences by the time we were fifteen years old if we count putting on our shoes as one experience, opening the door as another, stepping outside as another, being teased by the neighbor boy as another, and falling off a bike as yet another. From fifteen years of age to our current age there have been millions of experiences, more than we can name, count, or remember. We do not need millions of spiritual strategies to deal with these experiences. Actually, we may only need about one to two dozen tools if they are skills similar to the following:

- » Forgiveness
- » Listening skills
- » Prayer
- » Humility
- » Trust in God
- » Vulnerability
- » Willingness to change
- » Boundaries
- » Love
- » Acceptance
- » Identification of feelings
- » Patience

- » Faith
- » Ability to let go
- » Ability to turn fear over to God

Some of the toxic tools that keep us stuck and separated from God include the following:

- » Fear
- » Anger
- » Judgment
- » Criticism
- » Demands
- » Use of curse words
- » Blame
- » Control
- » Secrets

Spiritual strategies help us connect with God and ourselves. The negative baggage results in our being disconnected from ourselves and God. In Matthew 26:69–75, as Jesus is being taken away to be tried and condemned to death, the words "and Peter denied Jesus" appear when he was asked if he was a friend of Jesus. The English translation of the Hebrew word is *denied*. The Greek interpretation is not *denied*, but *disowned*, a much more powerful word. When we disown, we push away from the person, object, or part of ourselves that we want to have no connection with. We cut off or attempt to sever claims to that person, ourselves, or even to God. When we connect spiritually, we can give ourselves or be given what we need.

I truly enjoy going to Easter and midnight Christmas Eve services at my church. I enjoy them even though I usually end up tearful as I connect with God during the songs or rituals. My tears take the toxicity of my ego, expectations, and fear out of my body and open my body up to connection with God. We too often want black-and-white answers or to have someone tell us what to do. These things, if provided to us, keep us from thinking and making our own decisions after examining our deep, moral, and ethical barometers. I believe God gave each of us these barometers, and it is our job to discover them and to apply them to life in all of the varying situations presented to us.

I do not have the answers. I do not pretend to be God. You do not have all the answers, and you are not my God. But if what you do repeatedly does not work—does not bring you good consequences—then doing something different might work better. Many do not do the something different because it involves a significant amount of faith to overcome the fear of the unfamiliar. If we are afraid to do something other than what we have been doing, even if what we have been doing does not work, then the problem and the barrier are in our feelings, not in our intellect. It is most likely about fear and not about faith. The problem is not with the spiritual dimension. We need to ask God to do for us what we have not been able to do for ourselves.

INTERNAL TOXICITY

One of our primary emotions is fear, and we may have many fears within us. I was helping a patient examine internal peace and the means of its practice. When he returned after one of our sessions, he said, "When working to practice peace, it's weird to think I have resistance to myself from myself, inside of myself."

When we identify our fears and confront them, we move from our past into our present and prepare a better foundation for our futures. We humans have clothes, but our clothes change in style and wear out. The car we bought new no longer smells new or performs reliably. We do not keep clothes or a car twenty-five years and expect them to fit or to perform as they once did. But we may turn forty-five and use the same behaviors, philosophy, or theology that we did twenty or more years ago.

We need to update our wardrobes, our cars, and our habits and attitudes. Clothes change as a result of experiences—and so do we.

A woman I knew who was engaged to be married continued to meet with a male friend for lunch about three times per year. They used to work together. He had been married for thirty years, and they each paid for their own lunches. They liked each other's company, and they liked to catch up with each other. Her new fiancé was fearful of that relationship and wanted her to stop seeing her friend. He not only told her to stop seeing the friend, he pouted. He started saying "if we marry" instead of "when we marry," and he called her less often. His fears lead to these control strategies. He was not operating in faith with God or his fiancée. His insides were toxic.

My patient Anita had an adult son who was moving back home—again. He did not leave her alone in the house. He followed her to the kitchen and hung around her when she was on the phone. He asked her why his father wanted him to write down all of his expenses as he spent money. He did not help with any chores in the house. He stayed out late with his friends or brought them home. Anita did not want to be "mean" to him, so she kept her anger inside. Her insides were toxic.

Our stomachs can seem full if we eat dry sponges or dry leaves, but this is not the same as having a stomach full of nutritious food. Similarly, we can appear to be happy or content with our material goods, but we are not truly full until we allow ourselves to be filled with spiritual life so that all four parts of us are in balance.

The outside world and material goods cannot fill an inside hole. It has to be filled from the inside. Our emotions and our memories are inside of us and are ours to manage, poorly or well. If our spirits, heads, and hearts are not connected, there is no new car, house, or TV that can connect them, because it is an inside task.

CHAPTER 14

THE MYSTERY

When you come to the edge of all the light you know, and are about
to step off into the darkness of the unknown, faith is knowing
one of two things will happen: there will either be something
solid for you to stand on or you will be taught how to fly.
—BARBARA WINTER

WHERE WE HAVE BEEN IS important, and where we are going is
important. Where we are now is where we are living. The past
is a memory, and the future is a dream. The meaning you experience in
this life and the depths of peace you feel in this life are determined by
the journey of life, not by its conclusion. The conclusion is a different
journey, another life.

I do not know why I am still alive on this planet and why I have been
given what I have been given. But I am reminded of one of the verses of
the song "Amazing Grace": "Grace has brought me safe this far, and grace

will take me home." We do not need to know why and how. It will be enough to just accept *what is*.

Our lives are revealed to us a second at a time; they are not revealed to us except as we go through them. They are not revealed to us ahead of time. We do not know what the future will bring. So we are left to practice peace and acceptance with what is in front of us, right now. Our plans for the present and for our futures, if they are to bring us peace, must include the spiritual side of life, not just the material. After he had learned of his wife's emotional affair, a patient said, "I never had much fear about the future, because I always felt like I had a plan. Now I'm scared to death." Unfortunately, his plan involved mostly their house, his job, the cars, and his retirement money. It was a plan only for the material. The spiritual is a mystery. As such, it is not concrete, not obvious, and not touchable. So expect occasionally to be temporarily a bit lost and to be in need of redirection. The road is not marked. We learn the road and the direction as we walk forward on the paths of our lives. When you swim in a pool, lake, or ocean and stop in the water and turn around, you may see a few swirls of where you were, but you are no longer there. The water, or life, filled in behind you, and your life is now where you are. You can face forward, but you have not made any movement in the water in front of you. That is your life yet to be traveled.

Spirituality does not exist in a vacuum. It is connected to the other parts of ourselves. If your behavior is against your value system and you are operating with fear and guilt, then your spirituality may be disconnected from the other three parts. I knew a woman who had some financial difficulty including making the payments on her house. She said, "I have a friend who thinks I should just walk away from my house. She talked to a man who did that, and he lived in the house two years before he was finally evicted. But that is not my value system." This woman's behavior and emotions were connected to her spirituality. She was creating peace inside of herself using guidelines, some of which are similar to the following:

» We cannot control other people.

» Everything happens for some reason or purpose, and we can learn from every experience and everyone to grow and to overcome our blind spots.

» The only time we have is now. The past is a memory, and the future is a dream.

» You are also a child of God and as valuable as anyone else—and thus deserving of love and self-love.

» Most of what we fear never happens.

» Most behavior is learned; we are not born with it.

» The first ten years set the stage for everything else we learn. We cannot unlearn the first ten years, but we can learn healthier behaviors.

» The only person responsible for you is you.

» Life is simple.

» People are consistent.

» Forgiveness is good for you.

» We are never alone. God is always with us.

» We are all in this life together.

» Spend more time with people you love.

» Be of service to others.

» Take care of issues as they occur. Do not procrastinate.

» Plan to do one thing at a time.

» Have fun with the life God gave you.

» Want what you have instead of planning to have what you want—in the material dimension.

» Develop and cherish new relationships.

» Continue to surrender to God.

» Remember that your whole life can be an offering to God, and your behavior can be prayers to God.

The Bowl of Life

Look at the bowl we use to hold life. If we hold the bowl with peace and love, then the details inside the bowl—or the content of our lives—also have more peace and love attached to them. If we hold the bowl with resentments and fear, then the contents will reflect those. We grow with the emotions of peace, vulnerability, and love. We stay stuck with the emotions of fear, anger, and resentment. Because resentments and fear are about our pasts, we stay stuck in our pasts—forsaking the growth and the opportunities that are in our present and futures.

We humans are very capable of creating our moods and of altering them with food, chemicals, and much else that is external to ourselves. We may buy a new car and feel the excitement associated with the shine, the smells, and the gadgets. But after weeks or months, the excitement wears off. And later we buy another one and feel the same excitement and the same let down months later. Eventually, we may learn the excitement is not about the car. It is about how we create the excitement. And the car does not create it—we do. We often forget we can create and change our moods in the absence of the external agent.

Imagine the car, in the example above, as being in a large container, maybe a large bowl. The bowl may hold other things we have used to help generate excitement or mood shifts in our lives. In the bowl may be alcohol, other drugs, clothes, electronics, work, and exercise. But the quality of our lives is not determined by what is in the bowl. The spirituality and peace in our lives are not determined by the contents of the bowl. The quality of our lives is determined by what the bowl is made of. If the bowl in which we hold life is made of spirituality, our lives are much more spiritual. If the bowl is made of envy and jealousy, our lives have much negativity.

It is the same two hundred yards to hit a golf ball whether you are tense or relaxed. The ball does not care. It is the same dead cell phone battery whether you are relaxed or tense. The phone does not care. You are the common denominator among all the people you know, all the activities you are a part of, and all the places you visit. All these other things are not running your life, they are not communicating together or plotting against you, and they are often in very different places. You are running your life, poorly or well.

No matter which way you turn, no matter what choices you make, there will be consequences. So the issue is to learn to hold the consequences loosely, because life is a series of ongoing consequences. There is good news and bad news. The good news is that there are many people in the world for you to relate to, to talk with, to enjoy, to be challenged by, and to love. The good news is that there is weather outside to enjoy, lakes to splash in, and water for our plants. The good news is that there are many situations in life you can be a part of and enjoy. The bad news is this: you cannot control other people, you cannot control the weather, and you cannot control situations. The best you can do is respond well to people, weather, and situations.

Some people will be a challenge. They can be difficult to deal with. Some weather can be very hot, very wet, or even dangerous, in the case of hurricanes, blizzards, and the like. Some situations can be full of joy, such as childbirth, and some can be full of grief, such as a friend with cancer. However you view them, as sad or happy, joyful or painful, the truth is you cannot control them. So it is good to learn to have various ways to deal well with what life sends your way.

Hold life like you are holding an egg. Hold it gently, relax, and enjoy it. Even if you are on a rocking ship, hold it gently. It is in your attitude about the egg, about you, and about what is happening around you. Most times in life you are not on a rocking ship or in a tornado. Most times you can hold the egg gently and still deal well with what is happening around you. If you hold the egg too tightly—if you hold life too tightly—and react and overreact to situations that are usual, normal, and not life threatening, you will crush the egg. Hold the egg gently, and then you can decide what you want to do with it and when you want to do it. Holding it tightly will exhaust you and keep you stuck in your old behavior. You will not have peace.

Turning It Over to God

Turning it over to God involves several phases. First, we hold the problem up to God with an extended, open hand. Second, we turn it over to God as when we turn our hand over so the palm is facing down. Third, we let go of whatever it is we have been holding onto and attempting to control. We see it falling out of our downturned palm.

Too many people are afraid to do all three steps. Instead, they say they are handing a problem over to God—but they do so with a closed fist! When they turn it over to God, it is still with a closed fist, and they do not let go. And then they wonder why their faith life does not seem to be growing. It is not growing because they are not living in life but continuing to survive in control.

And this is where fear and the practice of the spiritual come into play. We hold up a problem, we turn over a problem, and we let go of a problem. But then with our fear habit we often take back the problem! Do not be discouraged by this when you do it. It just means you are a human with a history. You can change these habits. When you become aware of control, hold it up, turn it over, and let go. And keep practicing letting go to have less fear and more faith.

One of the biggest struggles is to let go of our mind-set about fear and to practice a mind-set of faith—that is, to weaken the neurological connections wired around fear and to increase the wired connections about faith. We can create the worst, or close to it, in our minds. And then we react to that as if it is real, and we become very fearful and immobilized. Fear, as it comes in the front door of our thoughts, pushes faith out the back door. Faith allows for building ourselves up, not for tearing ourselves down.

The gospel of Mark 10:50 describes Jesus healing the blind man who calls out to him from the side of the road, even though others rebuke the man and tell him to be quiet. The Bible says, "Throwing his cloak aside, he jumped to his feet and came to Jesus." Going toward Jesus could be interpreted as the faith that Jesus could heal him. And his cloak could be interpreted as what he was willing to leave behind, possibly his fear. He was cured because he wanted to be cured, because he believed he could be cured, and because he had made room in himself to be cured—by throwing off his old baggage. "Throwing off his cloak" can be seen in our lives as going inside of ourselves to learn who we are. We identify who we are, in part, by leaving behind all that is not truly us—such as our old roles, our unreasonable fears, and numerous other outdated habits.

On the radio one day I heard a story about elephants. Specifically, if you walk with an elephant through a market in India or Malaysia, the elephant will extend its trunk and grab a bunch of bananas and put them into its mouth. Walking on, it will grab oranges with its trunk and eat them. The elephant is taking advantage of what is around it. Before you enter the market, if you give the elephant a stick to carry in its trunk, it will walk through the market and touch nothing. Its focus is on the stick. Sometimes people are similar to the elephant with the stick. We go through life focusing upon fear and resentment, and we ignore and miss the opportunities to grab love and joy. Life is a buffet. Sample it. The stick that many people focus on is control, and that keeps them from experiencing the banquet of life. To move ahead, to change, we must drop the stick and leave it behind. That is an act of faith.

A patient once told me that in high school he was afraid of forgetting some football plays. He told this to his coach and asked what to do. The coach said, "If you forget, just tackle a guy wearing a jersey that is a color different than yours." The man then told me, "I think the coach was saying the worst thing to do when you are afraid is to do nothing." Wise coach!

The definition of life involves words such as *dynamic* and *changing*. Our job is to learn the tools, practice them, and deal well with the changes in our lives. It is our responsibility to put in the effort. The consequences are God's. This is not meant to rule out plans and to be in la-la land. Plans can give us safety, and we can also have faith in them—as long as they include God, our souls, and the spiritual core of life. Then we can follow the plan, be willing to change, and trust God as circumstances change.

Our psychology often involves the belief we can control outcomes, big outcomes. Spirituality involves a recognition and acceptance that we cannot control outcomes. Too often we become stuck in the psychology of our lives, in part, because we grew up with it. It is habitual, and it is physical. We do not "see" the spiritual—unless we open something other than our eyes. "I have a job and a family. I'm a realist," she told me. "I just can't let go of all these things." We are not letting go of the effort and of the intentions. We are letting go of the belief that we can control the outcomes and that we ought to rely just on ourselves.

Talk to yourself so you reduce your fear. Expect to have problems. Expect to be afraid of some of them at some level, but learn to handle them. Hold them or address them gently. When I work with couples, I sometimes tell them, "I hope you've had some problems this past week. It is a chance to practice resolving issues." When I talk with individuals, I tell them I hope they have had some problems in the time between sessions. When they ask why, I tell them, "You need the practice dealing with your fears." For example, I had a patient who told me, "I am less pleased with success than I am with the fear of failing." This person needed the practice of failing—such as "failing" to be on time or "failing" to pay a bill. He held himself to such a high standard; he needed the practice of letting go.

To change from the way we have been or from the way we are now, we must be willing to take the risk of making mistakes and trusting in God as we do so. We learn skills by practicing what we do not know and slowly becoming better at succeeding. Along the way we make mistakes; we can learn from those as well. If you are not willing to risk, where is your faith?

We tend to be given repeated opportunities in our lives to learn to deal with the issues, people, places, and situations we have learned to avoid. If we continue to avoid them, another situation or person will come into our lives again to give us another opportunity to deal with fear. Like a fear of conflict, if you do not learn to deal well with it now, you will have numerous opportunities to deal with it later. Do the best you can, at that moment, and that will be enough.

GODCIDENCES

God does constant work in our lives. There are no coincidences. These are times God is working anonymously in our lives. They might more accurately be called *Godcidences*. My patient Caitlin had a father who was dying; his body was shutting down. When she flew in and went to the hospital his blood pressure was 85/50, and he was not responding to her or to the nursing staff. She took his withered hand and began to talk soothingly to him. "You are my wonderful father, and this is your loving daughter. Thank you for all you have done for me and my family over these many years. I will always love you." Caitlin said these and similar statements for about an hour and then left to use the restroom. When she returned, the nurses were taking his pulse; his blood pressure was now 130/85. Then her father said, "I have always loved you, and I know you have always loved me. Your husband has been wonderful to you. Don't worry about me. I am fine." And then he went silent again. Caitlin later told me, "Those were the first complete sentences he has said to me in months—and they were his last."

Sometimes God answers prayers in ways we do not anticipate. For months my patient and I had been working on his addiction to the painkiller Vicodin. For months I had prayed God would take away my patient's addiction. He had been using up to eight pills a day. At the beginning of a session, he told me his insurance company had terminated his disability payments; after two years, he had been given the maximum amount of money under his agreement. He explained, "So now I barely have enough money to support myself. I should have been out looking for a job. I can't afford the Vicodin now. I have to get off it." And he did.

Another patient informed me that her ex-husband was entering a hospital. He became ill, but because he knew his ex and adult son already had trips planned, he told them to go. They had each booked their flights separately, hers to the coast and his to Europe, without coordinating with the other. When they landed on their return flights, they bumped into each other at the same luggage carousal at the same airport. And it was there they received a phone call from the daughter, who said, "He is dying. Come quickly." He died that evening, and they were all there.

Recently my wife and I agreed to pay for the wedding rehearsal dinner that my nephew and fiancé had in Cabo. My nephew said we could pay with a credit card, so I checked the balance of two cards and decided to pay down the balance due on one card just to be safe. As I transferred the money, I decided to pay down more than I had intended to. In Mexico, the caterers did not accept the first card, so I paid the bill with the second one. The amount due was twenty-six dollars less than the amount I had transferred. To me that is a Godcidence.

One year my wife and I discussed sponsoring a less fortunate family in our church. The previous year we had sponsored one family, and this time we decided to sponsor two. We bought presents for the children and food for the families and delivered them to church. That Sunday in church we were informed about other families who would not have a Christmas with presents and food if additional sponsors were not found. We volunteered again and were given the name of a seven-member family. We bought gifts, filled bags with groceries and a turkey, and delivered them to their two-bedroom apartment. We had done this knowing we had little money in the bank. I had already told my wife not to give me a Christmas gift but to donate money in my name to some of my favorite charities, including the MD Anderson Cancer Center. The day we received a thank-you letter from MD Anderson was the day we received a large and unexpected check from an investment we had made years previously. The check was for much more than we had spent on the families and the donation to the hospital.

Another time my wife and I were in the middle of an amazing day of contrasts, as if God was giving us a message that in spite of what was happening around us, we would be taken care of. It began on a Friday, the first day of our vacation to go skiing with friends in Nevada. At the airport, the staff was courteous and put our luggage on the conveyor belt. But one of the locks promptly got stuck between two conveyor belts and was broken. The suitcase was taped shut by the staff. This was a negative. The airplane flight was supposed to be full, but we had the only empty seat on the plane between us so we could stretch out a little. This was a positive. When we arrived in Reno, we saw that the other piece of luggage we had was partially open and the lock was broken. Another negative. The rental car we had reserved was not available, so the agency upgraded us to a much larger and more comfortable car. Now that was a positive. I rented a luggage cart at the airport, but the machine malfunctioned, so I lost two dollars. So that was a negative. By now, my wife and I were laughing and amazed at the balance of these events. We bought groceries on the way to our rented condominium. The clerk asked if we had a discount card. We said we did not have one for their chain of stores but that we did for a chain of grocery stores in Texas. She said that was acceptable and gave us a thirty-eight-dollar discount. Back to positive. The room was not ready at 4:00 p.m., the check-in time, so we were given vouchers for food in the restaurant. And that balanced out also.

I am amazed at how many things work out well in my life if I relax, have faith, and behave with the God-given gifts that I have. I had a friend in England who enjoyed all things Western, such as boots, saddles, and ranches. He could exercise his interest only when he visited us or when he watched movies. I knew he liked the old movies of the Cisco Kid, so I ordered one for him. When it arrived, it was a modern version, and not what he would like. I returned it and sent him another video for Christmas. During Christmas week, my wife and I did some house cleaning and took a load of clothes and other items to the Goodwill truck near our neighborhood. While helping the men put the items in the truck, I saw some videos. Out of curiosity I looked and saw that one was of *The Cisco Kid*—the original version! We offered to buy it, and the attendant said that we could have it. Life is a mystery.

"There is alcoholism in my family. My son and wife told me two weeks ago that I am drinking too much. I knew I was drinking way too much. I was missing the birthday parties for my wife and kids. I was out of control with my drinking. I stopped fifteen days ago on a Thursday. The following Monday I was randomly tested for alcohol and drugs by the oil and gas company I work for. If I hadn't stopped, I would have been fired that Monday." That was the first time my patient had been tested in six years.

Travis was in tremendous emotional pain regarding how to appropriately deal with his second wife, her children, and his children. He kept arguing with his wife, trying to get her to change, which is also what he had done with his first wife. We talked about his habit, how it was not working, and why he kept using it. On Monday evening after his morning therapy session, he went to a twelve-step meeting, and the topic was this: "How much pain do you have to have before you will do something different?" He returned the next week with a different attitude and said he thought God was giving him some strong messages. He was willing to listen.

I have a variety of self-help books that I read. Some are in the form of a reading, a meditation, and a prayer for each day of the year. Numerous times I have opened a book to the reading for the day and discovered that it was about an issue I was struggling with that day. These are also examples of small Godcidences in my life.

Living versus Surviving

Life is fluid like a river, not static like the water behind a dam. Learn to be content with the passing of time, your relationships, and your effort. Learn to be in the moment while still being aware you came from somewhere and are having those experiences and memories. Learn to be in the moment while recognizing you have a future. So keep paying your taxes—but be at peace where you are. If you are maintaining or avoiding your fears, you could be surviving instead of living.

Bad things happen to us. And our lives do go on. If you stay stuck in the event, you are not living—you just exist. If you are sad, give yourself permission to cry. And give yourself permission to live, to go on. You are not responsible for all that has happened around you. You did not create the world, so do not act as if you did. But you are responsible for what you do, whether it is lying, stealing, tax evasion, or child abuse.

We all have choices of some type to make in our lives. We can resolve our psychological baggage or ignore it. We can return to spirituality or not. Look at what you were given and what you've done with your gifts.

- » We were given peace, and we created conflict.
- » We were given compassion, and we hardened our hearts.
- » We were given openness, and we learned to hide.
- » We were given faith, and we learned to mistrust and to fear.
- » We were given a hunger for God, and we learned to hunger for money.

INTERNAL AND NOT EXTERNAL ORIENTATION

Fear is often an orientation to the external, rather than to the internal. A female patient of mine had a lot of fear (worry, anxiety) regarding what to wear to the gym because she wanted to look a certain way and was afraid of looking fat, poor, or somehow "out of place." Another patient of mine bought a piece of property even though he could not afford it. He bought it because he wanted to keep up with his friends (i.e., he was afraid of not fitting in). He was taking his cues for his actions and his beliefs from outside of himself.

Although our physiological and psychological development in our early years required us to focus on what was outside of us, as we aged and became wiser with experience, many of us realized that the external world would not bring us the peace and contentment we wanted. To have the spiritual gifts we desire, it is necessary to focus on the internal. The internal is where your feelings are, where your memories are, where meaning is, where peace lies, and it is where the power greater than you is. It is the inside, the internal, that we can change. We can change how we respond to what and who is outside of ourselves. It is the inside where we can change how we manage our emotions and our memories. It is the inside where we dialogue with God and with ourselves, where we ask for God's forgiveness, and where we begin the process of forgiving others and asking them to forgive us.

If you want to have more peace, you must learn to take more of your cues for your actions from inside yourself. For example, if you are in the right lane on a three-lane highway traveling at sixty miles per hour, this might be a speed where you are comfortable and safe. The drivers in the middle lane might be traveling seventy miles per hour, and the people in the far left lane even faster. Their speed is not your speed. At any time you can choose to go faster or slower. If someone is too close to your rear bumper, you can speed up, move to another lane, or stay at your speed. If the person behind you drives around you and gives you an obscene gesture, you can choose to say, "Peace is with you" or "God watch over you." Finding and maintaining peace is like finding your safe speed on the road and maintaining it. Others will go at whatever speed they want, and they may or may not find safety and peace while doing so. When we take our cues from inside, from God within us, we can have peace and courage to deal well with the external.

When you read newspaper articles about people who behaved heroically during a hurricane, flood, car accident, or fire, it is important to recognize these are people just like you and me who *knew* what the right thing to do was in a time of crisis. They quickly discerned this path by looking inward at their consciences and moral code. They did not sit down, think about what to do, take a vote of those around them, or make phone calls to the mayor's office. They were not in conflict, at least not for very long. They just knew. And we can have that *knowing* most minutes of most hours if we resolve our conflicts and are in intimate connection with God. Like Yoda said in the Star Wars movies, "Do or do not. There is no try."

One Sunday when we were in church, the priest stepped forward and asked us all to clap our hands on the count of three. He counted and we clapped. The he asked us to clap just once on the count of three. We clapped when he counted. And then he asked us to listen carefully, without clapping, to determine if we could hear anything after he counted to three again. We listened, and we could hear the sound of two coins dropping from his hand inside the sleeve of his robe onto the slate floor. Then he told us he had dropped two coins each of the times we had clapped our hands, but the noise had kept us from hearing the soft sounds. We must calm ourselves down and not be distracted by external noise if we are to hear God.

CHOOSE INTERNAL FREEDOM

There are different levels of freedom. A ten-year-old boy who is beaten by his father does not have much freedom to leave the situation. He may have few choices about where to go—to relatives or to the legal authorities. An adult may have more choices in a similar situation. But some adults are prisoners of their pasts because they do not see or are not aware of the choices they have. A relationship with God will set us free from our self-constructed, habitual, or learned prisons.

With freedom we can make a true commitment. We are not forced or obligated to do something. We do it because we want to. If we know we are free to choose, then we can choose acceptance instead of judgment, action instead of avoidance, faith instead of fear, and patience instead of an attempt at control.

Take care of today. If you wake up tomorrow, then take care of that day. I've learned to deal much of the time, but not all of the time, with what is presented to me in the current hour and day with the skills and faith that I have that day. I pray that as I go through life, however many days are given to me, that I learn more skills and have greater faith that God is doing God's work in my life. On the path of increased serenity and spirituality, bad events still occur, and people still might criticize or malign us. The difference on this path is how we handle the potential upsets.

Deep inside each of us is a moral blueprint for love and good. Our job is to find that moral blueprint and use it to construct our lives—just as a blueprint is used to construct a house. Deep breathing, relaxing, and being quiet for a few minutes help us to find our blueprint. As we become good at this, we will find it is easier to deal with the reality of life and to see opportunities to grow, even in stressful and challenging situations.

Where does peace come from? From other people, from cars, from clothes, from activity, from food? No! Peace comes from inside of us, not from the millions of distractions outside of us. Peace comes to us from the inside out. It does not come from our attempts to shove a car, food, or another person inside of ourselves.

God is inside of you, and you can hear God only if you are quiet, at peace, and willing to listen. God does not draw words in the sky or speak to us in a booming voice. God whispers. If we are distracted by people and by our numerous "toys," we will not hear God.

Fear and faith have many associated concepts that are opposites. The chart below shows the differences. Practice faith concepts to reduce your fears and to have more spirituality.

Fear	Faith
Focus on earthly power	Focus on spiritual power
Disrespectful	Respectful
Pride	Humility
Self-will	God's will
Focus on others	Focus on God
Control	Letting go
Rejection	Acceptance
Resentment	Forgiveness

Fear	Faith
Conflict	Peace
Making deals	Surrender
Closed	Open
Judgment	Love
Stagnation	Growth
Excuses	Commitment
Procrastination	Decisiveness
Seeking safety in the material	Safety in the spiritual
Compulsions	Freedom
Avoiding the unknown	Willingness to go to the unknown
Threats	Consequences
Self-centered	Self-care
Self-reliance	God reliance

OUR PRISONS

We are often prisoners of our emotions, fears, and habits. We have created the prison ourselves. Each prison bar is a fear or a habit such as avoidance. We build our walls to keep others, hurt, and fear out. There is a door to the prison, and it is locked. It is locked from the inside, and we have the key. Using the key requires a significant amount of faith. And faith is a spiritual issue.

Inside of our prisons, our habits, and our comfortable existences, we may feel safe, or at least safer. And we may feel safe because we keep repeating the same behaviors we know and that are familiar to us. The problem is that they may not help us grow. To grow, we must learn new behaviors and move beyond what is familiar and comfortable.

If you want to be free, you must leave the prison behind—and also leave behind the attitude of prisoners. One of my patients was a prisoner of his thinking because he compared himself negatively to his older brother and sister. He was also a prisoner to his fear of making cold calls and of being rejected in his career as a salesman—after he had made few cold calls, his business had deteriorated. He stayed stuck in a prison of his own making.

Some people are prisoners to their activity levels, maybe as a means to avoid addressing their fears. It was in Houston that a patient of mine was staying very busy with his job, his dating life, and his friends. He was also desperately afraid that his girlfriend was going to leave him. I asked him to imagine himself living alone in a log cabin in Idaho fifty miles from the nearest neighbor without a car. I then asked him what he would do. He said he would be busy chopping wood and fixing the cabin. He would also walk to the neighbors once a week (even though walking there would take twelve hours one way). "And I would want a dog as a companion," he said. "It's not good to be alone." He continued talking about his busyness at the cabin until I asked what he would do if all the wood was cut, all the crops were planted, and the cabin was airtight. Then he said, "I would listen to some good and loud music."

Now, this was a man who was afraid to be alone with himself and God. This was a man who was still very busy attempting to distract himself, even in a log cabin. He did not say he would relax and enjoy the time in the woods. He did not say he would sit quietly and listen to the sound of birds singing. Psychologically, the cabin is him, and he is uncomfortable and fearful of being with himself. He also did not understand that he could hear God only if he was quiet and listened very carefully. God speaks to us softly—as softly as the sound of butterfly wings.

Fear is a prison. Psychology provides a door out of the prison. Psychological strategies and interventions, including medication, can be used to address our fears, reduce them, and have them become more manageable. Spirituality is another door out of the prison. We can learn to open our minds and hearts up to a power greater than ourselves and find peace, freedom, and faith. The differences between fear and faith are many—we can choose which we want to practice and accomplish.

Inside of our jail cells we do not grow. We grow only when we push the walls out farther or open the door. True vulnerability is when we knock down the walls and doors to stand exposed. It is when we are vulnerable that we have the most opportunities to grow, to expand, and to move. This type of vulnerability and growing involves faith, and that is how the journey becomes spiritual. Vulnerability is a spiritual matter, while fears, walls, and habits are psychological matters.

A married man I know built his inside walls stone by stone over the years while he had difficulties with his wife. He built a strong gate, and he usually kept it shut. Inside his walls, he existed, but he did not live. Inside his walls, he protected himself from his wife, just as he had protected himself from his mother decades before he married. None of the stones he used to build his walls were necessary in the current time period. He could do much more and behave very differently if he would let himself grow. He is a prisoner of his past, and he does not have freedom in his present.

I asked him to consider an image to think about and maybe grow from. I told him to imagine that a diagnosis of liver cancer was given to his wife—a diagnosis that would most likely mean death in less than eight months. I asked him if he would relate differently to his wife. "Of course," he said, "who would not treat a person differently under those conditions?" I told him I agreed with him and then suggested that he notice that the capacity and skills to relate differently to his wife were already within him. If they were not, how could he immediately begin to behave more openly to his wife? And if he already had those skills, why did he continue to relate to his wife as if he were a ten-year-old boy in fear of his mother? He had no answers at that time, but he did become aware that he was a creature of habit, had not been growing in this relationship in years, and had not been using faith in God to grow spiritually.

Dorothy in *The Wizard of Oz* could have clicked her heels together anytime she wanted to return home, but she did not know this. We can create the kingdom of God anytime, anywhere, because it is within us.

There is no one and nothing so common, so ordinary, that it cannot be seen as sacred—if they are viewed as a means to move closer to God, to love, to acceptance, and to peace. My wife and I serve in our church as extraordinary ministers of Holy Communion. That is, we often serve the wine or host to the parishioners during Mass. When I hold up the wine or host, I look into the eyes of the person. Some of them keep their eyes open and look up; some don't. They are all sacred, so I look. I look, and sometimes I think I see angels. It is about my attitude, so I keep my eyes open so that they can also see me.

CHAPTER 15

FEAR, FORGIVING, AND FORGETTING

Whether you think you can or you think you can't, you're right.
—HENRY FORD

LET'S TALK REALITY ABOUT THE cultural adage "forgive and forget."
The truth is that forgetting is a neurological issue, and forgiving is
a spiritual issue. You forget when your brain is damaged. If a person
has traumatic brain damage, dementia, or Alzheimer's disease, he has
probably forgotten much. That is, neurological connections that were
in his brain for Aunt Helen or Richard Nixon—or even for yesterday's
lunch—are no longer present. And that is sad.

Forgiving is what you can choose to do even though you remember
the painful emotions you once felt. Not forgiving means staying stuck
in painful emotions and memories, stuck in the time period where the
action or inaction occurred. And that is sad.

Memories may be hidden but not forgotten. We may repress
traumatic memories by tucking them into a small, dark box in our minds

and covering them up. But they do not go away. That is why an adult may recall her own sexual abuse as a ten-year-old child when she hears that a neighbor's ten-year-old child is sexually abused. The memories were hidden, not forgotten.

According to *The Second College Edition of Webster's New World Dictionary*, the definition of the word *forgive* is the following: "(1) to give up resentment against or the desire to punish; pardon (2) to give up all claims to punish or exact penalty for (3) to cancel or remit (a debt)."

A patient of mine was hurt and angry with his wife for what he thought was an emotional and possibly physical affair with another man. "I'm angry and I can't forgive her," he stated. However, it was not an issue of "I can't," but rather "I don't want to." Two months into therapy, he said, "I've got my spirituality back. I've forgiven her." He had the ability to forgive, but his forgiving had been overwhelmed by his fear of doing so and by his hurt and anger. He also had a fear about what she had done and could do again.

In the process of therapy, I asked him several times what he would teach his children to do with their friends. Did he want to teach them to be resentful, unforgiving, and in constant conflict? If so, then that is what he could do for himself. However, if he wanted them to forgive, then that is what he ought to do for himself. Otherwise, he would be hypocritical and would disconnect his spiritual part from the other three parts.

His forgiveness did not just happen, and it was both psychological and spiritual. It occurred in the context of thoughts, emotions, memories, intentions, and ongoing everyday experiences with his wife. There are these physical and psychological realms to be aware of. His forgiveness was also a function of what he said to himself, what he saw in his head, and what he practiced. Concerning the spiritual, God was always present in his life offering forgiveness as an option. My patient was the one who built the wall of fear and resentment between himself and God. He did not initially hear God talking and encouraging him. He had been taking care of himself in an unhealthy and self-centered way.

His wall of fear, resentment, and self-centeredness did not change his wife or himself for the better. To change himself, my patient began to count his blessings. He said, "She's still here with me. We're talking more now." He began to count the negatives less often. He began to get what he practiced. "You know, forgiveness wasn't all that hard when I did it," he explained. True enough—and neither are typing, driving a car, speaking in public, and learning to tell jokes, if you practice them. This is a man who at some point along his recovery regarding his wife moved from self-focus to God-focus and from fear into faith. It did not just happen.

We use resentments to build up walls, to close our hearts to others, and to protect ourselves, because we have fear of being hurt again. To grow, we have to do something different from we have been doing with our fear habit. We must surrender to the possibilities for growth through forgiveness.

FORGIVENESS AND PRACTICE

Jesus was asked the following by Peter: "Lord, how many times shall I forgive my brother when he sins against me? Up to seven times?" Jesus then made the point about practice. "I tell you, not seven times but seventy-seven times" (Matthew 18:21-22, NIV). That is, we must forgive many, many times to become good at it. It may not change the other person, but you will most likely be changed. And if the other person sees you moving from a standpoint of fear and resentment to one of peace, he may want what you have and do what you have done. If you want more fear in the world, then practice fear. If you want more peace, then practice peace. Don't wait for someone else to do it first. You do it. Expect this to be a process—a slow accumulation of forgiving skills. It is a little different for each person. So be patient with yourself as you learn to forgive *while still remembering.*

"I can't forgive myself," Rosa admitted during one of our sessions. I suggested that she had been practicing how *not* to forgive for many years but that now she could learn to practice forgiving herself. She said,

"It's tough for a tiger to change its spots." I explained the neurological connections that happen with practice. "It'll take me another thirty years to learn," she answered with a sigh as she used the negative yet again. She was trapped in the negative and unforgiving jail of her own making and was not visualizing new possibilities. Practice the positives. Forgive yourself and others. You will create the kingdom of God within yourself.

"I didn't lose my ten pounds, and I was disappointed in myself. But when someone else did not lose I was not disappointed," Francesca said. Learn to give yourself what you give others. You already know how to forgive. It is also important to learn to give. The question is where to aim your forgiveness. God also forgives us, completely and as many times as is necessary. The personal presence of God is always with us. You might just be distracted from it or not notice God because of your other priorities and activities.

If you are twenty miles out at sea in a sailboat and your GPS shows land is twenty miles to the northwest, you can set your sails and go northwest. You will get there eventually if you stay on the same course. Or you could let your sails down and moan and groan about the hot sun and salty water and about how difficult life is. If you practice staying where you are, you will stay where you are. Do not allow your fear of change to keep you from practicing how to change.

RESENTMENTS USE UP ENERGY

There are many problems with resentments. One is depression. The resentments (or lack of forgiveness) within us have energy. An equal or greater amount of energy must be used to keep the resentments within ourselves. The energy drain used to deal with repressed emotions can make us depressed. One twig may not be heavy, but two hundred of them are unwieldy and weigh us down. Resentments operate the same way.

Another problem is the possible habit of adding to resentment. If every time you see a certain relative you think back with anger on something he or she has done, you will add to the resentment pile. This is a cumulative process, and the resentment may grow bigger. This is part of the "buildup to a blowup" cycle when we might say or do something with impulsivity and exaggeration. Resentment is dynamite in search of a blasting cap. It is also spiritual homicide. Resentment will keep us from connecting to the spiritual realm inside of ourselves, a place where we can feel at peace. That connection requires forgiveness and a willingness to do something different instead of giving in to the paralyzing fear of change. I know people who have lived the first year of resentment over and over again for thirty years in a row. Time has gone by and opportunities for change have arisen, but they have not taken advantage of the possibilities.

Forgiveness of someone does not release the other person—it releases you! It does not release them from their responsibility. It does not release them from any guilt. But it does release us from resentment and from the past so we can have joy and peace in the present. If you spread the seeds of weeds in your yard, water them, and pay attention to them, you will have more weeds. If you spread the seeds of grass in your yard, water them, and pay attention to them, you will have more grass. If you nurture resentment, you will have more resentment. And if you nurture forgiveness, you will have more forgiveness. You choose and you practice. It is your life.

FORGIVENESS AND BOUNDARIES

Forgiveness does not mean you have to tolerate the intolerable or bear the unbearable. It does not mean that you have to continue to see or spend time with the person who abused you. It does not mean you have to behave as a victim—that would go against common sense and healthy self-care. Forgiveness of yourself does not mean you will never have problems again in your life. When you forgive someone or yourself, you are not excusing what the person did or did not do. Everyone is responsible for what he or she does. Actions have (legal, moral, and ethical) consequences that extend into the future. Forgiveness allows you to stop dragging your past feelings about the person you are forgiving into both your present and future lives. Forgiveness requires vulnerability and love. Forgiveness releases you into growth. Consequently, you will have more available energy. You might then not be suppressed, repressed, or depressed.

Forgiveness is one of the tools God gives us to use to make our life journeys more peaceful. If you make a mistake, view it like you would a flat tire. Get out the tools you need, fix it, and go on your way; you do not need to stay preoccupied with the flat tire! It is not an emergency or crisis. Flat tires happen, so fix them. In life, you make occasional mistakes. Ask for forgiveness, forgive yourself, and move on.

Forgiveness is a worthy tool to have in our spiritual toolbox. One of my patients complained to me about her sister's self-centeredness; she gave me an example. She and her sister flew with their mother to another city to have some time together. Their departure flight was at 1:00 p.m. on a Sunday. My patient suggested that they leave the center of the city by 10:00 a.m. The sister agreed and then arrived late at the house. At the airport parking garage, an elderly couple in front of them was having difficulty figuring out how to get a parking ticket from the meter. My patient's door was blocked, and her sister refused to get out and help the couple. So they all sat there until the couple stumbled upon the right button to push. When the ladies finally arrived at the ticket counter, my patient went to the front of the line, making excuses all the time, and said, "We have to make the plane to Atlanta." She was told the plane was already taxiing away from the terminal. The sister became irate and made a scene as if the plane could not leave without her. My patient could forgive her sister. In the future, one option my patient might consider would be to travel without her sister.

FORGIVENESS AND MISTAKES

You cannot learn something new without making a few mistakes. There is a learning curve. If you do not make mistakes, by definition, it means you already know the material or have the skill. You cannot learn forgiveness unless you recognize that you did or said something that you or another person was injured by. You do not learn forgiveness in a vacuum. You learn it in the normal context of life—a life full of wonder, awe, mistakes, and pain. It is all part of your life, just as your fingers and toes are part of you. You are what you are made of, and that includes the spiritual, intellectual, emotional, and behavioral. Your life is what you live, and if you live all parts of it, then your life is bigger and fuller.

Life is like the weather: we cannot predict it very far out with any reasonable certainty. We might want to golf on a Saturday, but we also recognize it might rain, so we develop a backup plan—something that can be done indoors. If it rains we do not blame ourselves, say we should have known better, berate ourselves with words such as *stupid* and *inadequate*, or ask what is wrong with us. But we use these self-abusive behaviors with other issues in life—issues over which we have no control, just like the weather. We often believe we should not make any mistakes in our relationships with others even though they are much more complicated than the weather. We beat ourselves up when we do not anticipate other people's every need, move, and emotion. The first person we need to practice forgiving is ourselves. We are as human as anyone else we know.

People give us numerous opportunities to practice forgiveness. Rather than expect perfection from others and ourselves, we could practice seeing mistakes as opportunities to become accomplished in forgiveness. My sisters and I have a story about our mother, who went to a funeral home in our hometown to pay her respects to a friend who had died and to his family. But she went in the wrong room for the viewing. She soon realized she did not know the man in the coffin! As my mother turned around and was backing out, the grieving widow came over and said, "Thank you so much for coming." My mother said, "He was such a nice man." We all make mistakes, so we do not need to have incapacitating fears about forgiving ourselves.

Another story in my family is about my uncle who is a minister. He told us of the time he was in the church restroom just prior to performing a wedding. But when he zipped his pants, the robe got caught in the zipper. And at that moment the organist began to play!

If you do not make mistakes, it is because you are dead. When the air conditioner belt on your car breaks, you don't kick the car and leave it on the side of the road. When you make mistakes, don't abuse yourself and abandon yourself. You do most things in life well. You make few mistakes compared to the good you do. You would forgive your child for making a mistake, so forgive yourself. Your child is a child of God—and so are you. Because we have made mistakes in our lives and because we chose paths we later thought were not right, we probably all could use more than one lifetime. But one is all we are given, so it is important to accept what has happened to us and what we have done, to learn to forgive ourselves and others, and to be at peace. If you ask God for help with forgiveness, keep in mind that God will probably not give you ten pounds of it that you merely have to use. No, God will probably give you the circumstances, people, and opportunities to learn to practice forgiveness. If you ask for it, be prepared to practice it.

Forgiveness removes fear from within us. It may do so only temporarily until we become very accomplished at forgiveness. Then it can remove fear for longer periods of time and even remove it from our relationships with some people. The process of learning and practicing forgiveness is sometimes like the process of showering to clean ourselves. Usually within minutes, the bacteria on our bodies begin to accumulate again in large numbers. It looks like we are clean, but the bacteria are still there. The shower, like forgiveness, may not solve the problem of being physically or spiritually *dirty* completely. However, it sure improves the situation for yourself and for those around you who smell either your body odor or your nonspiritual scent.

Mistakes are often accidents. The wife of a patient of mine saw a pile in the garage so she went through it and threw much of it into the garbage. When he learned of this, her husband became upset and angry, because some of the items were mementos from his childhood. He feared losing them, so he went through the trash and retrieved them. She felt guilty and asked for his forgiveness even though her mistake was unintentional.

You will keep making some mistakes for many years. Then, one day or night, you will stop making them. You will be dead. In the meantime—until that end comes—it is good to learn to be kind to yourself when you do make mistakes. A man told me that "asking for forgiveness from someone seems like groveling [his ego]. It makes me highly vulnerable to ask for forgiveness. It's kind of like praying on my knees. I won't do it. I can pray just as well sitting up or lying in bed." It sounded like he was running away from some image in his mind or a past issue with pride or inadequacy. Asking for forgiveness, being vulnerable, and praying on his knees are so powerful that he avoided trying them.

FORGIVENESS AND RESPONSIBILITY

Taking responsibility for what you do and apologizing is related to, but not the same as, asking for forgiveness from someone. Forgiveness is for the spirit what taking responsibility is for the other three parts of us. So take responsibility (you did it, not someone else), offer an apology ("I'm sorry, and I will not do it again"), and ask for forgiveness ("Will you please forgive me?"). The problem with living in fear is it makes it difficult to apologize and ask for forgiveness. The fear often takes the form of not wanting to admit you did something wrong. You may have a fear of appearing mistaken, inadequate, or imperfect.

Life works better when there is no blame and no excuses. Life works best when there is only responsibility for our actions. No blaming of others, no excuse making—simply responsibility for speaking, for fixing what we have broken, and for cleaning up what we have messed up. Blame and excuses keep us stuck in the past. Taking responsibility for our actions allows us to move forward. Each of us is responsible for what we have done and for who we want to be.

If you have harmed someone else, by design or inadvertently, you can free yourself by asking for forgiveness from God, from yourself, and from the other person. As you ask for forgiveness, tell God, yourself, or the other person that you love Him, yourself, or him or her. Take the initiative regarding forgiveness. Take your cues from yourself rather than waiting for someone else to go first. This is your life. There is no one else in your skin but you. Use your time and your energy well. Asking for forgiveness takes the weight of the past off your shoulders so you can move forward.

Forgiveness and Ego

The following is a quote from a patient: "My father and I were not communicating well after he fired me from the family business. Then he sent me an article about forgiveness. He called me a couple of days later and was angry because I had not read the article right away." The father may need to read the article again. Our egos are often very grandiose—even when we want to help someone.

During a session, Monica asked, "When am I supposed to ask for forgiveness? I am not worthy of it. I am not important enough to get it." Her ego seemed to be swelling with pride about her uniqueness in the universe. She was so unique that she could not, as a human, be forgiven. Monica also called herself selfish and mean and began to tell me about all the times she was unkind to her brother. But those events were twenty years in the past. She also described her masturbation as an adolescent and labeled it "nearly addictive." Her obsessiveness about what she had done wrong strengthened her negative self-talk. It reinforced her self-abuse and not her forgiveness. I reminded Monica that we are incapable of comprehending the forgiveness that God gives us. Who are we to challenge God's forgiveness by saying we do not deserve it and that we will not forgive ourselves? I gave her my handout entitled "People and Incidences to Forgive." I asked her to write down the specific incidences in which she believed she had done something wrong and then to forgive herself for each one in a written statement. I also asked her to say the following to herself every time she looked at a clock, answered the phone, or used a restroom: "God forgives me, and I forgive myself." If you practice forgiveness, you will probably become more accomplished at forgiving.

People and Incidences to Forgive

People to Forgive	Incidence	Forgiveness Statement
	Who was present? What happened? What was said? What was felt? Be specific.	Write a detailed sentence in which you forgive the person (who may be yourself).
1.		
2.		
3.		

Think of the process of reading a book. After you have read it, you can place it on a shelf or give it away. But there is no value in dragging it around with you wherever you go. Keep what you like in your memory, and let go of the book. Carrying the book around with you will cause it to become physical or mental baggage. Dragging baggage can wear you out.

The book is like your experiences—some work out well and some do not. Keep the ones you like in your memory, forgive yourself for the mistakes, let go of the baggage, and move on into your future. Wounds can heal but scars remain. And we do not need to keep picking at a scar.

CHAPTER 16

FEAR AND EGO

You can change the outer aspects of your life by
changing the inner attitude of your mind.
—WILLIAM JAMES

I WAS ONCE IN A MEETING where the focus was on the concept of ego.
Several of us understood ego in the Freudian sense. I enjoyed the
intellectual stimulation offered when an older man who had been quietly
listening to us leaned forward and, speaking slowly, said that based on his
experience, ego ought to be understood as an initialism—in other words,
with each letter said separately. "I see it as EGO, and I think it means
'ease God out,'" he said. He went on to say more about his thinking, but I
did not hear most of the rest because I was recoiling from the power of the
concept he had just shared. I have thought about that concept for years
now and shared that gentleman's idea with many others. When there is
too much *I* and too many control tactics, the spiritual and accepting side
of life is pushed to the background. If you believe you can make things
happen, then you are a god in your mind and you don't need God.

A male patient of mine demonstrated easing God out when he talked with me about the stress and anxiety that resulted from his pushing to make a point at work. He said, "For two and a half years I have been pushing to get them to look at this problem. I know I'm right. I know what's going to happen. But they don't listen to me." I asked him what he was trying to prove or what he wanted people at work to say to him. He responded, "I want them to say I'm worthy and to know that I'm smart." We discussed his plan to help his company become more efficient, but we also discussed the price he had paid for his efforts. He wanted things on the job to go his way. He knew he was right. But during the two-and-a-half-year process, he had isolated himself at work, and coworkers avoided him because he was on edge and angry. His marriage and relationships with his children were suffering as well. This man put his interests, goals, and priorities above God. He tried to prove himself worthy by focusing on others instead of focusing on God. He behaved as if he believed he was not worthy in the sight of God or himself, but only in the eyes of others.

As we talked, it became apparent that this patient's current behavior was determined by the behaviors practiced repeatedly in his past. He had punished himself for about thirty years. He explained, "I've blamed myself for not going to medical school. I settled for second place." All these years later he was still trying to prove to himself—through the comments and approval of others—that he was intelligent. I asked him if he would punish his child for thirty years if she did not get admitted to medical school. Like her father, she might be late in recognizing that good grades in high school are important. "I wouldn't punish my child for thirty years. I love her. She did the best she could. It's her life, and she is worth more than a career and worth more than what she does," he said.

His thinking was accurate about his child, so we discussed his hypocrisy and control. He behaved hypocritically because he would do for her what he would not do for himself. He was afraid to forgive himself and relax because he thought he might give up, do nothing, and lose his job. He was also startled when I said he was placing himself above God. "How?" he asked. I explained, "You are willing to forgive your child for her mistakes, but you do not acknowledge that God can forgive you or already has forgiven you for yours. You say you know more than God does about yourself and spiritual matters and that you have decided you are unforgivable. You are attempting to place yourself above God." This man's ego and fear resulted in an intense focus on the material world and the *I* rather than the spiritual world and the *You* of God.

The ego can be defined partly as the awareness of self. The ego is at the junction, or the intersection, of the material world and the spiritual world. We grew up in the material world, and we learned the ways of the material world. The ego is usually defined in relation to the physical, the material. So the ego comes to mean not who we are spiritually but also who we are materially—what we own, how much money we make, which important people are our friends, what committees we are on, how busy we are, and what car we drive. When the ego is distorted, it is distorted in the direction of the material world. Unfortunately, too much emphasis on material things keeps us rooted in one spot, unmoving, just as if we have a huge anchor chained to our feet.

Our egos can lead us to create walls between God and ourselves and between others and ourselves. A distorted ego, one focused upon the material world, is often characterized by inflated pride, arrogance, judgment of others, and attempts to win and be right. If we were less afraid of losing something in the material realm, we would have a more balanced ego. As a patient of mine once said, "I never knew life could be this good until I got out of my own way."

Our culture can be caring and compassionate; it can show spiritual values. A careful examination will also show the many subtle and pervasive emphases on the material in our culture. Believing strongly in the adage "Where there's a will, there's a way" involves much ego with a focus on what one wants. The saying could be more God focused if it was "Where there's God's will, there's a way." The phrase carpe diem ("seize the day") could be less materialistically focused and more spiritually focused if it were interpreted as "God, seize the day."

Of the four parts of us, only two involve reasonableness or conscious choice. It is not the behavioral, because that is usually habit. It is not the emotional, because, by definition, emotions lack logic and choice. The intellectual can involve consciousness, but that consciousness is often about the self or the ego and how to help the self get what it wants, sometimes at any cost. This consciousness is often in the service of the ego. Without a balance, it can make us very self-centered and selfish. The spiritual part of us involves the most choice and the most consciousness. This consciousness is of God and not of us only. This consciousness is about choosing to behave for a common good—for a good greater than our materialistic and concrete desires.

Your ego is like an iron umbrella that you keep above your head as you walk on the beach. God is the sunshine that you do not bask in because of your ego and your defenses—especially the defenses designed to reduce your fears. I had a patient who was very damaged by the events of his childhood and by his years of perfectionism and work addiction. He often referred to himself as worthless, pathetic, or weak. He also talked about his fear of allowing himself to find out who he truly was inside without the defenses he had learned. I told him that if he were a car, he would have been built of stainless steel but was later told or had somehow learned that he was rusty. So he covered up what he believed was rust with a coat of paint. The paint, of course, was a role he played in his life. Then he was told that paint was not attractive or that the rust was leaking through the paint, he applied another coat of paint: another role or facade in his life. Now, because of his growth—his change—some of the paint was falling off in pieces, and he and I could see the stainless steel underneath. And stainless steel does not rust. His job then was to continue to take off the paint or to allow the paint to fall off completely so he would be free to be himself.

It is a paradox that the more we surrender, the stronger we become, and the more freedom we have. The more we let go of ego-based behaviors, the more we discover who we are and the more we love ourselves. In Matthew, Jesus was asked what the greatest commandment was. He answered, "To love your neighbor as yourself." When we judge others, we take the position that we are in the right or that our way is the right way. Immediately, our ego is in front of us. It is between us and the person or persons we are judging. It is also between us and God. If we do not judge and if we move our egos aside, we expand our own realities as we allow ourselves to interact and engage with others and accept their differences.

A patient, Jenny, told me that at about age thirteen, other girls in her guitar class teased her. Perhaps it was because she already knew how to play a little, thanks to her grandfather. The other girls even put a nasty note in her desk, but the teacher said Jenny had forged it. So she stopped taking lessons but played a little just for herself, by herself, over the years. In her forties she heard a voice say, "Play for me," and she began to play in public, starting with the singles group in her church. The faith that God had spoken to her—wanting her to use her gift in the present—overcame her fear from the past. When she was a child, her ego said, "I do not want to be hurt so I will stop playing." As an adult, Jenny could view herself differently and make other choices.

Another woman I knew had a father who was domineering and pushy. This lady had also learned to push to "make things happen." Pity the poor person who cut in front of her in a line or who was too slow in traffic. She had her ego invested in her identification with her father and with his behaviors. When she let go of thinking with the ego—"Get out of *my* way. *I* want this done *now*"—she began to explore and nurture other parts of herself that were more godlike in tone and appearance. Giving and accepting compliments became a part of her repertoire.

The ego and the fear of losing what the ego wants will keep us from our spiritual side. Most of us won't die driving an expensive sports car while on the way to the marina to hop onto our sixty-foot yacht. Many, if not most, of us will leave this world the way we arrived—in a hospital with family, friends, and a few medical professionals around us. Our banker, stockbroker, boss, or new-car dealer probably won't be there. I want to live my life the way I want my death to be—surrounded by loving family and friends, at peace, letting go, and preparing to meet God.

The nearness of God is not determined by our thoughts, feelings, actions, accomplishments, and bank accounts. God is always present and near. However, we can create the thoughts and feelings—especially the fear-based emotions—that keep us from experiencing God's nearness. We are creative and material people; we can create many priorities to place on a higher pedestal or in front of God.

Daily we encounter numerous situations that let us know we are not God and that we cannot control others. Yet we labor under the delusion that we can. Our lives can become worse and worse, more fearful and unmanageable because we do not pay attention to the small messages about our lack of control of the world. And then, for many of us, our little worlds collapse.

Do you have friends that often seem to want to argue with you? They do not want to discuss, compromise, or learn with you. They want to "win" or be "right." In their attempts to do so, they raise their voices and show anger. Do you notice how you keep moving farther and farther away from them, physically and emotionally? Now, you may not be close to or connected with them. Striving to win and to be right damages relationships with God, with ourselves, and with others. It is the out-of-balance ego that pushes to be right and show off. Underneath that ego is probably the emotion of fear—a fear of intimacy, connection, or inadequacy.

Ego and Priorities

In our three-part priority system, God is first. The rest of our lives will not work well unless we are connected with God. For example, to give away love, we must have love. God is the source of love, and it is given to us. Second on the priority list is us. To give away love, it has to be

228

within us, nurtured by us, and carried by us. Third on the priority list are spouses, families, friends, and everyone else.

Be friends with God and be friends with yourself. Then being friends with others will be much easier. Be humble with God. That is, move your ego out of the way so you can live in faith and not fear and know you are worthy. The keys to healthy relationships include not lying, cheating, or keeping secrets. In other words, tell the truth, create win-win situations with others, be fair, and seek justice. Then you will have little or nothing to prove to others about your innate worth as a human being. Get clear in your relationship with God and clear in your relationship with yourself. Then other relationships you have will become clear.

It is a paradox that life is not all about us, but at the same time, it *is* all about us. By itself the ego cannot resolve and live peacefully with this paradox. But the spiritual side of life can result in living in peace with the paradox. We do not make everything happen around us. We do not have that type of power. You might be angry with yourself if a traffic cop pulls up behind you in his car and signals for you to pull over. "What did I do now? What's wrong with me? Why are they after me?" But maybe you did not make it happen. To be ridiculous, maybe the cop had hemorrhoids and pulled you over because he wanted to get out of his car and walk around. On the other hand, it is about us because we have another opportunity to learn—maybe about authority figures if you have that issue, or about fear if you have that issue, or about patience, or about being gentle with yourself.

There is a positive aspect of the ego when it is in balance and when it is part of our gratitude, willingness, and positive self-talk. For example, we can say the following: "I am glad I have a job. God loves me. I have friends who care for me." These affirmations can be examples of healthy ego use. In recovery we do not want to destroy the ego—just to assist it in becoming part of a healthy balance.

When we have a distorted ego we are more likely to attempt control strategies. We attempt control because we have fear, and fear will nudge out faith. The ego is connected with thoughts such as these:

» I know what is right for them.

» I am right, and they are wrong.

» Something bad will happen if I change from what I've been doing.

» I'm too afraid to change.

» I won't change until they change.

The common denominator in these sentences is the focus upon the self and on what you believe you can make happen. It is not on leaning on God, noticing what is happening around you, and asking God for help. We often arrive at this point in our lives because we live in a material world. The people who raised us had their own flaws. We learned various behaviors with fear as a motivator. And we may still behave that way years later. We may resist change because of fear. We may hang onto the belief that we run the world. Ultimately, we do not hear God because we focus on what is screaming at us while God is whispering to us.

If you have ego, conflict, and fear, you are in good company. Elijah, the Old Testament prophet, also had them. In I Kings 19:11, we read he was afraid for his life because Jezebel, the wife of Ahab the king, had sworn to have him killed. Elijah ran into the desert and prayed he might die there. But an angel of the Lord spoke with him and gave him food, twice. Next Elijah walked to the top of Mount Horeb:

> Then a great and powerful wind tore the mountains apart and shattered the rocks before the Lord, but the Lord was not in the wind. After the wind there was an earthquake, but the Lord was not in the earthquake. After the earthquake came a fire, but the Lord was not in the fire. And after the fire came a gentle whisper. And God was speaking in a whisper.

Sometimes in therapy I have a patient who is a significant challenge to me. Sometimes, I just do not like some, or much, of his or her behavior. To deal with this, several years ago I wrote a note to myself and read it repeatedly. The note reads as follows: "These people who seem manipulative and want to be taken care of and who complain without changing are also children of God. It is important to move my ego, my vanity, aside, and to enter their world. They are not going to enter mine— that is unknown, unfamiliar, and frightening to them. With my vanity, my ego, and my one-right-way thinking out of the way, I can hear them differently, see them differently, and respond differently to them."

My wife developed a wonderful concept called "plan A is always God's." Now, you may be developing your own system, your own plan A, or your priorities. But this is important: the overriding plan A, including all that you do not know about, is not yours, but God's. If the big plan A was yours, your life would be and always would have been the way you wanted it. Your plan A did not include unexpected and unwanted pain, such as that of the death of someone close to you, disease, or accidents. The first plan that is in the world is not yours. In the process of recovery, the ego must learn to surrender to a power greater than itself.

I have learned that I do not know God's plan in advance. Sometimes I can see parts of the plan in my rearview mirror after I have gone through an experience. In order to do that, I have to move my ego out of the way, see, and listen. If I focus on me, what I wanted, or what I lost, then I do not see or hear.

A person may have a lot of money, many cars, and several homes. But it is important to realize that when that person wakes up at three in the morning, there is not a car or house in his brain. No one and nothing else is inside of you at three in the morning or when you are dying—just God and you. So it is good to be at ease with and have good relationships with yourself and God.

Jesus was tempted just as we are tempted, and we can learn from his temptations. In Mathew 4:1-9, we discover the three temptations of Jesus by the Devil. All three are related to the value many in the material world place upon pleasure, fame, and power. Jesus spent forty days and nights in the desert fasting when he was initially tempted. The first temptation was about physical satisfaction when the Devil said, "If you are the Son of God, turn these stones into bread." The second temptation took the form of fame when Jesus was taken to the wall of the temple and asked to jump. "If you are the Son of God, the angels will protect you," said the Devil. Angels jumping from the wall to rescue Jesus would have impressed the people below—and made Jesus famous. However, Jesus resisted, again. The third temptation was about the material world's focus upon power. Jesus was shown all the world from a mountaintop and was told by the Devil that "All this will be yours if you will simply prostrate yourself and worship me." Jesus again resisted temptation. Our struggles with pleasure, fame, and power may last longer than those of Jesus did. Even so, we can effectively deal with those struggles if we keep our ego in check and our eyes on God.

If we were to become Buddhist monks with no possessions and to beg daily for our food, we could possibly shrink our ego to a very small size. However, if you are reading this book, you live in a world where you have friends, a spouse, children, a job, or a car. You have possessions that are not you but that you interact with and have some responsibility for. If you are not careful, your ego will want you to have more and better things. That is where selfishness and self-centeredness come from. So in the real world, we are looking at balance, and that involves knowing who we are in relation to others and to those things we own.

Chapter 17

Acceptance

I am a great believer in luck, and I find that the
harder I work, the more I have of it.
—Thomas Jefferson

Before you go on a trip you must accept where you are. If you want to drive west to Los Angeles from Houston, but you refuse to accept that you are in Houston because you want to be in Denver, then when you head west, you will be looking and preparing for mountains that are not there.

If you live with an emotionally aloof spouse, accept that you are with him or her. Accept all of your feelings about the situation, and accept that your best efforts to change your spouse have not brought you the changes you wanted. Sit down, take a deep breath, exhale, and accept that you can only change yourself. This might bring you some peace even if your spouse does not change today. If you want to weigh 140 pounds, but you weigh 220 pounds, accept where you are now. Start where you are. You cannot start where you are not.

Acceptance does not mean you believe nothing will ever change and that you ought to do nothing. It does mean you accept where you are, now; with the thoughts and feelings you have, now; and with what is happening around you, now. Acceptance of the moment puts you on a better foundation from which to move forward. Fear, anger, resentment, and other control tactics do not change your spouse and do not help you move forward into change and growth. When we accept that we cannot control others, we are left in the wonderful position of being willing to live in faith. Acceptance thoughts look like the following:

» Acceptance brings peace. Fear does not.

» Your parents did the best they could with the tools they had.

» Your parents loved you as best they could.

» Your spouse loves you the best way that he or she knows how.

» Accept what was and is and move on into your future.

» Accept what and whom you do not like.

» Accept the past to live in the present.

» Accept what is, at the moment, so you can be open to a different future.

» This is the best I can do today—now.

» The progress I've made so far is the best I could do.

A patient of mine told me that her husband said he no longer loved her; he loved another woman. He said he would maintain her major medical insurance through his company and would also give her one thousand dollars per month until she reached Medicare age. He said he would not divorce her, but she feared he would not keep the agreements. She did not want to be divorced. She wanted a romantic relationship with her husband, not a business contract.

Accepting her situation instead of denying it puts her in a good position to grow. Her faith is involved in every step along the journey—the faith that she is making the right decision at that time, and that somehow the situation will work out okay. After all, she made it so far fairly well, up to nearly Medicare age. As we talked, she was reminded of a woman she had met through a friend the previous week. This woman had terminal pancreatic cancer, but her attitude toward the life she had and the life she had left was one of gratitude. "To hear gratitude from a woman that was terminal was very humbling," my patient said. We can practice gratitude or practice grumpiness. We get to choose, and we get to change if we want.

She went on to say, "Things are rolling along with me." That is true, and things have been rolling along for years. However, now she is handling and holding them with more of a spiritual point of view. The unfortunate events, such as her husband's behavior, are still there outside of her. Nonetheless, she has now reduced the fear inside of herself even though he has not changed. It is not her husband who has been and is determining her state of mind, gratitude, level of friendships with others, and peace.

She told me that with the contract behind her she could focus on other matters such as updating her will. Life is a process. There is always some thought following a previous thought, some action following a previous action, and something to take care of following a previous something to take care of. Because of this process, it is important to learn how to handle the somethings well, or you may not have any peace—even on a Hawaiian beach vacation. It is not the number or intensity of things around you that determines your state of mind; it is how you hold them that determine your level of peace and faith. Holding them with acceptance can bring peace.

Another patient, Margie, has a daughter-in-law in a distant city who appears to have some serious psychological problems. She restricts Margie's visits to see her only grandchild to one weekend every three months. Margie was initially very angry, hurt, and fearful about this situation. She was fearful because she believed there was something wrong with her and that a visit every three months would not be enough for the child to bond with her. Even so, just a year later, the boy had already bonded with her. Margie said, "He seems to have the same exuberance that I have, and actually I may see him more this way because we have a schedule." Accepting the situation, rather than fighting with her daughter-in-law, led to peace and recognition of the positives in the situation.

A couple I worked with utilized their son, who was a part-time real estate agent, to sell their house. During the six-month contract, the son moved to another city two hundred miles away. He had not sold the house, and he wanted his parents to sign another six-month listing agreement with him. They told him they would not do that; they signed with another agent and the house sold within two weeks! "But our son hasn't spoken to us in five months," they said, "We send him cards for holidays and his birthday. He'll get over it sometime." We all agreed he would at his own pace. The son seemed to be nurturing some dysfunction rather than feeding healthy thoughts and behaviors. My patients accepted the situation, accepted their son as he was, and were not fearful of losing him forever. They also practiced patience, love, and enjoyment of the life they were given day by day. The couple never gave up on their son. They prayed for him several times a day.

BEING PRESENT FOR OURSELVES

For many people, having the large house or expensive car or being around the right type of person is more important than living the day. That is, what is outside of the person becomes more important than the experience of what is inside the person.

If it takes four years to obtain a high school diploma or a college degree, it is important that you go to class, do the work, and enjoy the day in which these events and experiences occur. It will take four years whether you are impatient or enjoying the passing of time. It will take four years whether or not you accept the four years.

We are all handicapped somehow. Some people have poor eyesight, some have ADHD or another learning disability, some have impaired social skills, some have depression, and some have poor handwriting. Not one of us is perfect. We can attempt to hide the handicap from others (to survive in fear). We can try to keep it secret, but we know the truth. Hiding it or keeping it secret requires more energy and results in a greater toll on us emotionally and spiritually than accepting the truth.

I once had a patient with cerebral palsy who used crutches to walk. He was a young man, and at parties he would keep the crutches on the floor or behind a sofa. When he spoke with women, he had a fear of how they would react when they saw the crutches—when they learned the truth. Usually, it was a shock to the women, and they would move off to talk with someone else. As he and I worked together to examine his fear and how he kept himself a prisoner to it, he decided to lean his crutches against the sofa at parties and against his desk at work. He kept his handicap in full view of others and himself. He practiced accepting himself as he was, and he began to feel more relaxed. He explained, "I feel good about myself, not because a girl likes me. I feel good about myself inside of myself, even though things have or haven't changed outside of myself." He was learning to accept himself as he was.

In my own life, when I am frustrated or irritated with someone, I ask myself a series of questions. I would not ask myself these questions if I were not open and willing to change. The questions include the following: Why am I irritated? Does this person remind me of anyone? What can I do? What are my options? Does my irritation help the situation? If I deny or reject will there be any growth?

Our painful inner reality and our desire to avoid it can drive us. If you believe you have a large nose, you will function based on that belief system even with all the pain and conflict that it involves and even though you have many friends who tell you your nose is not too large. Not until we accept instead of reject our fears will we find peace and be at ease within our own skins so that we can move on.

I am a big believer in the power of self-help groups. Men and women in the program of Alcoholics Anonymous read and find inspiration in what is called the *Big Book*—the basic text of AA. Years ago, I memorized the first paragraph of page 449 in the book. I have quoted it to others and repeated it to myself hundreds of times. Each time I say or think about the passage it brings me a measure of acceptance and peace. It helps move me out of fear and control. This is the paragraph:

And acceptance is the answer to all my problems today. When I am disturbed, it is because I find some person, place, thing, or situation—some fact of my life—unacceptable to me, and I can find no serenity until I accept that person, place, thing, or situation as being exactly the way it is supposed to be at this moment. Nothing, absolutely nothing, happens in God's world by mistake. Until I could accept my alcoholism, I could not stay sober; unless I accept life completely on life's terms, I cannot be happy. I need to concentrate not so much on what needs to be changed in the world as on what needs to be changed in me and in my attitudes.

You can worry a great deal about your son who is married to a woman who creates much drama in his life and in his family. However, your worrying will probably not change either your son or your daughter-in-law. They are in their own habit cycles and may be afraid to change. So take care of yourself while waiting for them to change, and remember that worrying is not healthy self-care.

Take a close look at what you cannot control. Then work to accept it the way it is today, at this moment. Learn to take life one moment and one day at a time. Learn to live in the moment, because most of our fears do not happen anyway, and our worries do not change people or situations.

Many people—not just sports fans—do a lot of Monday morning quarterbacking. A sports fan may go over a play many times and say, "If only they had blocked that kick ... If only they had made that basket ... If only the referee had called that foul ..." The energy remains in the "if only" even though the game is long over. Sometimes people do the same thing with their lives. Instead of accepting and moving on, they worry and say, "If only ..." and keep the energy in their old memories. Accepting a person or situation the way it is, at this time, takes the energy out of it, at this time. It allows you to have room for acceptance and peace instead of being flooded with fear and worry.

CONFLICT

Conflict within ourselves occurs when we are not doing what we know deep inside, at the God-within-us level, we ought to be doing. If you want peace, you must resolve the conflict. Conflict occurs when we do not accept what is within us, in our thoughts, feelings, and memories. These are all ours. We created them. We have embellished and nurtured them. And we are responsible for them. No one else but us and God can change them. No one else is at fault, and there are no excuses—only responsibility.

If you have too much conflict or focus outside of yourself (i.e., if you take too many cues from others), you will have difficulty hearing God within us, who speaks in a quiet voice. God wants us to pay close attention to Him. So, unlike a loud commercial we take for granted or become bored with, God whispers to us.

A man I once knew told me this: "I have these big swings in my self-esteem that are based on how I think others see me. I went to the range to hit golf balls, and the manager gave me the senior discount. Because he gave me that, I worried I looked old, and then I did not hit the balls well." He was not accepting and he was not at peace. Stay updated with yourself. Learn to be at ease inside of you.

Sarah told me she thought she was like a weather vane: going every which way when someone blows a look or comment her way. And then she said, "When someone asks me my age, I tell them the age of my oldest child, and then I tell them how many years ago I got married. I figure they will do the math." By avoiding telling the simple truth, Sarah is nurturing her own fear. By avoiding, she participates in making the fear appear large and strong. "I am afraid people won't like me if they know my real age," she admitted. She avoids telling people the truth, gives cute answers, and gets laughs. People do not push to know her age, and she successfully dodges the question, which reinforces or strengthens the avoidance.

My Fears

My fears to claim or not to claim have their origins in my childhood, a time before I had gained much experience, developed a sense of self, surrendered to God, or knew freedom of choice. I do not blame my parents or make excuses for them or for me. These are simply some of the major dynamics of our family. My mother was full of fear, inadequacy, and guilt. My father was full of fear and anger. I was the oldest child and the only young male in the extended family for thirteen years. These have been some of my general fears:

- » Fear of authority figures
- » Fear of making a mistake
- » Fear of not fitting in with others
- » Fear of conflict
- » Fear of being a leader (and making a mistake)
- » Fear of saying no to others (and then being rejected)
- » Fear of displeasing others
- » Fear of having and enforcing boundaries (fear of rejection and conflict)
- » Fear of inadequacy

Claiming these fears as my own to address—and knowing no one else can do it but God and me—involved my willingness to enter what I saw and experienced as a very dark space inside of me. I preferred to go anywhere but there, and for years I went to many other places. My list of compulsive behaviors is long and includes the following: exercising, reading, being alone, focusing on money, and working. These behaviors distracted me from my fears for many years. They hid my fears from others as well. And they kept me from growing. As I learned to claim my fears—that part of me that I had disowned—I could more easily deal with my life. My compulsions never brought me peace, but accepting my fears began the process that resulted in increasing levels of peace.

My Whirlpool Story

When I was in college and also in seminary, I had a reoccurring dream that involved a huge whirlpool. I had the dream maybe seven times over as many years. The dream always started with a bird's-eye view of a whirlpool in an ocean. The center of the whirlpool was simply a deep and dark hole. There was usually no land anywhere around; the water and the sky were gray. The whirlpool rotated slowly in a counterclockwise direction. I watched it from above for what seemed long minutes and then would see a small figure drifting toward the whirlpool from the right. The figure was struggling to swim away from the swirling mass, but the effort was futile. I could then see and feel that the figure was me! The vortex pulled me in, and I began to rotate around the lip of the whirlpool—slowly at first but then faster and faster. I looked down into the darkness and could see nothing. Maybe halfway down the whirlpool—but I had no way of knowing if it was halfway—I began swirling very quickly. I could not hear my own screaming because of the noise of the rushing water. At that point, I always woke up sweating.

I clearly recall thinking after one such episode that I was tired of the dream. I did not want to have it in my life, and I did not want to go to bed fearful that the dream would reoccur that night. I told myself that if I had the dream again I would see it through to the end, whatever that would be. I had found strength and peace inside of myself, and I slept well for many months. And then one night I had the dream again. It was almost a relief to see the whirlpool—and I was not afraid. This time I did not fight the twisting waters as I was pulled into the vortex. This time I was relaxed as I sped up while plunging farther down. This time I was not afraid of the darkness at the bottom. I recall thinking that I wanted to see what would happen. I thought I might explode, die some other way, or be okay. I did not scream as I was pulled right into the blackness. I was there for a brief instant, and then the whirlpool disappeared. It was replaced by bright sunlight, and I had a bird's-eye view of the ocean again—this time with only small waves and no whirlpool. I never had the whirlpool dream again after that night.

ACCEPTING OUR FEARS

If we are to accept our fears, we must be willing to know them intimately. When we massage someone's back, we do not do it by keeping our hands five inches above their back muscles. We must put our hands on the muscles. Our hands must be in contact with the flesh to know which muscles are tense and which are relaxing. We must do the same with our fears; we must *massage* them, touch them, and be in contact with them.

A female patient, Rosa, has an issue with boundaries. Recently, her boss sued her when she left because he believed that she had stolen some patients. Rosa denies the charge and has witnesses to back it up. She says, "At times I am clear and strong, and then two days later I'm all emotional and I doubt myself." It is important that she claim her strength and doubt, because they are both part of her—not part of someone else. Her husband complains she is "too emotional," but being emotional is part of her to accept. She wants her husband to accept her as she is, including her emotionality, and she needs to accept that about herself. She does not want her husband to push away or disown her emotionality, and she ought not to push it away either. Rosa does not want to be in conflict with him regarding her emotionality—her sensitivity—and she doesn't need to have the conflict inside of herself either. To manage her emotionality differently, she needs to know it, be in touch with it, claim it as her own, and not avoid it.

We must experience conflict to build more character. So do not look down upon or avoid conflict—it can lead to wisdom, awareness, change, and growth. The seeds of the lodgepole pine tree require intense heat, such as from a forest fire, to be released from the pinecone so they can grow. With us, conversion experiences are the heat that can free us for a new life.

Learn to Accept All Four Parts of Yourself

In order to accept all parts of ourselves, we must go inside to God within us, and then we will come to know what to do even if we cannot adequately explain it. The calm knowing is powerful and allows us to break old habits and move forward in faith.

A patient told me that he had a fear of not getting all of his work done at the office and not having enough time to help his daughter with her homework. Therefore, he consistently rushed through both lunch and dinner. "When I was a boy," he told me, "I had four brothers, and I had a fear of not getting enough food. So I ate fast. Now, the fear is about not getting chores done, not having enough time." I suggested that he accept his fear rather than avoid it by using his old habits. I asked him to eat both lunch and dinner slowly for six months, taking between thirty and forty-five minutes to eat. He was afraid and had old images from his past flash in front of him. Even so, by staying in his lunch or dinner chair, he came to accept his fear. In the process he also learned to manage it differently. Only one month was required for him to become significantly at ease with himself, with his food, and with his family while eating. He learned to have all four parts of himself remain at the table rather than having only his body sitting there while his spirit, thoughts, and feelings focused upon the past or the future.

Acceptance and Surrender

If you are late, surrender to lateness. Fighting it and being angry will not cause time to go slower so that you will not be late. Fighting it will not cause traffic to go faster so you will not be late. If you leave late for the office, you can be angry and impatient on the way, but it will still take maybe half an hour. Alternatively, you could drive peacefully and patiently, and it will still take about half an hour.

The journey to the office is similar to the journey of life. If you are forty-six now, you will be forty-seven next year. You can be tense or relaxed on the journey to forty-seven. It will take the same amount of days to turn forty-seven whether you are tense or relaxed. You choose the mood on the way.

Repression and nonacceptance of reality do not work well. Imagine you have a cube of Jell-O in your hand. It is your Jell-O, not someone else's. But you may pretend it is not there. Because you do not begin at the beginning, acceptance of reality, you might be the only one pretending you do not have Jell-O in your hand. Other people can see it. You can try to squeeze it down to the size of a marble in an attempt to hide it, but then it will ooze out somewhere. Our emotions operate the same way. When we attempt to repress and deny them, they ooze out somewhere.

By the time we become adults, we are sensitized (highly reactive) to a variety of issues, people, and situations. Some individuals are sensitized to small spaces, criticism, not being liked, big men, or women who sound like their mothers. We can also be sensitized positively—to rainbows, puppies, and gentle touches. The positives do not cause us problems, but the negatives do. It is important that we desensitize ourselves to negative issues, to release ourselves from their grasp, and to not continue to spend our energy trying to run from a concern or repress it. It is not an issue of letting things be the way they are. They already are the way they are, and it was not up to you. It is now an issue of you letting yourself be at peace while you notice the way things and people are.

Acceptance is a platform from which you can manage life. This is today. It is not yesterday, and it is not tomorrow. Live in what you have. If I start with today, life is simple. If today is a Tuesday morning, it is a good platform from which to consider what the afternoon and the weekend might be like. But be sure to live the Tuesday morning, because that is where you are. At this moment, you are the way you are. This afternoon it might be different, tomorrow it might be different, but at this moment, start with where you are.

A woman I know has a father who treats her autistic son as if he has no neurological problems. He will refer to his grandson as "wimpy" and a "poor sport" if he does not do what he wants him to do. The man does not understand the severe social limitations and few social skills the grandson can draw upon. She says her father was like this when she was a child. She says she wants him to be different and wants him to change, but now realizes that she has choices. She can accept the way her father is and not hold a grudge or be resentful. At the same time, she can protect herself and her son from his verbal abuse if it occurs. She is no longer the child. As an adult, she has many choices.

It is important that we learn to accept all answers, not just the ones we want to hear. We can learn to accept experiences other than the ones we want. Life will probably not work out your way. So, given that it is not your way, your job is to have a variety of tools to deal well with what is presented to you during your lifetime.

Acceptance involves the process of admitting the present reality. John told me the following about his wife: "I do want her to be happy. If I could just go back ten years and do it differently, she would be happy now." Just because he wants it for her does not necessarily mean that she will be happy. That is not in his control—even if he could go back in time. Ten years is a long time. There were many decisions, interactions, thoughts, and crossroads for his wife. These would be measured in the hundreds of thousands, and any one could have resulted in a consequence other than what he wanted for her. It is good that he is compassionate, but he is not in control of her or her happiness. And he does not accept the current situation if he is dreaming and fantasizing about another situation. Without acceptance his peace could be postponed.

ACCEPTANCE AND UNDERSTANDING

We will not truly *understand* many events, experiences, and people in life. There are just too many variables, or things in the distant past. I described this once to a female patient who was busy attempting to understand why her relatives behaved as they did. She complained that they often said *mean* things to her. She believed that if she understood, she could change them, and that then her life could begin or she would then be happier. I gave her an example to consider. I asked her to imagine she was on a freeway and had a flat tire. She could try to understand why the flat happened, or she could change the tire and continue moving on down the road. She could work to understand why the family members said mean things to her. Or she could just accept that is what they do and move on down the road.

This woman's relatives all had their own issues. If her father had a flat tire, he would have cursed the road and been mean to it. If her father-in-law had a flat on the road, he would somehow have attempted to sexualize it. If her mother had a flat, she would have blamed the manufacturer. This is what these people do in their relationships with this woman, and she had been unsuccessful in changing them for over twenty years. I encouraged her to stop that behavior and do something else that might have a higher chance of success. If she accepted the way the family members were, she would then have that much more energy available to change herself.

Accepting a behavior does not mean condoning it or learning to like it. It is, however, the recognition of what the current reality is. Acceptance keeps us out of denial and daydreams. It allows us to be in the present. Acceptance comes in many forms. A patient of mine initially resisted his diagnosis of ADHD and did not use his medication. With some encouragement and his continued difficulties with attention and memory, he began the treatment. "I've started the medication. I take it sometimes. I don't know if it's helping. By the way, I didn't take it today," he said as he wiped some dirt from his shorts. With some embarrassment, he said, "Awww, these are my dirty shorts. I put on the wrong shorts. Maybe I need that medication even more than I thought."

Another man was very angry at one of the security guards where he worked because "she had a surly attitude and didn't really care about others." His attempts to control her and get her to change did not work, so he practiced an attitude of not fixing her. "I just don't feel compelled to fix her, and now she's getting fixed." The guard may change a bit because she does not see his unconscious threatening behaviors. She no longer protects herself by being surly.

You will have a hard time managing the five fingers on your left hand if you pretend you do not have them. You can manage your emotions, memories, behaviors, and thoughts if you know them well and accept them as yours. They are no one else's.

ACCEPTANCE, NOT CONFLICT, WITHIN YOURSELF

I enjoy working with alcoholics in my clinical practice. I once worked with a young alcoholic who had been in several treatment programs, but he relapsed to drinking after each discharge. I met him after he had been sober for several months but had just returned to drinking. He had lost his job and his marriage. "I am so sick of myself," he said. "I know what I ought to do, but I sabotage myself and end up drinking by myself, alone in my car in a parking garage." He looked very sad, and I asked him, "When was the last time you cried deeply, even sobbed?" He told me he did not know, but he said that one time he had cried a little in a treatment program. He had not accepted his pain and was avoiding it. He was negative in his comments about himself. He did not accept his uniqueness among the seven billion people on this planet. I asked him if he talked in AA meetings. "Rarely," he said. "I don't want to give people information they can use to judge me." He did not accept that he needed to purge himself of the stress, fear, and anger he had repressed. We discussed his perfectionism, his fears, and what he called his arrogance, which was really a cover-up for his fears. "This has happened before," he said. "I'll be okay in a day or two."

"You remind me of a ship," I said to him, "a ship that looks good on the ocean but that has small holes in the hull that slowly allow water to come in. Next the ship is sabotaged and sinks. You have many small holes in your psychology and in your spirituality. You just told me that somehow the ship will be raised, and the water will be pumped out—but the holes will not be fixed. You are that ship. You are preparing to return to doing what you have been doing, and that doesn't work very well. You could accept your fears and begin to plug the holes." He was still looking at me as if I had suddenly grown two more eyes. I figured that as long as I had his attention, I would tell him more. "You need to go to AA meetings and plan to talk briefly during each one. You need to manage your fear. Look in a mirror and begin to talk to yourself as the unique and worthy person you are. Otherwise, I am concerned you will continue to patch up your life and that you will sabotage yourself again."

Chapter 18

Specific Spiritual Plans to Practice

Faith is to believe what we do not see; the reward
of faith is to see what we believe.
—Saint Augustine

I F YOU WANT TO BECOME more accomplished at spiritual matters, you
will need to practice. Because we are in the physical world, we must
do physical activities that are symbolic of the spiritual. So practice Bible
reading, go to church, and write about forgiveness. To connect with the
invisible world, we can use the thoughts, feelings, and behaviors of the
visible world. Keep in mind that following this plan is not about ability
but about availability. Are you willing to practice and to be open to
receive?

1. **Spiritual Practice: Prayer Exercise.** For one month, thirty days,
pray on your knees at the side of your bed in the morning when
you get up, and do the same at night before getting into bed. Two
times a day for thirty days is an appropriate number of practice

sessions to see what the consequences might be once you get past the embarrassment or fear of being seen. In the morning, part of your prayer might be to ask God for guidance, strength, and humility during the day. At night, you might pray and ask for forgiveness for the times that you did not behave with humility or kindness that day. You might also thank God for the times during the day when you did show compassion and acceptance of others. The morning prayer prepares you for the day, and the evening prayer prepares you for a restful sleep.

2. **Spiritual Practice: Positive Self-Talk.** Because we become better at what we practice, it is important to find the positive in yourself, in others, and in the world. Make a list such as this one: God loves me, this other person is also a child of God, there is good in everyone, I am not a mistake, and I am here for a reason.

3. **Spiritual Practice: Pray for Others.** Pray for those who have a disease, have lost someone to death, do not have a job, will have surgery, or have a compulsion. These other people, like you, are children of God. Pray for their healing and for their peace. As you do this over and over, you participate in the process of strengthening them and strengthening yourself. As you focus on peace for others, you will increase the peace within yourself and reduce your self-centeredness and selfishness.

4. **Spiritual Practice: Joining or Forming a Prayer Group.** There is power in a group. We learn from others, and they learn from us. We all support each other. They help us in ways they may never know. And what you say and do may help them in ways you will never know. As is stated in the gospel of Matthew 18:20, Jesus said, "For where two or three come together in my name, there am I with them."

5. **Spiritual Practice: Forgiveness.** Since we are human, we all make mistakes. Do the exercise below, not just in your head, but also on paper and in detail.

FORGIVENESS EXERCISE

People to Forgive	Incidence	Forgiveness Statement
	Who was present? What happened? What was said? What was felt? Be specific.	Write a detailed sentence in which you forgive the person (who may be yourself).
1.		
2.		
3.		

6. **Spiritual Practice: Deep Breaths.** As you exhale, say, "Please, God, take away my fear." Say it over and over, and look for the calm that comes from believing what you say.

7. **Spiritual Practice: Closing Your Eyes.** Once they're closed, practice seeing yourself surrounded by angels. You may know some, such as your grandmother. Learn to look for and to trust others. Then practice seeing yourself surrounded by angels while keeping your eyes open. Feel their embrace and nurturance. You are not alone.

8. **Spiritual Practice: Telling Yourself It Is Okay to Be Different from Others.** God knows you are different from others, and you

are loved as you are. Embrace yourself as you are. Not everyone can run one hundred yards in ten or eleven seconds. You run it or walk it at your pace. It is okay to live your life at your pace.

9. **Spiritual Practice: Holding Life Gently.** Since you don't control the earth, it will do what it does. Be a part of it and do your part--while holding it gently. See yourself playing a guitar. You are not the guitar, but you do your part to make music and hold the instrument gently as you do. If you squeeze the neck tightly you cannot move your fingers easily. You will develop cramps and have to stop playing too soon.

10. **Spiritual Practice: No Swearing for One Month.** Bite your tongue or pinch your fingers together, but do not swear for one month. Swearing is a shortcut and does an end run around logic, effective communication, and spirituality. Swearing is fueled by the power in our habits. Swearing maintains the disconnection between the emotional, the intellectual, and the spiritual.

11. **Spiritual Practice: Make a prayer list.** Have a book or notepad where you can write details about who and what you are praying for. And pray for them daily.

12. **Spiritual Practice: Prayer Partners.** Find someone to meet with routinely as well as at special times. When we know someone is waiting for us, we are more likely to meet with him or her than if we pray alone. Just as with exercise, it is a way to hold ourselves accountable.

13. **Spiritual Practice: Carrying a Small Bible or Meditation Book.** There are small Bibles that will fit easily in a pocket or purse. Refer to it when you want direction or need a comforting prayer.

14. **Spiritual Practice: Weekly Prayer Breakfasts.** Meet at the same restaurant or at someone's house before work. Have breakfast and then follow an agenda of praying for each other or for a person who has a request.

15. **Spiritual Practice: A Chair for God.** When you sit down at a table to eat or at a desk to do work, pull out a chair for God or imagine God is standing beside you. Teach yourself to experience God's presence more directly.

16. **Spiritual Practice: Recognition That Some People Are Stuck in Childhood or Adolescence.** To increase your patience and acceptance, look in her eyes and see her as a child. See her fears. This will result in you being triggered less often by her comments and behaviors. You will learn to react less and respond more.

17. **Spiritual Practice: Music.** Listen to music that touches your soul and changes your mood. Make a CD or download songs to your phone. I like to listen to some of Mahalia Jackson's songs, such as "Lord, Don't Let Me Fail." My favorites also include "Amazing Grace," "Ave Maria," "Just a Closer Walk with Thee," and "One Day at a Time." Memorize the words and repeatedly sing to yourself while working, folding laundry, or driving your car.

18. **Spiritual Practice: Rewriting the Lord's Prayer in Your Own Words.** For example, "The Lord is my Holy Father; I am given all I truly need. God gives me pleasant and restful places and walks with me by quiet lakes ..." This practice can help you find gratitude and peace.

19. **Spiritual Practice: Lists.** Make a list of people in your life who are nurturing and supportive of you. Then make a list of those who are critical and unaccepting. It is important to practice repeating to yourself what the supportive and loving people say and not what the nonsupportive and critical people say.

20. **Spiritual Practice: Reflection on Listening to God.** Write down the times you listened to God within you about a particular decision and what the consequences were.

21. **Spiritual Practice: Your Personal Mission Statement.** People in business write mission statements—statements that briefly

summarize what the business provides. Your personal statement could be the following: "I am here to provide service to others to the best of my abilities," or "I am here to show love and compassion to others."

22. **Spiritual Practice: Religious Charms.** Buy a religious charm or charms and carry them with you or put them where you see them many times each day, such as on your desk, dashboard, or bathroom mirror.

23. **Spiritual Practice: Humming.** Teach yourself to hum phrases such as "thank you" or "be patient" or "life is good." Hum these while walking, driving in the car, or showering, for example.

24. **Spiritual Practice: Saying Thank You.** A wonderful priest I knew said that when he went to bed, he repeated "thank you," sometimes for up to five minutes, as a way to put himself more in touch with the spiritual. He would then, sometimes for another five minutes, repeat "help me" as a way to acknowledge that he was not in charge of the universe.

25. **Spiritual Practice: Statements from God.** God created you. Write ten statements God might have said to you or about you as you were being created. Memorize them.

26. **Spiritual Practice: Refrigerator Notes.** Post this on your refrigerator: "I have attempted to change and to control many others, and I have learned I cannot. They still do what they want, what they choose, or what they have a habit of doing—whether it is drinking alcohol, taking drugs, spending, swearing, abusing others, being grumpy, not talking, smoking, or being late."

27. **Spiritual Practice: Mirror Notes.** Tape this to your mirror: "I can change and control only one person. With God's help, I can change that one person. That one person is the one who looks back at me in this mirror."

28. **Spiritual Practice: Ego Check.** Each time you look at your watch, ask yourself if your ego is getting in the way. Do you have

something you believe you need to protect that is bigger than your connection with God? Do you want people and things to be the way you want them?

29. **Spiritual Practice: Asking for Forgiveness.** Several times per day examine what you are doing and ask for forgiveness if appropriate. Look at whom you may have harmed and consider making amends to him or her. That is, clear up problems soon after they are made.

30. **Spiritual Practice: Bible Meditation.** Pick a Bible verse and meditate on it. Sometimes all you need to do is open the Bible and begin to read. A verse will seem to jump out at you. Meditate on that one. Ask yourself what the verse might mean for your life.

31. **Spiritual Practice: Integrating Your Four Parts.** Say a prayer that will help you integrate all four parts of yourself. For example, "Lord, please, please grant me, your servant, clarity of mind, purity of heart, and moral strength."

32. **Spiritual Practice: A Wall of Crosses.** This wall will be a religious symbol of your faith. My wife and I have a wall that has about thirty crosses of various types on it. Friends know of our shared spiritual journey and have given us most of them.

33. **Spiritual Practice: Seeing God in Others.** We are all made in the image of God—every one of us. Learn to look at others; learn to look into their eyes and see God. Learn to let others look into your eyes and see God.

34. **Spiritual Practice: Practice Cards.** Carry a three-by-five card with you and write a message on it for yourself that you want to practice. "I choose to live in faith today knowing that God has taken me safely this far, and I trust God to take me further. I will live in faith and turn other people over to God."

35. **Spiritual Practice: Fear Cards.** On one side of a three-by-five card write down a fear of yours, such as, "I have fear today about

my job, my car, and my salary." On the other side write, "I choose to live in faith about my job, my car, and my salary." Practice the faith statement.

36. **Spiritual Practice: Relationships.** The three levels of relationship, in order of priority, are relationship with God, with ourselves, and with others. Write examples of what you want your relationship with God to look like. Then write about what you want the relationship with yourself to be like. And do the same for your relationships with others.

37. **Spiritual Practice: Your Faults and Their Opposites.** Write down your character faults along with examples. Next to them write down the opposite characteristic. For example, if one of your character faults is pride, give an example of it, and also write the opposite of it—humility. Then give examples of humility. If the fault is judging others, the opposite may be acceptance. Then practice humility and acceptance.

38. **Spiritual Practice: Bowing.** Learn to bow—to lower your head. It is an act of deference and humility. Bow before you pray and before a cross.

39. **Spiritual Practice: In-Home Altars.** Create a small altar at home. Put a Bible on it, hang a cross, put your special prayers and intentions on it, and light a candle.

40. **Spiritual Practice: Prayer Requests.** Ask others to pray for you and tell them what you want help with.

41. **Spiritual Practice: Wishing Peace.** When others cut you off on the road or are grumpy on the phone, just say to yourself, "peace be with you."

42. **Spiritual Practice: Phrases and Frequent Actions.** Pair up saying a phrase such as "Not my will, Lord, but Your will be done in my life" with some frequent behavior such as turning on a faucet, looking at your watch, or turning the directional

signals on your car. Find a phrase that you would like to use and repeat.

43. **Spiritual Practice: Imagining God.** Imagine that God is walking by your side and God's hand is on your shoulder. Put a large piece of tape on your shoulder, on the skin, so when you feel the tug during the day, you can say, "I know you are with me, Lord. Thank you."

44. **Spiritual Practice: Connecting the Material and the Spiritual.** When you talk with others, imagine you are holding a copy of *Time* or your newspaper in one hand and the Bible in the other. Talk about the material world, but relate it to spiritual principles and lessons. The Bible is relevant as a guide today.

45. **Spiritual Practice: Fear Identification.** Identify all of your fears and write them down in sentences. Take just one per day, but refer to it numerous times during the day. You could say, "Lord, I am turning this fear of mine over to you. Please help me to have more faith and less fear."

46. **Spiritual Practice: Mealtime Questions.** At breakfast, lunch, and dinner ask yourself the following:

    » Am I spiritually vulnerable and open to growth?

    » Do I have clean thoughts?

    » Do I have peace in my heart?

    » Do my behavior and my appearance show love and peace?

47. **Spiritual Practice: Active Listening.** God is calling you always. God is crazy about you, His creation. Practice active listening to God's messages and learn to say, as Samuel did in the Old Testament, "Here I am, Lord." Listen; you are not alone.

48. **Spiritual Practice: Missions.** The missionary work begins when you leave your church building or your home. Remember, religious ritual without actions containing love is empty.

49. **Spiritual Practice: Charity.** Do charity work, serve others, and

give of your time, talent, and treasure. Volunteer to serve food to the hungry—not just at Thanksgiving. When you buy groceries, buy a bag of basic food items and give it to a food pantry or take it to your house of worship for distribution to the poor. What you have was given to you by God. Give some back.

50. **Spiritual Practice: Learning to Listen.** God does not spell out messages to us by forming clouds into words. God speaks in a whisper.

51. **Spiritual Practice: Eating with Others.** In both the Old and New Testaments of the Bible, sharing food was part of a ritual that could seal deals, help heal social wounds, and bind people together into community. So when you eat with God and others, plan to talk and connect with them. Do not create conflict over food.

52. **Spiritual Practice: Living in the Here and Now—Day by Day.** If we could look into the future and see when others we love will die, how they will die, and when we will die, then our lives would probably become intolerable and overwhelming. We cannot see the future, but we do not need to. The present time, what we have one day at a time, is sufficient. Write and memorize some phrases that will help you live in the here and now, such as "I cannot see the future. I will live today," and "I trust God to take care of my future and of those I love."

53. **Spiritual Practice: A Gratitude Journal.** In it, list all that you have to be grateful for. Carry it with you.

54. **Spiritual Practice: One Thing at a Time.** Do one activity at a time as best you can. This helps to keep all four parts of you in the same place. Learn to be in the here and now. Practice doing only one activity at a time instead of being proud of multitasking. Learn to listen to one person at a time and to answer one phone call at a time. Learn to value others and relationships, and show respect by giving attention.

55. **Spiritual Practice: Playing with Children.** Be present for little children and play with them. This practice will help you learn to be in the here and now without burdens and old fears.

56. **Spiritual Practice: Internal Peace.** Your peace is within you. It is not floating around in the air or behind a fence waiting for you to find it. So get quiet and go inside.

57. **Spiritual Practice: The Rule of Two.** Ask yourself how important an issue will be in two months, two weeks, two days, two hours, two minutes, or two seconds. If you are angry at someone, will it be a big deal two weeks from now? If you are afraid to own up to a mistake, will it be running and ruining your life two years from now?

58. **Spiritual Practice: Your Values.** Decide what kind of person you want to be. Write down the image you see for yourself. Put it somewhere you will see it several times each day. Consider telling another friend or two of your commitment—somewhat like Lent. And then practice those behaviors that support your values and goals.

59. **Spiritual Practice: Retreats.** Enroll in a retreat such as Road to Emmaus. There are many that are deeply and spiritually based and that facilitate growth and change.

60. **Spiritual Practice: Plan A.** Admit that plan A is always God's plan, not yours. This will help foster humility and the priorities necessary for spiritual growth. You cannot see into the future to connect the dots, but if you look carefully in the rearview mirror, you might begin to see how some dots do, in fact, connect.

61. **Spiritual Practice: Imagining the Deaths of Loved Ones.** If you knew someone you loved was going to die within the next sixty days, what would you do differently with him? Would you have less irritation and more patience with him? Would you spend more time with him? Would you pray with him? Would you talk about God and heaven and death with him? Put into

practice what you would do differently with him if you knew he was going to die soon.

62. **Spiritual Practice: Writing Yourself a Letter as if It Were from God.** Write a letter to yourself, in the first person, that explains why God loves you. For example, "I love you because I created you. You are wonderful. I gave you many talents. I am always with you." Put the letter in an envelope, address it to yourself, put a stamp on it, and mail it. Take a few quiet minutes to open it and read it when it arrives back at your house.

63. **Spiritual Practice: Self-Compassion.** Be gentle with yourself as you move through the learning process. As we behave differently and attempt to have more balance in our lives, we are likely to go to some extremes or "to do it wrong." That is okay. You are learning. You do not know how to do it well yet. That is why you are practicing—to make progress.

64. **Spiritual Practice: The Process of Discernment.** Knowing what to do about a situation is about a wisdom process and a balance deep inside. Not everything is a big deal, and you do not need to do everything. Ask yourself, "What am I being called to do?"

65. **Spiritual Practice: No Criticism.** If you stop teasing and criticizing others, you will find over time that you are teased and criticized less—particularly by yourself.

66. **Spiritual Practice: Praying Aloud.** When you are in your car driving to work, pray out loud to God rather than silently within your head. Hearing yourself talk gives the words more power; you will view yourself more appropriately and with more awareness.

67. **Spiritual Practice: Imagining Your Will.** Look at your possessions and decide whom you want to give them to when you die. Who gets your jewelry? Cars? Clothes? Furniture? Artwork? Put a sticky note on them with the name of the person you want

to receive them. Now, if you knew you would die within the year, how important would these things be? Would something else be more important, like relationships?

68. **Spiritual Practice: Daytime Prayer.** Pray during the day, not just at the bookends of the day when you wake up in the morning and when you go to bed at night.

69. **Spiritual Practice: Gratitude for Little Activities.** Be thankful for the little activities in your life that you might take for granted. Think back on a time you were ill and could not get out of bed or sit at a table. Now, when you sit at a table, say, "When I had the flu last year I couldn't sit here. So I smile as I sit here now."

70. **Spiritual Practice: Caution Signs.** Make a sign that says "Caution! Spiritual Life under Repair!"

71. **Spiritual Practice: Confession.** Confess all in your life to at least one other person. It does not need to be your spouse or a family member. Share with a priest, minister, or therapist. Tell at least one other person about all you have ever done that you consider bad, evil, and sinful. When another human being looks at us with acceptance and love, in spite of all we have told them, the bonds of dysfunctional fear that keep us from peace are weakened.

72. **Spiritual Practice: Receiving with Gratitude.** Teach yourself to receive as you cultivate and practice an attitude of gratefulness. God has given you more than you can ever repay to Him. The scale is always tilted toward us. Learn to be on the receiving end of God's grace—and be at peace with it.

73. **Spiritual Practice: Goal Contracts.** Make a written contract with yourself and maybe one other person using the contract form below. The value of this practice is that these contracts are visual and can be touched. Writing down what you plan to do will help you focus and give the plan more priority in your life.

> » My Goal: I want to be close to God.

» What I will do: I will pray at least twenty times per day, and I will complete my forgiveness list within two weeks.

74. **Spiritual Practice: Effort and Consequences.** Repeat this to yourself often: "I make the effort, God creates the consequences."

75. **Spiritual Practice: Self-Analysis.** Analyze yourself more than you analyze others. Take your own inventory, not others'. You can change only yourself, not them.

76. **Spiritual Practice: Eating Slowly.** Slow down your eating, and enjoy the food and time spent with it. Slow down your speech, and enjoy the time and relationship with the other. Slow down your driving, and enjoy the time, the drive, and the sights.

77. **Spiritual Practice: Consistent Behavior.** Behave the same in the dark as you do in the light. Behave the same in private as you do in public. This helps to connect the four parts of yourself.

78. **Spiritual Practice: Sitting in the First Row.** When you go to your house of worship, sit up front. This is not about ego. Have as few distractions, such as people's heads, as possible between you, the leader, and the symbols. You will have a clear physical view, and that will help you have a clear spiritual view. We often run our daily lives as if we are sitting in the last pew in the church, and we are often distracted from what we say are our priorities. Our compulsions and addictions are distractions from our view of the front of the church, from the altar, and from the cross.

79. **Spiritual Practice: Prayer Places.** Find a quiet, special, and safe place to pray. I have a patient who prays in her closet.

80. **Spiritual Practice: Prayer Request Books.** In a notebook, write the names of the people you are praying for and what you are praying for for them.

81. **Spiritual Practice: Godly Jewelry.** Wear a ring or another piece of jewelry that has special meaning. Have a priest, or other religious person, bless it to give it special meaning. And when

you need help, as when you are with someone difficult to be with, hold onto the jewelry or rub it to receive the special power and help.

82. **Spiritual Practice: Godly Self-Life.** Ask yourself these questions: "Do I see myself the way God sees me?" and "Do I love myself the way God loves me?"

83. **Spiritual Practice: Understanding God's Love.** Think of someone who would look at you with eyes of love and acceptance. And then imagine God looking at you with that type of love every minute of the day, always.

84. **Spiritual Practice: God Outside the Church.** God does not live in the church, and neither do you. You live outside of the church. Therefore, encounter God outside of the church, share God outside of the church, and talk about God outside of the church. Answer these questions: "How can I live the spiritual life each day even when I am not in church?" and "Am I a missionary for God?"

85. **Spiritual Practice: God's Gifts.** Imagine God giving you something to show that you are loved—really and completely loved—by Him. What would that object be? Think about buying yourself a bracelet and having it inscribed with "I love you now, and I have always loved you."

86. **Spiritual Practice: Forgiving Yourself.** Look at yourself in the mirror and say, "I forgive you for ..." Even if you have acted out sexually, been abusive, or stolen from others, you can still forgive yourself and be healed. There will probably be scars at some level, but they do not have to interfere with the process of having a spiritual life.

87. **Spiritual Practice: Inhaling God and Exhaling Fear.** As you breathe in, say to yourself, "God in." As you breathe out, say, "Fear out."

88. **Spiritual Practice: Texting God.** Start your message with a statement of gratitude such as "Thank you God for my health."

89. **Spiritual Practice: Turning Control Over to God.** Put your hand on a Bible and say, "I relinquish my attempts at control over others. I willingly turn them over to You. My attempts at changing others have failed. I will practice living in humility and in faith. I do want the world to be different, and I will begin by changing myself."

90. **Spiritual Practice: Cultivating a Sense of Awe.** Be in awe of babies, sunsets, flowers, and birds. Be in awe of the wonderful gift that you are.

91. **Spiritual Practice: Imagining Yourself on a Beach.** As you walk with the water on one side and dry sand on the other, look ahead in front of you and notice someone walking toward you in the distance. As the person comes closer, you see that he is wearing a long, very white robe that reaches from his shoulders to his feet. As the figure continues to approach, you observe that he is a man. As the distance between you becomes even smaller, you feel drawn to the man; you are not afraid. You notice that you are even anticipating talking with him. When you are close, you recognize that the man is Jesus. He opens His arms to you as He walks, and you open yours to Him. He puts His arms around you, and He says the words you have long wanted to hear: "You are my wonderful child. I love you. I have always been with you. Wherever you were, I was there also. You were never alone, and I was always watching over you. I will always be with you." He looks at you with a deep gaze full of love. You relax and sink into his embrace and love. Then he says that he must go and meet others. You let go of Him as he lets go of you. He walks off along the beach. You are simultaneously sad, joyous, and relieved as His image becomes smaller and then disappears. You smile as you continue your walk along the beach.

CPSIA information can be obtained at www.ICGtesting.com
Printed in the USA
LVOW120358130313

323939LV00003B/5/P

9 781449 782443